THE AGE OF DECEPTION

MOHAMED ELBARADEI served as Director General of the International Atomic Energy Agency from 1997 to 2009. He was awarded the 2005 Nobel Peace Prize, together with the IAEA, and has also been honored with the Indira Gandhi Prize for Peace, Disarmament and Development; the Nile Collar; and the Roosevelt Institute's Four Freedoms Award. Founder of the Egyptian opposition movement the National Association for Change, ElBaradei lives in Cairo.

THE AGE OF DECEPTION

NUCLEAR DIPLOMACY IN TREACHEROUS TIMES

MOHAMED ELBARADEI

BLOOMSBURY

LONDON · BERLIN · NEW YORK · SYDNEY

First published in Great Britain 2011
This paperback edition published 2012

First published in the United States in 2011 by Metropolitan Books,
Henry Holt and Company, LLC, 175 Fifth Avenue, New York, New York 10010

Bloomsbury Publishing Plc
50 Bedford Square
London WC1B 3DP

www.bloomsbury.com

Bloomsbury Publishing, London, Berlin, New York and Sydney
A CIP catalogue record for this book is available from the British Library

ISBN 978 1 4088 2224 1
10 9 8 7 6 5 4 3 2 1

MIX
Paper from
responsible sources
FSC® C018072

Printed in Great Britain by Clays Ltd, St Ives plc

To Maya, my three-year-old granddaughter,
in the hope that we will leave her a better world

CONTENTS

INTRODUCTION

"Help us help you."

The man on the other side of the table smiled, but it was not happiness that I read in his expression. His eyes softened, and the corners of his mouth drooped. Was it sadness? Fatigue? I wasn't sure.

It was February 9, 2003. It had been more than a dozen years since the UN Security Council had first issued sanctions on Iraq. In a little more than a month there would be yet another U.S.-led invasion. Saddam Hussein had recently readmitted UN weapons inspectors to Iraq, and Hans Blix and I, the leaders of the international teams, were making our third visit to Baghdad. This was our last evening. The Iraqi foreign minister, Naji Sabri, had invited us to dinner, along with our principal experts and an assortment of Iraqi counterparts.

The restaurant was the finest the city could still offer. Baghdad's infrastructure was worn at the seams, showing the effects of the sanctions. But the dinner service was elegant, the waitstaff gracious, the dark red linen tablecloths spotless. There was plenty of grilled fish, fresh from the Tigris River. The skewers of lamb kebab were spiced to perfection. And the table bore another treat: wine. That was a surprise. Alcohol was forbidden in public in Iraq, under an edict passed in 1994. But for this evening, for their out-of-town guests, the Iraqis had made an exception.

The man across the table was General Amir Hamudi Hasan al-Sa'adi, chief scientific adviser to Saddam Hussein. The title of "general" was essentially honorific. An urbane, charismatic negotiator with a PhD in physical chemistry, al-Sa'adi was equally eloquent in English and Arabic and preferred tailored suits to military uniforms. Although not a member of the Ba'ath Party, he served as the scientific front man for the Iraqi government.

Blix and I had steered the dinner conversation toward a critical theme: the need for more cooperation, more documentation. You insist you have no weapons of mass destruction, we said. You tell us you have not revived any of your prior WMD programs. But we cannot simply close the file where your records are incomplete. We need more evidence. The more transparency you show, the more documentation and physical proof you can produce, the better it will be for Iraq on the world stage. What else can you provide to resolve the gaps in your information? *Help us help you.*

Sitting beside al-Sa'adi was Husam Amin, the head of Iraq's UN interface group. He leaned forward to answer. "Let us be frank," he said. "First, we cannot give you anything more because there is nothing more to give." His glance shifted to Blix, then back to me. "But, second, you cannot help us, because this war is going to happen, and nothing you or we can do will stop it. We both know that. Whatever we do, it is a done deal."

He sat back. Al-Sa'adi nodded but said nothing. The sadness remained in his smile.

Despite Amin's view, I refused to believe that war was inevitable. The International Atomic Energy Agency, the UN agency responsible for the nuclear weapon inspections, which I headed, had been making solid progress. This included following up on every intelligence lead we were given—and finding nothing. In my report to the UN Security Council on January 27, I had stated, "We have to date found no evidence that Iraq has revived its nuclear weapons programme." This statement had garnered strong criticism from Western officials and media pundits who had convinced themselves otherwise—but these critics were pointing to circumstantial what-ifs and characterizing them as proof. What I had said was the truth.

The IAEA was not yet in a position to issue Iraq a clean bill of health. But I had urged the council to allow the inspections to run their course.

A few more months, I had proposed, would constitute "a valuable investment in peace." If the justification for a preemptive invasion of Iraq rested on Saddam Hussein's reconstituted WMD programs, then where was the evidence? Where was the imminent threat? If Amin was telling the truth, and Iraq had "nothing more to give," then the implications were significant: there was no threat.

A war without justification was certain to drive a divisive wedge into the already fractured relationship between the nuclear "haves" and "have-nots." Both the United States and the United Kingdom had nuclear weapons and showed no signs of giving them up; yet they were threatening Iraq for allegedly seeking to acquire such weapons. For many in the developing world, and particularly in Arab and Muslim societies, this was both ironic and grossly unfair. Saddam Hussein enjoyed relative popularity among the Arab public for his stance against Israel's treatment of the Palestinians and his defiant attitude toward the West. He was not a favorite among the mostly pro-Western Arab rulers, particularly after his 1990 invasion of Kuwait; but still it rankled to watch Iraq being treated with such disregard for its sovereignty. If a war were actually to occur, and particularly one hinging on trumped-up WMD charges, the sense of outrage across the Arab and Muslim world would escalate sharply.

Still, as the weeks wore on, with all my faith in the inspection process, I had a growing sense of unease. The rhetoric emanating from the United States and the United Kingdom was increasingly strident. Just four days before the dinner in Baghdad, U.S. secretary of state Colin Powell had made his case to the Security Council: he had played audio tapes of intercepted telephone conversations and had shown satellite photos of Iraqi facilities. These records, he declared, demonstrated "disturbing patterns of behavior" on the part of Saddam Hussein and his regime, "a policy of evasion and deception." To the inspection community, his presentation was primarily an accumulation of conjecture, an alignment of unverified data interpreted according to a worst-case scenario. Nowhere was there a smoking gun. But to many listeners, and particularly to nonspecialists, Powell's argument was compelling.

During the six weeks that followed, no amount of inspection

progress or diplomatic intervention would prove sufficient to avert the impending crisis. The IAEA revealed that key intelligence documents, purportedly linking Saddam Hussein to attempts to purchase uranium from Niger, had been forged. But the discovery made little impact. An emergency summit of Arab leaders in Sharm el-Sheikh, instead of developing a solution or even a unified position, ended in disarray. A last-ditch proposal by the British to avoid military action fell flat.

Early on the morning of March 17, I received the call from the U.S. mission in Vienna advising us to move our inspectors out of Baghdad. The invasion was about to begin.

"If a danger exists in the world, it is a danger shared by all; and equally . . . if hope exists in the mind of one nation, that hope should be shared by all." These were the words of U.S. president Dwight D. Eisenhower in 1953, in the "Atoms for Peace" speech that, four years later, gave birth to the International Atomic Energy Agency. It was an extraordinary message, delivered in the midst of an expanding nuclear arms race, to an international community that had not forgotten the devastation of the Second World War.

Eisenhower's Atoms for Peace concept—the notion that both the benefits and insecurities of nuclear science must be addressed cooperatively by the international community—is the core principle of nuclear diplomacy. It would become a near-universal commitment to foster technological cooperation in peaceful uses of atomic energy and to prevent the spread of nuclear weapons—a dual commitment enshrined in the IAEA Statute and the landmark 1970 Treaty on the Non-Proliferation of Nuclear Weapons (NPT).

As a young Egyptian lawyer and professor of international law in New York in the early 1980s, I felt a resonance with the Atoms for Peace ideal. I joined the IAEA in 1984 and became its legal adviser three years later. By the time of the 2003 Iraq War, I had been the IAEA Director General for more than five years and part of the Agency for almost two decades. I had immersed myself in the Agency's nuclear diplomacy mission. For a war to be fought over unsubstantiated WMD charges—and for the IAEA's nuclear diplomacy role to be pushed to the side, serving as merely a fig leaf of due process—was for me a grotesque distortion of everything we stood for. It went against nearly half a century of painstaking labor by committed scientists, lawyers, inspectors, and public servants from every continent. I was aghast at what I was witnessing. The thought that would not leave my head was the certainty that nothing Blix or I had seen could possibly justify going to war.

General Amir al-Sa'adi, my melancholy dinner partner, turned himself in to coalition forces on April 12, 2003, after he learned that he was number thirty-two on the list of the most-wanted Iraqis and the seven of diamonds in the infamous deck of playing cards. He asked the German television station ZDF to film his surrender. Speaking into the camera, he announced, "We have no weapons of mass destruction, and time will bear me out." It was clear to me then that our provisional conclusion regarding nuclear weapons was correct, because by that time al-Sa'adi had no reason to lie.

In the years since, multiple sources have confirmed that the premise for the March 2003 invasion—the charge by the United States and the United Kingdom that Saddam Hussein's WMD programs represented an imminent threat—was groundless. The U.S.-appointed Iraq Survey Group would later spend billions of dollars to verify that the international inspectors were correct: Iraq had not revived its WMD programs. Nor, apparently, was the alleged WMD threat the real motivation for the U.S. and U.K. aggression. The famously leaked "Downing Street" memo from July 2002 was one of several sources indicating that the decision to go to war had been taken well before the inspections ever began.

To this day, I cannot read such accounts without reflecting on the thousands of soldiers who have died, the hundreds of thousands of Iraqi civilians killed, the millions maimed or displaced, the families disrupted, the lives ruined—and I am astonished that there has not been more self-examination, more introspection on the part of the principal players. The shame of this needless war obliges us all to consider what went wrong in the case of Iraq and to reflect on how the lessons of this tragedy might be applied to future crises.

The tensions over nuclear developments that are now agitating the world, particularly in relation to Iran, suggest that we could yet repeat the Iraq catastrophe, with even worse ramifications for global security. When I consider the challenges still confronting us, I often come back to the scene of our February 2003 dinner in Baghdad, because it so epitomizes the core aspects of the dilemma we face as a global community in search of an enduring and collective security: the increasing distrust between different cultures; the corrosive effects of a long-standing system of nuclear haves and have-nots; the folly of nuclear brinksmanship; and the certainty of doom if we are unable to learn from our past mistakes. That dinner scene is also important for what it is missing: the principal players—in this case the United States and the United Kingdom—whose decisions would actually determine the result. Their absence would become a recurrent motif in the years to come, particularly in Iran: the United States overshadowing negotiations from a distance, shaping the outcome while refusing direct participation. Nuclear diplomacy is a hands-on discipline requiring direct engagement, restraint, and long-term commitment. It cannot be performed by remote control. If dialogue is to be used as a tool to resolve nuclear proliferation tensions, it cannot be limited to a conversation between the inspectors and the accused country. The United States and its allies must be genuinely engaged in the discussions, speaking with their perceived adversaries, demonstrating by more than lip service their commitment to a peaceful resolution of the underlying insecurities. All parties must come to the negotiating table.

The dinner in Baghdad—which some of my colleagues have wryly dubbed "The Last Supper"—was only one of multiple crises unfolding in early 2003. North Korea had just expelled the IAEA inspectors monitoring the "freeze" on its nuclear facilities, and declared its intention to withdraw from the Nuclear Non-Proliferation Treaty. We were just beginning to probe the extent of the Iranian nuclear program and, with several IAEA colleagues, I was about to make my first visit to a nuclear enrichment facility under construction in Natanz. Libya soon would begin making overtures to the United States and the United Kingdom about dismantling its WMD programs. And the first vague outlines of an illicit and shadowy nuclear supply network were just starting to appear; eventually, we would find traces of its activity in more than thirty countries.

We now know more, a great deal more, about each of these cases of real or potential nuclear weapons proliferation. The circumstances in Iran and North Korea, in particular, remain fluid and unpredictable. What we still do not have is a practical, responsive approach for dealing with these or future cases. What we need is a commitment to nuclear diplomacy.

The First Nuclear Age was a race for the A-bomb, a competition among relatively few countries who either possessed the necessary technological sophistication or were able to obtain clandestinely the science needed to make a nuclear weapon. The climax of that race, the destruction of Hiroshima and Nagasaki, marked the United States as the winner. But the other contestants did not give up. Within a few years, four other countries had managed to acquire the bomb.

What we remember as the cold war was the Second Nuclear Age. While several countries possessed nuclear weapons, and others continued to work on the technology, this was really the era of two giants: the United States and the Soviet Union, each amassing tens of thousands of warheads, in a philosophy known as MAD, Mutually Assured Destruction, masquerading as "nuclear deterrence."

The Third Nuclear Age, the current era, dawned after the Soviet Union fell apart. In the vacuum of power that followed, the political community failed to capitalize on the opportunities for nuclear disarmament. As a result, more and more countries began to consider if not a clandestine weapons program, then at least a full nuclear fuel cycle that would render them capable of rapidly producing a nuclear weapon if their security situation so warranted.

The primary danger at this moment is not the MAD scenario, massive, silo-emptying exchanges of nuclear arsenals wiping out the major metropolises that house capitalism and communism, but the threat of asymmetrical atomic warfare: the acquisition and use of nuclear weapons by extremist groups or a "rogue" country headed by an aggressive dictator, or the use of a nuclear weapon by a major power against a non-nuclear-weapon state.

This situation is inherently unstable, and the developments of recent years have only exacerbated this instability. We have witnessed aggression where there was no imminent threat (in Iraq); inaction and vacillation while a real threat emerged (in North Korea); and a protracted stalemate fueled by insult and public posturing instead of meaningful dialogue (in the case of Iran). Along the way, we have uncovered an illicit and thriving nuclear network ready to supply clandestine nuclear programs. Meanwhile, the continued reliance on nuclear weapons by a few countries is a constant incentive for others to acquire them.

This growing instability means that we are at the twilight of the Third Nuclear Age. One way or another we are on the cusp of significant change. If we do nothing, attempting to maintain the status quo of nuclear haves and have-nots, the change will likely take the form of a veritable cascade of proliferation, or worse still, a series of nuclear exchanges. The signs are already apparent, most revealingly in the reactions of neighboring countries as real or perceived nuclear weapons threats emerge. The recent surge in the number of countries across the Middle East talking about or beginning to acquire nuclear technology and expertise is but one example. The suggestions by senior Japanese officials to open discussions about a Japanese nuclear weapons program in response to North Korea's first nuclear weapons test is yet another.

There is also an alternative. We could change course and embrace a different approach: a resolution of the asymmetry through genuine progress toward global nuclear disarmament. A new weapons reduction treaty between the global nuclear giants, to be followed by a forum in which the nuclear-weapon states begin to take responsibility for their need to disarm—these are the pathways that could lead us toward a more secure future. If we can heed the lessons of the recent past and confront the real threat that is just ahead, we might yet avert mutual annihilation and ensure that the dawn of the Fourth Nuclear Age will be marked by the resolution of nuclear tensions, the laying down of nuclear arms, and an enduring peace.

1

IRAQ, 1991–1998

Unmasking a Hidden Program

To appreciate the nuclear landscape of 2003 requires a return to the early 1990s, when two clandestine nuclear programs came to light: first, Saddam Hussein's secret program to develop nuclear weapons, discovered in the aftermath of the 1991 Gulf War; and second, North Korea's diversion of plutonium and concealment of nuclear facilities, which the IAEA uncovered the following year.

In the case of Iraq, what the Agency knew about the country's nuclear program at the outset of the first Gulf War was essentially limited to the Tuwaitha Nuclear Research Center, a short drive southeast of Baghdad. In its dealings with the IAEA, Iraq had declared two research reactors[1] located at Tuwaitha, as well as a small fuel fabrication laboratory and a storage facility. Twice a year, the Agency inspected those facilities, to verify that none of the declared nuclear material had been diverted from peaceful use to weapons development.

In the aftermath of the war, IAEA inspectors would find evidence of other, unreported nuclear activities at Tuwaitha and a series of other illicit nuclear sites across the country. The IAEA was faulted for not having detected earlier these clandestine aspects of Iraq's nuclear program. But the blame is mostly due to the limitations placed on the

---

1 The IRT-5000, a water-cooled, pool-type research reactor supplied by the Soviets; and the Tammuz-2, a French-supplied pool-type research reactor.

IAEA's inspection authority. The Agency was only expected to verify what a country declared. We had little authority, and few mechanisms, to search for undeclared nuclear materials or facilities.

If this sounds frighteningly naïve, it was. For regimes that chose to conceal their illicit activities, the IAEA was a beat cop with a blindfold. Nonetheless, the questions multiplied: Why had the IAEA not challenged the Iraqis on the completeness of their declaration? Why had there been no calls for special inspections? How could the IAEA have "missed" Iraq's broader nuclear ambitions?

These questions have good answers. In addition to the limitations on the Agency's authority, there was little solid intelligence at the time about Iraq's clandestine nuclear programs—or at least, if such intelligence existed, it was not shared with the IAEA. But to truly understand the situation requires additional perspective: (1) a few points regarding the Nuclear Non-Proliferation Treaty, from which much of the IAEA's verification authority derives; and (2) a rudimentary overview of the nuclear fuel cycle, to correct a common misconception or two.

The NPT, or the Treaty on the Non-Proliferation of Nuclear Weapons, was brought into force in 1970. For all its faults, it remains among the most widely subscribed-to treaties in history. At the end of 2010, 189 states were party to the NPT. Only three countries—India, Pakistan, and Israel—have never been party to it, and North Korea has withdrawn.

The NPT is built around three "policy pillars" agreed to by the parties to the treaty. Together, these pillars comprise a delicately balanced bargain.

First, NPT member countries that do not have nuclear weapons, also known as non-nuclear-weapon states, or NNWS, pledge that they will not pursue or develop such weapons. Each such member country is obligated to conclude a legally binding bilateral agreement with the IAEA, known as a comprehensive safeguards agreement. Under this agreement, the country promises to place all its nuclear material under IAEA safeguards, to ensure through physical controls and rigorous accounting procedures that the material will not be diverted for use in nuclear weapons. The safeguards agreement gives the Agency the authority to verify the country's compliance.

Second, all NPT members pledge to pursue negotiations "in good faith" to lead toward nuclear disarmament.[2] This includes, significantly, the five states that are acknowledged in the NPT as possessing nuclear weapons: China, France, Russia, the United Kingdom, and the United States, referred to as nuclear-weapon states, or NWS.[3] The NWS also agree that they will not in any way help NNWS acquire nuclear weapons.

Third, all treaty members agree to facilitate the use of nuclear energy for peaceful purposes in all member countries, and with particular consideration for the needs of developing countries. This includes exchanging relevant equipment, materials, and scientific and technological information.

There are plenty of flaws with the treaty. As I have already pointed out, it is weak on execution: the IAEA for decades was expected only to inspect, or "verify," what NPT members had declared. The disarmament aspects of the treaty are even weaker: there is no mechanism to verify the pledged progress on disarmament negotiations, nor a designated oversight body, nor a penalty for failure to comply. Finally, the treaty contains an apparent paradox: by complying with the third part of the bargain—by facilitating the exchange of nuclear equipment, materials, and information for peaceful purposes—NPT members are simultaneously increasing the capability of NNWS to pursue nuclear weapons, particularly when certain nuclear fuel cycle technology is involved.

This dilemma relates to the dual potential of nuclear science and technology and lies at the heart of nuclear diplomacy. Nuclear science is an extreme example of a classical quandary: human societies are able to

---

2 The exact quote from Article VI of the NPT: "Each of the Parties to the Treaty undertakes to pursue negotiations in good faith on effective measures relating to cessation of the nuclear arms race at an early date and to nuclear disarmament, and on a treaty on general and complete disarmament."

3 Article IX of the treaty defines a nuclear-weapon state as "one which has manufactured and exploded a nuclear weapon or other nuclear explosive device prior to 1 January 1967." At the time, the Soviet Union was one of five such states; but after its break-up, only Russia retained its status as a nuclear-weapon state. The three other former Soviet Union countries that had nuclear weapons relinquished them.

use their technological advances for good or ill. Whether the end use is a mushroom cloud or a cancer-curing medical isotope, much of the underlying science and technology is the same. It is the intent that differs: Will the acquired nuclear knowledge be used for military aggression and vast destruction? Or for the host of nuclear benefits that citizens of industrialized countries take for granted: energy and medicine, for example, or agricultural productivity, pest control, groundwater management, or industrial testing? It is one thing to deny additional countries nuclear weapons; but denying them the use of nuclear science for peaceful ends has no justification, and it would have meant no NPT at all.

Now for the nuclear fuel cycle. Terms such as *enrichment*, *uranium conversion*, and *plutonium separation* have slipped into the common lexicon, cropping up in mainstream press articles and public policy documents. Yet I constantly run into misconceptions regarding the nature, intent, and legality of these nuclear processes. To understand the stakes involved in the nuclear diplomacy of recent years, a layperson should have at least a rudimentary grasp of the overall fuel cycle and which parts of it are most vulnerable to weapons proliferation.

That said, it is a risky proposition for even the most well-versed lawyer to expound on nuclear technology, so I will confine my explanation of the nuclear fuel cycle to a simple series of steps.

1. **Mining:** Uranium ore is extracted from the ground. As it occurs in nature, uranium is predominantly made up of the uranium-238 isotope. Only about 0.7 percent is uranium-235, which is "fissile," meaning it can sustain a nuclear chain reaction.
2. **Milling:** The ore is processed, by grinding and chemical leaching, to produce "yellowcake," a uranium concentrate.
3. **Conversion:** The yellowcake is transformed, through a series of chemical processes, to uranium hexafluoride (UF_6) gas, the feedstock for centrifuge enrichment. The UF_6 at this stage is still considered "natural uranium," since the relative concentrations of U-238 and U-235 have not changed.

4. **Enrichment:** As the UF$_6$ is fed through centrifuges, the concentration of U-235 is increased, correspondingly decreasing the concentration of U-238. Enrichment makes the uranium more capable of generating nuclear energy.

5. **Fuel fabrication:** The enriched uranium is converted into powder, processed into ceramic pellets, and inserted into fuel rods, which are then arranged into fuel assemblies that will power a reactor core.

6. **Storage:** After being used in the reactor, the depleted nuclear fuel—now mostly U-238, with not enough U-235 remaining to sustain the reaction—is usually stored in a "spent fuel pool." Depleted fuel also contains about 1 percent of fissile plutonium, created as a by-product in the reactor.

7. **Reprocessing:** Since only a small percentage of the nuclear energy is used up in a normal reactor cycle, some countries recycle the spent fuel, recovering (or "separating") the uranium and plutonium for reuse.

The gas centrifuges used in uranium enrichment[4] resemble tall, skinny metal cylinders with inlet and outlet piping attached. They spin at enormous speeds—more than twenty thousand revolutions per minute, fast enough that the atoms of uranium-238, three nucleons heavier than uranium-235, move to the outside of the tube and can be separated out as they exit. When multiple centrifuges are lined up in a row, or in a "cascade," the UF$_6$ gas passes from one to the next and is gradually "enriched" to a higher percentage of U-235. Since U-235 makes up only a tiny percentage of natural uranium, it takes a very large volume of incoming feed material to produce even a very small volume of enriched product. This requires the centrifuges to spin for weeks and months at a time, which means they are not easy to design or construct and can be made only of special metals that can withstand the stresses.

Most light water reactors, which use nuclear fuel to produce electricity, require uranium enriched to about 3.5 percent U-235. "High-enriched uranium," or HEU, refers to any enrichment level above 20 percent.

---

4 The use of centrifuges is just one of several techniques for enriching uranium.

Uranium enriched to 90 percent or greater is usually considered weapons grade; however, many research reactors worldwide also use 90 percent enriched uranium fuel for peaceful purposes, such as to produce medical isotopes.

Contrary to the most common misconception, steps 1–7 are all elements of a peaceful nuclear fuel cycle. Despite what is at times implied in the press, uranium enrichment (or, for that matter, plutonium separation) does not inherently signal the intent to develop nuclear weapons. Since plutonium and HEU are the nuclear materials that can be used most directly in nuclear weapons, the two most proliferation-sensitive aspects of the fuel cycle are correspondingly reprocessing, in which plutonium is separated, and enrichment, which can make HEU. But both HEU and plutonium can also be used in reactor fuel, to generate electricity. Thus none of these fuel cycle operations is "illegal"; they are all within the rights of any member of the NPT. There are, of course, caveats: the relevant facilities and activities must be "declared," or reported, to the IAEA, and safeguards must be in place to verify that the nuclear material involved is accounted for and has not been diverted for use in weapons.

Roughly a dozen countries have significant nuclear fuel cycle operations. A fair number of non-nuclear-weapon states therefore have stockpiles of plutonium (separated out through reprocessing spent nuclear fuel), or HEU, which could readily be applied to a nuclear weapons program. And as more countries industrialize and nuclear knowledge spreads, still more governments are likely to consider the economic and other strategic advantages that come with owning the nuclear fuel cycle.

This is where the plot thickens. With the spread of nuclear technology comes an increased proliferation risk. Thus those states that already have the nuclear fuel cycle do not want to give it up but would prefer that no other countries acquire it. The have-nots resent this stinginess. And indeed, under the NPT bargain, the haves who possess peaceful nuclear knowledge and technology are obliged to share it. The have-nots resent, most of all, that the nuclear-weapon states have failed to keep their part of the bargain, to negotiate "in good faith" and "at an early date" toward nuclear disarmament. The haves enjoy a status that other countries might well envy, since nuclear weapons have become synonymous with political clout and power and an insurance against attack.

In hindsight, the emergence of the first clandestine nuclear programs in Iraq and North Korea in the early 1990s perhaps should have been no surprise. With the cold war winding down, the balance of power between the Soviet Union and the United States could no longer be relied on to maintain a relative peace. Countries not explicitly protected under a "nuclear umbrella," such as that provided to members of NATO or other U.S. allies, might understandably have been experiencing an increasing sense of insecurity. What better insurance policy than to develop nuclear weapons in secret?

This was the context in which Iraq's nuclear program was discovered at the end of the 1991 Gulf War. While the United States had mentioned Iraq's emerging nuclear ambitions as one of many reasons for military action,[5] in fact very little was known about Iraq's actual nuclear capabilities before the war. Some in the U.S. intelligence community reportedly presumed that Iraq had nuclear weapons ambitions—based on, among other indications, attempts made by Iraq to acquire nuclear enrichment components and other nuclear technology from a number of European countries.[6] No such information, however, had been presented to the IAEA. In the month or two before the war, a number of media outlets began making wild and unsubstantiated reports about Iraq's specific nuclear capabilities.[7] But perhaps the best indication of the extent of prewar Western intelligence is that the United States was reported to have

---

5 Soon after the bombing commenced, on January 16, 1991, President George Herbert Walker Bush said the following on national television: "We are determined to knock out Saddam Hussein's nuclear bomb potential." Quoted in David Albright and Mark Hibbs, "Iraq and the Bomb: Were They Even Close?" *Bulletin of the Atomic Scientists,* March/April 1991.

6 "Early Western Assessments: What Did We Know and When Did We Know It?" Federation of American Scientists, retrieved at www.fas.org/nuke/guide/iraq/nuke/when.htm.

7 A good example was that of William Safire, claiming in the *New York Times* that, among other things, Iraq's scientists were enriching uranium with twenty-six centrifuges. Referenced in David Albright and Mark Hibbs, "Hyping the Iraqi Bomb," *Bulletin of the Atomic Scientists,* March/April 1991.

had only two nuclear sites on its list of targets to bomb, whereas, in the postwar inspection, as many as eighteen nuclear sites would be identified by the IAEA. In fact, it was Saddam Hussein's invasion and occupation of Kuwait that provided the primary justification for the U.S.-led coalition to invade.

On April 3, 1991, less than two months after the end of the war, the UN Security Council issued a sweeping set of terms with which Iraq was to comply. Naturally, this included obligations such as respecting the Iraq-Kuwait boundary, returning Kuwaiti property, and compensating Kuwait for injury, damage, and loss. But a major part of the resolution was devoted to the council's demands that Iraq rid itself of weapons of mass destruction.

In the nuclear arena, Resolution 687 called on Iraq to come clean—to declare fully all of its nuclear facilities and its weapons-grade nuclear material. It asked the IAEA Director General to carry out immediate inspections based on Iraq's declarations and to develop a plan within forty-five days to destroy or remove from Iraq any nuclear-weapon-related capabilities. The resolution also established UNSCOM, the United Nations Special Commission, which was charged with a similar mission related to Iraq's biological and chemical weapons programs and long-range missile delivery systems.[8]

Both the IAEA and UNSCOM were given carte blanche "anytime, anywhere" authority to search out and eliminate Iraq's WMD programs. From an inspector's perspective, this sounded idyllic. But it worked only because Iraq was a freshly defeated country, with no military recourse. No other country would have accepted such conditions.

The first IAEA inspection team, led by Chief Inspector Demetrius Perricos, landed in Baghdad on May 14, 1991, and headed directly for the Tuwaitha nuclear site. Aerial photographs had led the team to anticipate a scene of destruction, in the wake of the Gulf War. And indeed, every major building at Tuwaitha had received a direct hit from the bombing.

---

8 Iraq was known to have used chemical weapons during the 1980–1988 Iraq-Iran War.

The inspectors' first objective was to locate and secure the high-enriched uranium fuel designated for the two research reactors. The Iraqi technical experts appeared eager to assist. As it turned out, to the inspectors' surprise, the irradiated fuel had been moved at the height of the bombing, according to the Iraqis. They had reburied it in hastily constructed concrete pits, in featureless farmland in the nearby Garf al Naddaf district, to avoid the fuel being destroyed and radioactivity dispersed. With the Iraqis' assistance, the inspectors were readily able to locate and begin verifying nearly all the nuclear material in question, based on the declared prewar inventories.

However, achieving the second primary objective—to uncover any previously undeclared nuclear activities—would prove far less straightforward. It appeared that, beyond the destruction inflicted by the bombing, the Iraqis had done even more to dismantle the buildings. Some appeared to have been stripped of equipment. There were signs that operational records and other documentation had been burned. Verifying the purpose of the Tuwaitha facilities that had not been covered under previous IAEA inspections was difficult.

Similar observations were made at another site, north of Baghdad, Tarmiya, where nuclear activity was rumored. The Iraqis said the Tarmiya facilities were used to manufacture electrical transformers. But in the judgment of the IAEA team, this explanation did not match certain facts: for example, the massive electrical loads Tarmiya had required, and the volume and arrangement of electrical distribution equipment. When these discrepancies were pointed out, the Iraqi counterparts could not or would not offer plausible explanations.

Even during this first inspection, the challenge facing the Agency safeguards inspectors was beginning to take shape.

Here, again, it is important to correct a common misconception. IAEA inspectors are not detectives, nor are they security officers or police. They are accustomed to looking for and pointing out quantitative and qualitative discrepancies—including deliberate cover-ups—and they do not shrink from confronting the party under inspection with the evidence. But their style is respectful, whether the country being inspected is Canada or South Africa, Japan or the Netherlands—or, in this case,

Iraq. For my part, I firmly believe that this respectfulness, a hallmark of IAEA inspections, has repeatedly proven to be a key Agency asset.

Furthermore, the IAEA is not a spy agency. Our inspectors do not engage in espionage or use deception to get at the truth. We do not have access to the databases of police forces, Interpol, or national intelligence agencies, unless these organizations choose to make relevant information available. Nor do we provide the confidential results of our inspections to these agencies. The information is disseminated within the IAEA, on a need-to-know basis.

In the early 1990s, in Iraq, North Korea, and elsewhere, the relationships between the intelligence agencies and the international inspection organizations took on the look and feel of an awkward dance. In exchange for sharing their privileged information with the IAEA and UNSCOM, the intelligence agencies wanted as quid pro quo to have privileged access to the inspection results. It was perfectly clear why they might want this: the IAEA and UNSCOM inspectors had much greater on-the-ground access and were therefore able to make highly efficient use of the intelligence, uncovering and reporting the facts in a way that the intelligence agencies could not. But the IAEA would not agree to such an arrangement. The flow of information was, by necessity, one way: to maintain its integrity and legitimacy, the IAEA could not afford to pass privileged information as a favor to a national intelligence organization.

The Agency was adamant about its independence, which sometimes put it at odds with individual states. This was evident during the negotiation of Security Council Resolution 687, when the United States had tried to place UNSCOM in the driver's seat of the inspections, over the Agency. To me, the motives were transparent. UNSCOM was new; by necessity, it would be an ad hoc body, a subsidiary organ of the Security Council, whose major players would be able to exercise a good deal of influence over its operations. UNSCOM's inspectors were culled rapidly from national government agencies and laboratories, where the necessary skills (familiarity with biological and chemical toxins and with long-range missile technology) resided. UNSCOM would thus be easier to infiltrate than the IAEA, an established organization with independent nuclear expertise.

As the Agency's legal adviser at that time, I was in New York during the negotiation of the resolution. I had several meetings with Robert Gallucci, a sharp, smooth American diplomat and academic and future deputy executive director of UNSCOM. The IAEA tried hard to insist on its independence in handling the nuclear file. For the most part, we succeeded. Gallucci later admitted that there was some internal dis-agreement in certain U.S. government circles where great anxiety was expressed about whether the IAEA was up to the task. Others, by con-trast, worried that giving UNSCOM primary authority would damage the IAEA's credibility.[9] The compromise language in the resolution sounded quite mild: the IAEA was to accomplish its mission "with the assistance and cooperation of the Special Commission." But in Galluc-ci's view, the language ensured that UNSCOM would have its "camel's nose under the tent" of the IAEA.[10]

Of course it was important that the two agencies cooperate, particu-larly on logistics. Since many of the facilities we needed to inspect had been bombed, there were safety hazards associated with unexploded ordnance. UNSCOM had hired explosive ordnance disposal experts to accompany teams from both agencies. For its part, it had much to learn from the organization and discipline of the IAEA teams, who had been working together for years and, in some cases, were familiar with their Iraqi counterparts and Iraqi ways of doing business.

The personalities involved undoubtedly influenced the relationship between the agencies. Hans Blix, at that time Director General of the IAEA, was a former Swedish foreign minister. Rolf Ekeus, who was appointed as the director of UNSCOM, was also a Swedish diplomat. In foreign service terms, Blix outranked Ekeus, and he clearly did not appreciate receiving instructions from Ekeus in areas where UNSCOM had been given the lead. Nor did it help that UNSCOM was based in New York, where they received the bulk of the media attention, while the

---

9 "Reflections on Establishing and Implementing the Post–Gulf War Inspections of Iraq's Weapons of Mass Destruction Programs," transcript of an address by Robert Gallucci at the Institute for Science and International Security, June 14, 2001.
10 Gallucci, "Reflections" address.

IAEA was rather obscure at that time. Relations were eased, in part, by Maurizio Zifferero, a congenial Italian scientist who served as head of the IAEA's Iraq Action Team and who was effective at smoothing difficulties between the two organizations.

By the time of the second Iraq inspection, from June 22 to July 4, 1991, the stage was set for drama. An intelligence agency had shared reconnaissance photographs with the IAEA showing a surge of Iraqi activity immediately after the departure of the first inspection team, in an area just outside the Tuwaitha site. A number of large metallic discs had been unearthed from where they apparently had been buried and taken to a new location.

Information had surfaced also about an alleged enrichment program the Iraqis had been conducting in secret, through a technique called electromagnetic isotope separation, or EMIS. This method used a machine called a calutron: a type of mass spectrometer positioned between oversize electromagnets, invented at the University of California. The process is not very efficient, and it consumes enormous amounts of electricity. Specialists with insight into the calutron program of the Manhattan Project[11] had evaluated the IAEA inspectors' photographs and reports from the Tarmiya site and believed the evidence pointed to EMIS enrichment operations.

The Iraqis were continuing to deny that they had an undeclared uranium-enrichment program, so it was important to track down the equipment as evidence. Early on, the second inspection turned into a chase. The new location of the unearthed discs, which were suspected to be magnets for the EMIS process, was said to be a specific military camp. When the IAEA team arrived, as scheduled, they were denied access. Protests were made to the upper echelons of the Iraqi government, and three days later, access was authorized. By then, however, the equipment was gone.

---

11 The U.S.-led effort to develop the atomic bomb during World War II.

Three days after that, the team received word of the new location: another large military camp. This time a group of IAEA inspectors showed up without warning. Admission was again refused at the gate. But two members of the team climbed the outside ladder of an adjacent water tower; from the top, they could see a convoy of trucks moving off from the rear exit of the camp. Two other members of the team gave chase in a UN vehicle, weaving chaotically through local markets until they could find the proper highway. Their persistence was rewarded: when they found the convoy, they discovered close to a hundred vehicles loaded with what appeared to be nuclear equipment, much of it not even covered in the haste to escape. Catching the Iraqis in this blatant attempt at concealment was a significant breakthrough.

In early July, Blix and I made a trip to Baghdad. We were part of a high-level delegation put together by the UN secretary-general, Javier Pérez de Cuéllar. The delegation was headed by Ekeus, much to Blix's displeasure. Our goal was to pressure the Iraqi government to stop obstructing the inspection process and to come clean with a full declaration of its nuclear program.

Initially, the Iraqis continued their denial. The chairman of Iraq's Atomic Energy Committee, Dr. Human Abdel Khaliq Ghaffour,[12] urged Blix and me to accept what the Iraqis were saying. Riding in the car together, he swore to us—despite the mounting evidence to the contrary—that Iraq had conducted no undeclared enrichment activities. Iraq's nuclear program, he insisted, was entirely peaceful.

But international pressure was growing. The UN Security Council set a deadline, making clear they were ready to authorize additional action. Still another IAEA inspection team had arrived, ready to pursue new leads.

On July 7, the Iraqi authorities yielded, providing the IAEA with an extensive new list of equipment and its location. This new declaration covered not only EMIS enrichment, but also centrifuge and chemical enrichment activities and the reprocessing they had conducted to

12 Ghaffour would later become the Iraqi minister of higher education and scientific research.

separate out a few grams of plutonium. The declaration also gave a list of manufacturing and support facilities. It revealed the existence of almost four hundred tons of non-enriched uranium, some of which had been imported from Brazil, Niger, and Portugal, but which had never previously been declared to the IAEA.

One scene from that visit stands out vividly. Blix and I had accompanied members of the inspection team, including both UNSCOM and IAEA personnel, to a location in the middle of the desert. The Iraqis were showing us what they claimed was calutron equipment they had destroyed and buried, to avoid detection. We were well into the Iraqi summer, and temperatures were through the roof; it was clear that our inspectors, measuring and cataloguing these huge chunks of metal, faced a grueling task.

Rather abruptly, David Kay[13]—a former mid-level manager in the IAEA's Technical Cooperation Program, with little to no prior experience in safeguards inspection—decided that one of the senior Iraqi scientists should be interrogated on the spot. Raising his arm melodramatically, he shouted, "Let the investigation begin!" Blix and I were embarrassed. We promptly called Kay aside, to let him know that this was not the way we performed inspections. Our aim, in this case, was to work toward full cooperation on the part of the Iraqis. Intimidation and humiliation were not, in our view, useful tactics.

Kay's appointment as an IAEA safeguards inspector was at that time a mystery to me. He had, to my knowledge, no scientific or technological expertise; his educational background was in international affairs. I knew him as a bright, courteous, and articulate person. But once the IAEA assigned him to its Iraq Action Team, he seemed to undergo a metamorphosis. We had traveled together to New York at the time that the implementation of Resolution 687 was under discussion. Without consulting me or letting me know, Kay had scheduled his own meetings with U.S. officials, a sharp and noticeable departure from normal IAEA practice.

---

13 David Kay would later be appointed by President Bush, in 2003, to head the Iraq Survey Group.

In retrospect, it is quite possible that U.S. intelligence was working through Kay to pass along information, to be acted on by the IAEA's Iraq Action Team. His assignment to the IAEA team was initially for administrative and managerial purposes, yet somehow he was asked to lead two of the more crucial inspections. Whether Blix or Zifferero knew of any ties Kay may have had to U.S. intelligence I do not know.

Kay's inspection style—which even Robert Gallucci referred to as that of a "cowboy"[14]—was fortunately uncommon among the IAEA inspectorate, but the case was different with UNSCOM. On the same trip to the desert, I witnessed a senior Iraqi scientist weeping in frustration at the treatment he was receiving from an UNSCOM inspector who had accused him publicly of lying. Later, on the bus ride back from the desert, I took a look around. The bus was full of Americans. Many of them had come from U.S. national labs. They were highly qualified technically, but they had no clue about how to conduct international inspections or, for that matter, about the nuances of how to behave in different cultures. From their brash conversation, it was clear they believed that, having come to a defeated country, they had free rein to behave as they pleased.

I spoke to some of the people sitting next to me on the bus. I explained the basics of the IAEA's approach: professionalism marked by tenacity and respect. I noted that this professionalism was characteristic of our inspectors and had been developed over years of experience. I was critical of UNSCOM's abrasive behavior.

The result was stunning. A distorted version of the conversation was passed along and gained traction. Eventually, it made its way into the *New Yorker*, as a purportedly factual account in an article by Gary Milhollin, the director of the Wisconsin Project on Nuclear Arms Control:

> ElBaradei, fresh on the scene, embodied the tradition of the IAEA. Before an incredulous group of inspectors, he declared, as Kay recalls it, "The Iraqis do not have a uranium enrichment program. I know so,

---

14 Gallucci, "Reflections" address.

because they are my friends and they have told me that they don't."
ElBaradei was wrong, of course. But he was following the line laid down
by his IAEA superiors.[15]

I had said no such thing. The Iraqis had already begun to admit to
their work with calutrons, and we had just been returning from seeing
what they claimed were buried calutron components. Evidence of Iraq's
enrichment-related components and facilities was beginning to show up
from multiple angles. I would have to have been rather thickheaded to
insist that these programs did not exist. But this did not affect what was
published or the spin-off stories that alleged IAEA incompetence.

Some UNSCOM inspectors would continue to use their authority
excessively, without regard for religious and cultural sensitivities. They
barged into mosques and churches, without evidence, to inspect for concealed WMDs. They inspected on local religious holidays, when there
was no urgency to do so. They later insisted on inspecting Saddam Hussein's palaces, not because of solid intelligence leads, but apparently just
to show that they could. I sometimes wondered how they would have felt
if the tables had been turned.

Although the majority of Iraqis loathed Saddam Hussein for his ruth-
less governing style, they saw these actions—as did much of the Arab
world—as an affront to Iraqi dignity and a humiliation. Far from encouraging cooperation in Iraq, the inspectors' invasive "cowboy" behavior
naturally caused a buildup of resentment on the part of the Iraqis, particularly since these arbitrary intrusions never yielded any results.

As the summer of 1991 wore on, we still had no hard evidence of Iraqi
nuclear weapons intentions. That Iraq had concealed their uranium
enrichment and plutonium separation activities was clear. But they continued to claim that their program was peaceful.

The turning point came in late September, during the IAEA's sixth
inspection. Once again, useful intelligence information had been passed
along, this time pinpointing two buildings in the center of Baghdad,

---

15 "The Iraqi Bomb," *New Yorker,* February 1, 1993.

offices of the Ministry of Industry and Military Industrialization. A security lapse on the part of the Iraqis had left a sizable cache of records in these buildings. When the inspectors showed up unannounced, they were able to view, and take possession of, many of these documents.

The Iraqis refused to let the team leave the site with the papers, however. The inspectors, led by David Kay of the IAEA and Robert Gallucci of UNSCOM, refused to give in, camping out in the parking lot. The standoff lasted three days and nights and was broadcast on live television. The scene became famous as the "parking lot" confrontation.

In the end, the Iraqis yielded. The seized documentation included a progress report that outlined the Iraqi efforts in weapons development. While it showed them to be still a year or two away from constructing a nuclear weapon, it demonstrated clearly the intent of the Iraqi government and proved that this aspect of their nuclear program was extensive, well organized, and well funded.

Later in the year, when Kay received an Agency award, the Iraqi ambassador to the IAEA, Dr. Rahim al-Kital, submitted a formal complaint to Blix. The complaint alleged a range of specific actions—for example, throwing official documents on the floor and treading on them, or threatening to call in U.S. warplanes. According to al-Kital's memo, members of the inspection team were said to have broken down fences, cut telephone lines, and "appeared nude in the yard of the building in full view of the surrounding residential apartments."[16]

These accusations were never corroborated. But it was clear that Kay and others on the team believed they needed to be aggressive to get the Iraqis to cooperate. While in the case of the parking lot confrontation, it could be argued that a certain degree of intimidation was warranted, and effective, in general I believe that the use of such tactics is ultimately counterproductive. An aggressive, overbearing approach destroys

---

16 Robert Gallucci's description of this particular inspection makes it clear that, while it had to be an IAEA-led inspection, only three of the forty-two team members were IAEA inspectors. The others included individuals with "special skills," whose expertise was not in nuclear science or WMD at all; the implication is that they were assigned to the team to ensure the documents would be retrieved by whatever means needed. As Gallucci said, "The team was very, very special." See Gallucci, "Reflections" address.

cooperation in the long run. Irrespective of its motive, the team's behavior left an enduring impression, particularly in Iraq and in the Muslim world. The Iraqis, having just lost a war, had no choice but to accept these behaviors.

However, the most damaging action was the decision of Kay and Gallucci to send the critical papers to the U.S. State Department before either the IAEA or UNSCOM had received them. Gallucci insisted that they did so because that line of communication was "more reliable."[17] But the result hurt the reputation of both the IAEA and UNSCOM, not only in the eyes of the Iraqis, who accused the Agency of turning into "an intelligence body in a scientific guise under the tutelage of the United States and its allies," but also throughout the international community. Despite broad international support for the inspections, Member States were paying close attention to how the inspections were being conducted, and many were very sensitive to any implication that the international inspectors were in cahoots with U.S. or other national intelligence agencies. This perception would continue to plague UNSCOM, in particular, and eventually would lead to its downfall.

The ensuing series of Iraq nuclear inspections ran along three parallel tracks. One sought to flesh out our understanding of the weapons aspects of Iraq's nuclear program, including identification of intended high-explosive test sites. A second track began preparing for the removal of high-enriched uranium from Iraq.[18] A third track focused on the destruction of the accumulated enrichment equipment. Centrifuge rotors were crushed. Magnets were cut into pieces using specialized plasma cutting tools. Devices used to handle nuclear material, such as hot cells and glove boxes, were rendered useless with the severing of control cables and the filling of the containers with cement.

After less than a year on the ground, the fulfillment of the IAEA

---

17 According to Gallucci, "I was not confident about my interlocutor in New York, so I decided to go through the State Department." Gallucci, "Reflections" address.

18 The removal from Iraq of the clandestinely produced six grams of plutonium had already been arranged as part of the fifth IAEA inspection, in mid-September.

mandate in Iraq under Resolution 687 was well under way. The origins of Saddam Hussein's nuclear weapons program had become clear—as had, in large part, the motivations. The clandestine aspects of the program had begun in 1982, shortly after Israel's 1981 bombing of Iraq's research reactor at Osirak, which was under IAEA safeguards before it started operation. Whatever prior inclination Hussein and his colleagues might have had to pursue WMD had only been intensified by the humiliation of that experience. The perceived security imbalance in the region, with Israel as the only possessor of nuclear weapons, was starkly highlighted. The Security Council's condemnation of Israel's action as a clear violation of international law had resulted in no follow-up whatsoever. Israel merely ignored the council's demands that it provide Iraq with compensation and that Israel place its own nuclear facilities under IAEA safeguards. So Saddam Hussein had taken it upon himself to address the problem. We were witnessing the result.[19]

In the aftermath of the discovery of Iraq's clandestine nuclear program, I made a couple of visits to Washington, meeting with many people from Congress and the executive branch. The question on everyone's mind was why, over the years, had the IAEA missed the buildup of Iraq's undeclared nuclear program. I was candid about the flaws in the system. I emphasized the Agency's need for additional legal authority. The time was ripe. Nobody could argue that the NPT safeguards system was working properly. Iraq's program had been uncovered only after a military defeat.

Back in Vienna, at the IAEA Secretariat, we had begun work on the concept of a Model Additional Protocol to make the Agency's in-country verification authority more robust and explicit. As conceived, the

19 Saddam Hussein had long been viewed as an asset by the United States, Europe, and the Arab States, who had encouraged, supported, and financed his 1980–1988 war with Iran, as a way to "contain the Iranian revolution." This of course had added to Iran's distrust and resentment of the West, and is viewed by many as having been the genesis of the Iranian nuclear program, following Iraq's use of chemical weapons during the Iran-Iraq War.

Additional Protocol would be an add-on to the safeguards agreement each NPT member country was required to make with the IAEA.

It was a complex endeavor: a mix of technical, legal, and policy considerations. A frequent focus of discussion was how much inspection Member States would tolerate. This was not a new question. At the time of negotiating the NPT, a key sticking point had been the unwillingness of countries to give the IAEA too much oversight authority.[20] The deliberate deception carried out by Iraq had made clear that conducting international safeguards by "honor code" was no longer adequate; nor was it enough to inspect only what a country declared; nor was the IAEA authority sufficient. But these realities, while widely recognized, gave us no guarantee that Member States would subject themselves to more intrusive oversight.

Unfortunately, the process of developing the Model Additional Protocol led to a disagreement between Hans Blix and me. I argued for the involvement of Member States. Blix favored keeping the development of the protocol in the hands of the Secretariat. We had the necessary expertise, he argued. The IAEA staff should write the draft, bring it for consideration to the Board of Governors—comprised of representatives of thirty-five Member States—and continue a review and revision process until it was approved. Blix believed that putting the initial drafting in the hands of Member States meant that the protocol would go nowhere.

It soon became apparent that Blix's approach was not working. In order to gain Member State buy-in for the Additional Protocol concept, they needed to be involved in its creation. I proposed to Blix that we create a working group, with Board member involvement. Blix was completely resistant to the idea.

A number of Member States began to see their exclusion as a lack of openness on the part of the IAEA in developing what would clearly become a critical and influential policy mechanism. Representatives from a group of ten Western countries, a group we referred to as the "white

---

20 The focus of IAEA verification at the time was large industrial countries, such as Japan, Germany, Italy, and Canada, since most developing countries did not have significant nuclear infrastructure.

angels" because of their staunch support for nonproliferation, came to see me. They asked me to tell Blix to let go of the Secretariat's "hold" on the Additional Protocol and to allow the Board to get engaged. Of course I spoke to Blix about it, and of course he did not appreciate that they had not come to him directly.

This rather trivial incident marked the beginning of palpable tensions that would continue between the two of us. Perhaps he thought that I was working behind his back. In any case, it was unfortunate—especially since it had been Blix who had first recruited me to work for the Agency and under whom I quickly moved through the ranks from legal adviser to assistant director general for external relations.

The struggle continued behind closed doors. Eventually, the chairman of the Board at that time, Canadian ambassador Peter Walker, simply informed Blix that he was taking over the task and asked for the Secretariat's support. Richard Hooper, a director in the Safeguards Department who was quite adept on safeguards concepts, was made the lead technical person. I was made the lead on legal and policy issues. The Board chairman also chaired the working group. Blix did not attend any of the sessions. It was a long and complicated exercise, with many governments on the defensive. The toughest battles were political; success was in large part due to deft diplomacy by a number of key players.

Finally, on May 13, 1997, the Model Additional Protocol was adopted by the IAEA Board of Governors. It was a breakthrough legal instrument that would strengthen the effectiveness of the NPT safeguards system. So what had changed? In countries that accepted the Additional Protocol, IAEA inspectors had more freedom on the ground, with more access to information and sites, and could now search more effectively for undeclared nuclear material and facilities. In the past, the IAEA could theoretically invoke the right to look for undeclared material and facilities through a "special inspection" mechanism. But special inspections were arduous to invoke and had almost never been used. The Additional Protocol enabled greater access as a routine matter.

The adoption of the Model Additional Protocol, a major milestone in the history of nuclear safeguards, had the potential to effect great change. For countries that had only a safeguards agreement in place, the

IAEA was expected to provide assurance that declared nuclear material and facilities had not been diverted for non-peaceful purposes. But for those that brought an Additional Protocol into force, the IAEA could provide, in addition, the equally important assurance about the absence of *undeclared* nuclear material and facilities.

There was only one catch: whereas the safeguards agreement was compulsory for NPT members, the Additional Protocol was a voluntary mechanism. It remains so today. NPT members are not obliged to accept it, whatever the amount of prodding by the IAEA or from fellow Member States.

Here lies another major tripping point in the public understanding of the IAEA's role. The Agency is, in a sense, at the mercy of those it oversees. It can exercise only the authority it is given. When I began traveling in Arab countries as the IAEA Director General, for example, it was common for me to take strong criticism for the IAEA's failure to "do something" about Israel's nuclear program. I could explain as often as I liked that we had no authority to inspect Israel's facilities: Israel, while a member of the IAEA, has never signed the NPT, much less concluded a comprehensive safeguards agreement with the IAEA.[21] The aggravated Arab public, however, couldn't have cared less; as far as they were concerned, we were biased and shirking our responsibility.

In fact, if the general public fully understood the continuing unevenness of the IAEA's authority, I believe there would be even greater concern. The challenge is how to raise that public awareness.

Consider the present circumstance. At the end of 2010, thirteen years after the introduction of the Model Additional Protocol, many NPT member countries have not even brought into force their required comprehensive safeguards agreements with the IAEA.[22] And out of 189

---

21 This is often a point of confusion. By joining the IAEA (becoming a "Member State"), a country pledges to uphold the principles of the IAEA statute and thus gains access to proliferations discussions. However, this does not obligate that country to accept IAEA verification of its nuclear material and facilities. That legal obligation comes with joining the Nuclear Non-Proliferation Treaty and, pursuant to the treaty, concluding a comprehensive safeguards agreement with the IAEA.

22 While it is compulsory for countries party to the NPT to conclude safeguards agreements with the IAEA, the Agency has no power to penalize those who fail to do so.

members of the NPT, just 103 countries so far have brought an Additional Protocol into force. For the large number of countries remaining, when it comes to providing the international community with the assurance it desires, the IAEA's hands remain tied.

Could another Saddam Hussein be out there, undetected, busily at work on clandestine nukes? The answer is that, for those countries that have not accepted the Additional Protocol, we really don't know.

Throughout the mid-1990s, the IAEA and UNSCOM continued their work in Iraq. All weapons-usable nuclear material was shipped out of the country, and all other nuclear material—roughly five hundred tons of natural uranium in various forms, and nearly two tons of low-enriched uranium dioxide—was verified to be under IAEA control. Similar steps were taken with biological and chemical weapons stocks.

By October 1997, the IAEA had completed a series of thirty major inspection campaigns in Iraq. Roughly five hundred site inspections had been completed, involving more than five thousand person days of inspector time. IAEA inspectors had supervised the destruction of more than fifty thousand square meters of nuclear facilities, approximately two thousand fuel cycle or weapons-related items, and more than six hundred metric tons of special alloys. As an example, the facilities at Al-Atheer, designed for nuclear weapons development, testing, and production, had been destroyed by explosive demolition under IAEA and UNSCOM supervision. All uranium enrichment equipment and facilities had been dismantled.

Gradually, as the work mandated under Resolution 687 was completed, the focus of both agencies had shifted away from dismantlement of equipment and removal of material and toward monitoring and verification. The IAEA's task of eliminating Iraq's nuclear program under Resolution 687 was essentially complete. But the Americans, acting through the State Department and other parts of the administration, urged the IAEA not to report this conclusion to the Security Council. They wanted the pressure on Saddam Hussein to continue unabated.

To this end, the United States suggested that the IAEA should wait to report the completion of its work until UNSCOM could do the same. Of course there was no logic to this—as Blix argued in his discussions with the United States. He said they should think of UNSCOM and the IAEA as two horses running, and that there was nothing wrong with one reaching the finish line before the other.

Blix made his final report to the Security Council as the outgoing Director General in October 1997. He felt that since he was leaving, he would have an easier time resisting pressure from the United States, and he reported to the council that the IAEA had pretty much completed the "disarmament phase" in Iraq and had moved to the next phase. The report stated that the Agency was now dedicating most of its resources in Iraq to "ongoing monitoring and verification," with only a few minor disarmament issues remaining.

The UNSCOM situation was considerably more complicated. From the outset of the Iraq inspections, the IAEA and UNSCOM had diverged sharply in both their composition and their styles of inspection. But a more disturbing difference emerged later in the 1990s. The Iraqis charged that UNSCOM was a de facto spy agency of U.S. and Israeli intelligence, trying to collect information outside its mandate—in effect, using WMD disarmament as a cloak under which to gather and pass along information regarding conventional weaponry and military capabilities, which Western governments could then use to develop military targets.

These charges from Baghdad intensified after Richard Butler, an experienced arms control diplomat from the Australian Foreign Service, took over from Rolf Ekeus as director of UNSCOM in 1997. Butler, Scott Ritter, one of the chief inspectors, and other UNSCOM officials were specifically accused by the Iraqis of cooperating with the CIA to spy on Saddam Hussein's military apparatus. Not only were accusations coming from Iraq, but Butler and Ritter themselves began to take potshots at each other.

Two years later, both the *Washington Post* and the *Boston Globe* wrote that members of UNSCOM had cooperated with a U.S. electronic eavesdropping operation that allowed intelligence agents to monitor military communications in Iraq.[23] And Scott Ritter himself admitted how much UNSCOM was being manipulated.[24] In 2002, in an interview with Fox News, he said:

> Richard Butler allowed the United States to use the United Nations weapons-inspection process as a Trojan horse to insert intelligence capabilities into Iraq, which were not approved by the United Nations and which did not facilitate the disarmament process, but were instead focused on the security of Saddam Hussein and military targets. . . . Richard Butler facilitated American espionage in Iraq. Richard Butler facilitated American manipulation of the inspection process. . . . On four occasions, from March 1998 until my resignation in August 1998, I wrote Richard Butler a memorandum saying, "Boss, if you continue down this path you are facilitating espionage. This is not what we're about and you can't let this happen." He received this memorandum and disregarded my warning and ultimately, in the end, let's ask ourselves why the inspectors aren't in Iraq today.

Butler strongly denied these accusations, saying that Ritter's claim "that I sold the store to the CIA is dramatically untrue." Butler said he had actually scaled back on the degree to which UNSCOM used intelligence, because of concerns about reputation and the need to protect "the independence of multilateral disarmament activities." He admitted that UNSCOM members had, on occasion, reported back to their home governments, but he categorically denied that UNSCOM had been dominated by the United States, calling Ritter's charges "quintessentially ludicrous."[25]

What seems clear is that Butler had very decided preconceptions about Iraq and about the intentions of Saddam Hussein's government.

---

23 Barton Gellman, "U.S. Spied on Iraq Via U.N.," *Washington Post*, March 2, 1999. A similar story appeared in the *Boston Globe*.

24 Ritter would later become known for his criticism of U.S. foreign policy. In March 2003, he would argue publicly that Iraq possessed no significant WMDs.

25 "The Lessons and Legacy of UNSCOM: An Interview with Ambassador Richard Butler," *Arms Control Today* 29, no. 4 (June 1999).

Before Rolf Ekeus left his post in 1997 as the first director of UNSCOM, he had reported that most of the UNSCOM mandate—as it related to disarming Iraq of its chemical and biological weapons—was near completion.[26] Richard Butler disagreed. He routinely insisted that Iraq had undisclosed WMDs. His report to the Security Council on December 15, 1998, presented a harsh picture of Iraq's lack of cooperation. It was perceived by many as imbalanced and unfair.

Butler's report became the justification for the 1998 U.S. bombing campaign known as Operation Desert Fox. Notably, the United States suggested that UNSCOM withdraw its inspectors, for safety considerations, on the very same day that Butler delivered his report—a not-so-subtle indication that the United States knew what it contained.[27] Butler gave his order to withdraw the UNSCOM inspectors on December 15, at midnight New York time. By the time the diplomats woke up in the morning, the withdrawal of the inspectors was a fait accompli.

At this point, I had taken over from Hans Blix as the IAEA Director General. Early on the morning of December 16, Vienna time, I was woken by a call from John Ritch, the highly regarded U.S. ambassador to the IAEA. Ritch told me of his government's advice to withdraw the IAEA and UNSCOM inspectors and noted that Butler had already moved to take that advice. Because the IAEA relied on UNSCOM for logistical support, we really had no option but to leave.

After talking to Ritch, I called the UN secretary-general, Kofi Annan, who was in Morocco, waking him up to discuss Butler's action. I was shocked to learn that Annan was not aware of the decision.

---

26 S/1997/301, report by the executive chairman of UNSCOM, April 11, 1997. In his conclusions to this report, Ekeus wrote, "The accumulated effect of the work that has been accomplished over six years since the ceasefire went into effect, between Iraq and the Coalition, is such that not much is unknown about Iraq's retained proscribed weapons capabilities." Ekeus wrote further that the efforts from October 1996 to early 1997 were focused on getting the "major outstanding issues to a manageable quantity" and cited overall satisfaction with missile and chemical weapons issues. He noted that Iraq's presentation in the biological weapons area remained "rather chaotic."

27 In Butler's book *Saddam Defiant: The Threat of Weapons of Mass Destruction, and the Crisis of Global Security* (New York: Weidenfeld and Nicolson, 2000), he says it was U.S. ambassador Peter Burleigh, acting on instructions from Washington, who suggested that Butler pull the UNSCOM team from Iraq in order to protect them from the forthcoming U.S. and British air strikes (p. 224).

The inspectors left that day. The four-day bombing campaign commenced immediately, reportedly targeting various Iraqi military sites, including weapons R&D installations. Officially, the bombing was characterized as a response to Iraq's continued failure to comply with UN Security Council resolutions and its interference with the work of the UN inspectors.

UNSCOM was discredited. The Butler report was decried as patently unfair. The Chinese, French, and Russian governments were angered by the undue U.S. influence on UNSCOM as an international inspection body. UNSCOM was no longer trusted to serve the international community as a credible representative of the United Nations.

In January 1999, I wrote a non-paper[28] entitled "Arms Inspections in Iraq" for the Security Council, laying out the parameters of how to restore and maintain the integrity and credibility of a WMD verification system. I spelled out the need to decouple the inspection body from the Security Council, to avoid politicization. I recommended staffing the organization with international civil servants, rather than relying on "experts" on detail from their governments, who might put their national loyalties first. I recommended clearer rules for the inspections, with more defined technical objectives. I explained the importance of a geographically diverse technical inspection staff. And I explicitly called for the organization to respect the religious and cultural sensitivities of the inspected country, on which UNSCOM in many cases had trampled in Iraq.

Kofi Annan congratulated me on the non-paper, as did the Russians and others. The U.S. State Department, however, was furious that I had not consulted with them before circulating it. John Ritch came to warn me that some U.S. officials were threatening to ask William Safire, Charles Krauthammer, and other conservative columnists to launch an attack on my credibility.

With regard to Iraq, though, UNSCOM's standing no longer mattered. The damage had been done. Within the year, the Special Commission

---

28 In diplomatic parlance, a non-paper is a written proposal or set of ideas put forward informally, without commitment and often without formal attribution, as a way of engendering discussion or suggesting a basis for negotiation.

was dismantled by the Security Council, to be replaced by UNMOVIC,[29] a new agency with different rules of operation. But following Desert Fox, Saddam Hussein would not agree to readmit the IAEA and UN inspectors for four years. That absence laid the groundwork for suspicion that Saddam Hussein was reconstituting his WMD programs—which, in turn, would form the pretext for another war.

Although the IAEA's successful dismantling of Iraq's nuclear program silenced many of its critics and detractors and was a testimony to the Agency's effectiveness, from an Iraqi standpoint, the inspection process had culminated in Desert Fox, sending them a harsh message. To them, the Americans were not interested in the elimination of Iraq's nuclear program. The Iraqis understood that there would be no light at the end of the tunnel, no matter what they did. Desert Fox convinced some that the goal was not WMD disarmament, but rather regime change. In any case, their distrust of the inspection process only grew.

Four years later, when the inspections resumed, we saw this bleak sentiment expressed in the dispirited eyes and cynical statements of our Iraqi counterparts.

---

29 United Nations Monitoring, Verification and Inspection Commission, created by Security Council Resolution 1284 in December 1999.

2

NORTH KOREA, 1992–2002

The Case of the Missing Plutonium

When I arrived in Pyongyang, North Korea, on December 4, 1992, my first thought was to be grateful that the flight had landed safely. My colleagues and I had traveled from Beijing to Pyongyang on Air Koryo, the North Korean airline, our aircraft an aging Soviet model. It hadn't escaped my notice that, before departure, the pilot had checked the air pressure by kicking the tires with his foot.

Our handlers bundled us into government cars—old 200-series Volvos—and we headed into the city. It was midafternoon on a Friday. We were told that the basic mode of transportation for the common person was walking; there was a subway, but it did not connect the whole city, and most people were too poor to afford bicycles. We were permitted to walk about, but we saw few people on the streets. Pyongyang was a ghost town. The overall feeling of the place was eerie, the public spaces dominated by huge statues of Kim Il Sung, the "Great Leader" (and father of the current "Dear Leader," Kim Jong Il). On Saturday morning, we were told, every North Korean official would be attending the party headquarters for "education."

They put us up at the Hotel Koryo, the best hotel in town. Creature comforts were limited; the hotel was excessively expensive for what it offered. There was little to no presence of electrical lighting. The food was very basic, with few choices: noodles, meat, and kimchee; no fruit or salad. If you wanted an orange, you could get it only at the hotel's tax-free shop, paying with hard currency. And despite it being winter, the heating at the hotel was at a minimum. We had to pile on layers during the night.

In my room, I turned on the television. It was an old black-and-white model. The only channels I could get were showing films about World War II and the Korean War, with a heavy emphasis on the suffering and killing of North Koreans at the hands of the Americans and their allies.

The next evening, our hosts took us to the opera for an evening of entertainment. It was a series of staged patriotic songs. Each one ended with the Korean soldiers killing their American counterparts. It reminded me of a similar opera I had attended in Beijing in 1977, just after the end of the Cultural Revolution.

This 1992 visit to Pyongyang was a result of serious concerns regarding North Korea's nuclear program. North Korea had signed the Nuclear Non-Proliferation Treaty in 1985, but it had taken seven years to complete its obligatory comprehensive safeguards agreement with the Agency enabling the IAEA to verify the country's nuclear program. The safeguards agreement had gone into effect in April 1992. On May 4, North Korea had, as required, submitted its initial declaration of nuclear materials to the IAEA. According to the declaration, North Korea had seven sites and about ninety grams of plutonium subject to IAEA inspection. As in every safeguards agreement, the Agency was now charged with verifying that these nuclear facilities and materials were intended exclusively for peaceful purposes.

But by midsummer, questions had begun to emerge. According to North Korea, the plutonium had resulted from a single reprocessing of defective fuel rods in 1989. Of the ninety grams of plutonium produced, sixty grams were verified by the Agency during its first inspection. The North Koreans claimed that the remaining thirty grams had not been successfully extracted and were present in the waste. But the analysis of environmental samples taken by the IAEA inspectors said otherwise.

The root of the discrepancy was this: the composition of the plutonium evident in the waste samples did not match with the plutonium product presented for verification. Blix, with his customary skill in using metaphors, likened the situation to finding a pair of gloves that did not match. From a technical point of view, this meant two things. First, there had to be another collection of waste, somewhere, that matched the verified product. Second, there had to be a stash of additional plutonium somewhere that we had not seen. A key problem was that we didn't know what kind of quantity of "additional" plutonium we were looking for— grams or kilograms.

The North Koreans were clearly surprised by the sophistication of the Agency's analysis. Our environmental sampling techniques had helped us to determine not only the correctness of the North Korean declaration but also whether it was complete.

Their story began to change. North Korea acknowledged that they had performed "one small experiment," to which they attributed the mismatch shown by the IAEA analysis. But this explanation didn't fit technically. The reactor in question, a five-megawatt experimental Magnox reactor of Soviet design, had begun operation in August 1985. From their forensic study of the samples, Agency experts were able to determine that the reprocessing of fuel from the reactor to separate plutonium had taken place over a longer duration and with more complexity than the North Koreans were admitting. The inspectors concluded that, during the seven years of the reactor's operation, North Korea had probably reprocessed spent fuel on as many as three to four occasions, and certainly more than the "one small experiment" they were suggesting.

A second area of discrepancy had to do with the concealment of nuclear facilities. The Magnox reactor was located at Yongbyon, a site about one hundred kilometers north of Pyongyang, a 2.5-to-3.5-hour drive through villages, depending on the weather. The Agency was aware of a nuclear waste storage facility at the same site, referred to as Building 500. In addition, we had seen a series of satellite photos, provided by the United States, that showed the progressive concealment of a two-story building believed to be an additional nuclear waste facility. The North Koreans had ultimately placed the entire facility underground, covering it and planting the area with trees. Two high-explosive test sites also had been identified, one near the reactor at Yongbyon and another at a site twenty kilometers away.

In late August 1992, with anxiety mounting about the inadequate answers the North Koreans were providing, another inspection was conducted. Once again, the result was a mixture of cooperation and obfuscation.

The visit was coordinated by military personnel, much of it handled personally by the commandant of Yongbyon. The North Koreans seemed to be testing the inspectors, to see how much they knew. Our initial request to inspect the two waste sites and high-explosive test sites was met with a flat refusal; then the North Koreans relented and agreed to allow the inspectors to visit the Building 500 waste site as well as the high-explosive test sites. Full cooperation, however, proved elusive. On one occasion the handlers took the inspectors to the wrong location, and then appeared upset when the inspectors pointed out the error. In the end, our North Korean counterparts denied even the existence of the second waste location, insisting that it was only military bunkers and refusing access to the Agency inspectors.

During September and late October, with tensions rising, the IAEA held a number of meetings at its headquarters in Vienna with the North Korean minister of atomic energy, Choe Hak Gun, and the North Korean delegation. Each time the IAEA gave North Korea numbers that reflected the Agency's analysis, the North Koreans would adjust their declaration accordingly. However, they still did not come up with what we considered a complete and correct declaration.

Finally, Blix decided to send me on a mission to Pyongyang, to lay out the discrepancies, press the North Koreans to be fully transparent, and urge them to bring a new, accurate declaration of their nuclear program to the IAEA, including the nuclear material and facilities we believed they had not yet revealed. In short, we were asking them to uphold their obligations under their safeguards agreement with the Agency; otherwise, we would have to call for a "special inspection," the Agency's tool of last resort to get access to suspect sites.

Thus the December 1992 visit was not exactly a friendly call; we had our work cut out for us. By that time, I had moved into the position of the IAEA's director of external relations. I was accompanied by Sven Thorstensen, the Norwegian safeguards director responsible for North Korea, and Olli Heinonen, a Finn who worked for Sven at the time and who had been heavily involved in the initial inspections.

The discussions were torturous. The North Koreans proved to be formidable negotiators. There was a good cop/bad cop division of labor among the members of their delegation. Some accused us of being U.S. agents, and when I reacted sharply to this, they mumbled an apology. Others took a softer approach, and when that didn't work, they yielded once again to their harsher colleagues. This routine was repeated on various topics. In the meantime, the North Korean media began attacking Blix and me, and the Agency as a whole, accusing us of being stooges for the Americans.

This continued for three grueling days. Each night, I called Blix from the hotel phone to tell him we were not making progress; and he answered that we needed to request a special inspection. We were certain that our hosts were eavesdropping on our conversations, so we discussed a special inspection as a way to put pressure on them.

By the final evening, it was clear that our visit had failed to achieve a breakthrough. We were invited to dinner with Deputy Foreign Minister Kang Sok Ju, where the North Koreans served us each a hamburger topped with a fried egg.

At the outset of the conversation, I asked the deputy foreign minister a question that was meant to be more conversational than provocative: "Why is it that your country has so much resentment toward the United States?"

The response was anything but casual. It turned into a forty-five-minute harangue, an extended history of North Korean relations with the United States dating back to the arrival of the USS *General Sherman* on the Korean Peninsula in the mid-1800s. The ship had steamed up the Taedong River to the outskirts of Pyongyang. In what was viewed as a heroic victory against foreign invaders, the locals burned the ship and killed all its crew. The great-grandfather of North Korea's Great Leader Kim Il Sung had reportedly participated in that attack.

And so it went: while our food sat before us, untouched, the deputy foreign minister recounted every U.S.–North Korean interaction since that time. When he finally paused, I asked him, out of courtesy, a simple follow-up question. He continued for another fifteen minutes. The obsession was clear: North Korea was deeply entangled in a long-running struggle with the United States, certain that the Americans were bent on trying to change the regime.

At the end of this exchange, I looked down. Our fried eggs had turned a questionable shade of gray. But diplomacy offered little choice. We began to eat.

Back in Vienna, after further consultation, Blix made the decision to request a special inspection. This was an extremely rare move on the part of the Agency. It had been done only once before, in Romania, shortly after the fall of Nicolae Ceaușescu, when the new Romanian regime had itself requested a special inspection in an effort to further discredit the former Communist president.[1] In the case of North Korea, calling for a special inspection of the disputed waste facility would send a clear signal that the IAEA was upping the ante.

As expected, the North Koreans refused. They insisted they would not provide the Agency with the requested access.

The IAEA Board of Governors called for a special session. The event was memorable, a closed-door session with restricted attendance. The Agency's concerns about North Korea's nuclear program were presented in three parts: first, the technical background, in terms of the discrepancies as observed and analyzed; second, the arguments justifying additional access; and third, the evidence of concealment.

The concealment portion involved the presentation of satellite imag-

---

1 Following Ceaușescu's ouster, the new government requested a special inspection to show that, under Ceaușescu's rule, Romania had reprocessed one hundred milligrams of plutonium without informing the IAEA.

ery supplied by U.S. intelligence. Until this point, the satellite imagery
of North Korea's facilities had been made available to us only during
briefings at the U.S. Mission, with a security officer, an elderly chap,
stationed at the door of the briefing room—presumably to ensure that
the IAEA inspectors would not run off with the images. The United
States had altered the resolution of the images somewhat, in order to
disguise their actual surveillance capability. Still, the windows of the
buildings could clearly be discerned.

This was the first time in the history of the IAEA that the Secretariat
had shared information supplied by Member State intelligence in a
Board setting. Member States had historically been very uneasy about
the Agency's use of any information obtained through national intelligence agencies. The case of Iraq was an exception, but the Iraq inspections had been conducted under the extraordinary mandate of Security
Council Resolution 687. This Board meeting on North Korea thus served
as a quiet milestone: in subsequent years, referring to the use of intelligence would become much more routine.

Five weeks later, a Board resolution was proposed to refer the North
Korean noncompliance to the UN Security Council. The response from
Pyongyang was swift and decisive. Kim Il Sung's regime issued terse
edicts that restricted the Agency's inspections, making it nearly impossible to investigate further the history of their nuclear program. However, North Korea remained in the NPT, and the Agency maintained its
ability at least to verify North Korea's declared nuclear material.

Possibly this opening remained because the Security Council did not
take forceful action. China, with its emphasis on dialogue and restraint,
refused to endorse certain steps, such as the imposition of sanctions or
the adoption of a resolution demanding that North Korea agree not to
make nuclear weapons and not to withdraw from the NPT. Because of
China's opposition, the resolution that was finally adopted "called on"
but did not "require" North Korea to permit additional IAEA inspections. Resolution 825 was approved in May 1993, with China and Pakistan abstaining.

A stalemate now set in and continued through most of 1993. IAEA
inspectors had to negotiate every inspection, even when merely servicing

the Agency's monitoring cameras and checking the film. Finally, in the spring of 1994, the situation came to a head. North Korea announced that they would begin removing the entire core of the reactor at Yongbyon—a total of eight thousand rods of spent fuel—for storage and potential reprocessing. This was a critical moment. By taking a specific array of samples at this stage, Agency inspectors would be able to verify the history of the reactor's operation. The key question was whether this was still the original reactor core or whether an earlier core had at some point been removed and replaced but not reported to the IAEA. Since reactor operation produces plutonium, an unreported core of spent reactor fuel could already have been reprocessed in secret to separate the plutonium. By analyzing the material in these samples, the IAEA would be able to determine the amount of spent fuel (and by extension, the amount of plutonium) available to North Korea for possible diversion to weapons.

The North Koreans were uncooperative, at one point discharging so much fuel that the IAEA lost the continuity of this history. Once again, this confrontation generated a report to the IAEA Board; once again, the Board debate led to a report to the Security Council. This time the Board's resolution was harsher: in particular, it ordered cutbacks to the technical cooperation the Agency had traditionally given North Korea, such as assistance with medical, agricultural, and other humanitarian applications of nuclear technology.

North Korea shot back by relinquishing its membership in the IAEA and declaring that it would withdraw from the NPT. This withdrawal was then "suspended," at the urging of the United States, just one day before it was to go into effect. Nonetheless, cooperation with the Agency was deteriorating rapidly.

In the summer of 1994, the United States began negotiating directly with North Korea, in Geneva, on a bilateral arrangement intended to improve the situation. Former president Jimmy Carter was heavily involved, as a private citizen; his meetings with an aging Kim Il Sung in Pyongyang helped move the negotiations along. The result was the so-called Agreed Framework: an ad hoc, one-of-a-kind agreement that would remain in place for years to come.

The Agreed Framework was based on "action for action," according to a preset timeline. The primary provisions were that North Korea would freeze the operations of its existing nuclear program, including the existing five-megawatt research reactor and nuclear fuel reprocessing facility at Yongbyon and two new facilities under construction, a fifty-megawatt reactor and a two-hundred-megawatt reactor. In compensation, Pyongyang would be given two one-thousand-megawatt proliferation-resistant power reactors, at no charge, with crude oil supplied to meet energy needs in the meantime. The "action for action" would culminate in North Korea resuming its full participation in the NPT, in return for a commitment to normalize their relationship with the United States.

Put simply, the Agreed Framework was designed to buy off the North Koreans. According to Robert Gallucci, the U.S. official who negotiated the agreement, it was the best deal he could get. The hope was that the North Korean regime would implode from within before full implementation of the agreement.

My initial reaction to the Agreed Framework was rather critical. The IAEA had not been part of the negotiation regarding how nuclear verification would take place. Legally, since North Korea had "suspended" its decision to withdraw from the NPT, the IAEA was supposed to resume comprehensive safeguards inspections. However, under the terms agreed between North Korea and the United States, the Agency could not do so during the initial stages of the Agreed Framework.

This put North Korea in an automatic state of noncompliance. The IAEA would be able to reestablish its verification of the North Korean nuclear program only at a much later stage, after the United States and North Korea had followed through with their commitments and the North Koreans had returned fully to the NPT. For the IAEA, accepting this arrangement was politically and legally awkward. Moreover, it did not resolve the plutonium discrepancies in North Korea's declaration or answer IAEA questions about undeclared facilities. From a technical standpoint, the limitations imposed on our inspections under the Agreed Framework could make it impossible for IAEA inspectors later to retrace the development of North Korea's nuclear program.

The Agency's role consisted of monitoring the freeze—the shutdown state—of the nuclear facilities at Yongbyon: most important, the repro-cessing facility and the five-megawatt reactor. But we could not inspect, for example, the other two reactors under construction. The most important aspect of our monitoring role was to make sure that the spent fuel at Yongbyon was not reprocessed to extract the plutonium that could be used for weapons purposes. To monitor the freeze, the IAEA inspectors installed tamper-sensitive seals, used video surveillance, and conducted inspections on short notice.

Technically, there was no need for our people to stay in the country all the time; that would have been like watching grass grow. However, some Member States, including the United States, believed that our presence was important politically, so we maintained two or three inspectors in residence. Decent meals were available at the guesthouse for hard currency; but the inspectors were unable to get away from their immediate surroundings, so it was like being in a detention camp. We rotated inspectors every three to six weeks, to keep them from going stir crazy.

The discovery of discrepancies and plutonium concealment in North Korea was a success for the IAEA's verification program. What is less clear, in hindsight, is whether the Agency's request for a special inspec-tion in 1993 was the right approach. We were fairly certain that North Korea would reject the request, and that a confrontation would be the most likely result. From past experience, we could have anticipated that the Security Council, charged under the IAEA statute with ensuring compliance, would not take strong action. Thus, the IAEA and the inter-national community might have done better to continue negotiations with North Korea and push for incremental progress.

The only trump card at the North Koreans' disposal was their nuclear capability; clearly, they would play it to the greatest possible effect. The regime's belief that the United States was bent on its overthrow was a recurrent factor influencing the nuclear negotiations. Pyongyang did not place a high priority on the welfare of its people nor on the humanitar-ian impact of any potential repercussions from its nuclear activities; its sole priority was the survival of the regime. Accordingly, there was little to be accomplished by using penalties to apply pressure to North Korea, let alone the threat of force as an option: Seoul, just thirty kilometers from the border, could well be pulverized. In any case, it is the last time the Agency ever tried to resort to special inspections as a verification tool. We would remain limited in our ability to verify undeclared activities until the arrival of the Model Additional Protocol in 1997.

After the special inspections approach failed, the only sensible path available to the international community was gradually to rebuild trust with North Korea, and then try to buy out its nuclear option, keeping tensions to a minimum while waiting for the regime to change. This was what the Agreed Framework tried to achieve. However, that framework was ultimately undermined when the United States failed to live up to its commitments with North Korea, most notably by not delivering the promised power reactors. The North Koreans clearly read this as evidence of a lack of good faith on the part of the Americans.

The Korean experience can be seen as a textbook case of the short-comings of treating only the symptoms of insecurity, instead of developing a comprehensive, long-term approach designed to defuse the causes of tension. Security guarantees and development assistance are always more effective than punitive measures that inevitably escalate the tension.

3

IRAQ, 2002 and After

A Needless War

By 2002, the security landscape had markedly altered. The September 11, 2001, attacks in the United States had changed many assumptions about the capacity of terrorists to stage complex, suicidal operations. Extremist groups had expressed specific interest in acquiring and using weapons of mass destruction. In response, the IAEA had overhauled and greatly expanded its programs for helping countries secure their nuclear materials to prevent illicit use. As an agency, we, too, had changed. A decade of dealing with challenges such as Iraq and North Korea had made us more resourceful and more confident. We had considerably more legal and technological verification tools at our disposal.

The landscape had been altered also by the Bush administration's approach to nuclear arms control. In December 2001, Bush had uni-laterally withdrawn the United States from the Anti-Ballistic Missile Treaty—a cornerstone of U.S.-Soviet nuclear détente since 1972. In May 2002, Bush and Putin signed the Strategic Offensive Reductions Treaty (SORT), an agreement referred to jokingly in diplomatic circles as "sort of" a treaty, because: (1) it included no verification of its pledged reduc-tions in nuclear arsenals; (2) the reductions called for were not required to be permanent; and (3) withdrawal from the treaty required a mere three months' notice.

To nuclear policy experts, the signals from these actions were clear. The United States was not serious about following through on its disarmament obligations under the NPT. Rather, it was intent on retaining and even reinforcing its privileged nuclear weapon status, with minimal accountability. At the same time, it was determined to come down harder on potential WMD proliferation by other countries.

This was the context in late 2002, when the crosshairs began to focus on Iraq. A rash of statements had appeared in speeches, political talk shows, and press articles. They ranged from hints to outright declarations that Saddam Hussein had ties to Al-Qaeda or that his hand had been present in the terrorist attacks of September 2001. Of specific interest to the IAEA were the U.S. and U.K. claims that they possessed conclusive evidence that the Iraqi leader had failed to dismantle his WMD programs. The Agency had been absent from Iraq since our hurried departure just before the 1998 Desert Fox bombing, which had severely limited our ability to stay current on developments there during the intervening four years.

President Bush was one of those making bold assertions. A speech in Cincinnati, Ohio, on October 2, 2002, was a typical example:

Eleven years ago, as a condition for ending the Persian Gulf War, the Iraqi regime was required to destroy its weapons of mass destruction, to cease all development of such weapons, and to stop all support for terrorist groups. The Iraqi regime has violated all of those obligations. It possesses and produces chemical and biological weapons. It is seeking nuclear weapons. It has given shelter and support to terrorism, and practices terror against its own people. The entire world has witnessed Iraq's eleven-year history of defiance, deception and bad faith.

Later in the speech, Bush continued:

The evidence indicates that Iraq is reconstituting its nuclear weapons program. Saddam Hussein has held numerous meetings with Iraqi nuclear scientists, a group he calls his "nuclear mujahedeen"—his nuclear holy warriors. Satellite photographs reveal that Iraq is rebuilding facilities at sites that have been part of its nuclear program in the past. Iraq has attempted to purchase high-strength aluminum tubes and other equipment needed for gas centrifuges, which are used to enrich uranium for nuclear weapons.

With statements like this—replete with information that was inaccurate, unproven, and misleading—the United States began pressing openly for regime change.

The aggressive rhetoric was no empty threat: crippling sanctions had been in place for a decade; the United States and its allies had recently demonstrated, in Afghanistan, their willingness to take decisive military action. And indeed, the pressure on Iraq appeared to produce results. While denying that the country had rebuilt its WMD programs, Saddam Hussein wrote a letter finally inviting the UN weapons inspectors to return. After much discussion, on November 8, the Security Council unanimously approved Resolution 1441, authorizing a new round of Iraq inspections.

The action behind the scenes was both less coherent and more revealing. A good example was the process of drafting Resolution 1441. The initial draft was not made public. As formulated by the United States, it would have put the five permanent members of the Security Council squarely in the driver's seat of the inspection process.[1] It proposed the use of military escorts to accompany the inspectors in the field, a departure from the past. It also proposed that representatives of the P-5 be part of the inspection teams, and worse, that the UN inspectors report their findings directly to the country that requested the inspection of a particular site or the interview of a particular Iraqi. In short, it suggested a return to the same orientation and mechanisms that had led to the discrediting of UNSCOM.

In early October 2002, before the vote on the final, reworked resolu-

---

1 The shorthand reference to the five permanent members of the UN Security Council—China, France, Russia, the United Kingdom, and the United States—is the P-5. Not coincidentally, these also are the five countries named in the NPT as the possessors of nuclear weapons.

tion, Hans Blix and I were invited to a meeting at the U.S. State Department. Colin Powell was our host. Condoleezza Rice, Paul Wolfowitz, and Lewis Libby[2] rounded out the group. I was just completing my first term as Director General of the IAEA. Blix had come out of retirement to become the executive chairman of the successor organization to UNSCOM, UNMOVIC, which had been somewhat dormant since its creation because of the lack of access to Iraq. UNMOVIC would focus on chemical and biological weapons and missile technology.

The atmosphere was tense. It was obvious that the Americans were in sharp internal disagreement about the best way to proceed. Powell was advocating for the United States to use a typical UN inspection process, while Wolfowitz and other hardliners wanted to sidestep the UN altogether, or like Rice, create a UN cover for what would be, in essence, a United States–directed inspection process. Rice even went so far as to suggest that the person manning intelligence in UNMOVIC should be an American. "We trust our people," she said. Blix balked, saying that a Canadian had been designated and would be in charge.

It was starting to feel like 1992 all over again.

Their goal in this meeting was to try to persuade us to accept some of the clauses in the draft resolution to which we had taken exception. Blix was blunt, telling Rice that he was not going to act as a "façade" for a U.S. operation. "If you want a U.S.-led operation simply blessed by the UN, you can have [one] modeled after the South Korean operation in the '50s.[3] But if you want a UN operation," he declared, "you cannot have people on the teams that are not under the authority of the heads of the inspecting organizations."

Rice was unambiguous in her views of the UN system. At one point in the meeting, Blix stressed the need for the draft resolution to conform

---

2 Rice at the time was the national security adviser. Wolfowitz was the deputy secretary of defense. Libby was the chief of staff to Vice President Cheney.
3 The United Nations Command (Korea) of the early 1950s was a command structure that combined military forces from multiple countries, to provide assistance to South Korea in repelling North Korean hostilities. Security Council Resolution 84 recommended that UN member countries contributing troops and other assistance make them "available to a unified command under the United States of America."

to UN standards and for the inspections to be perceived as a "legitimate" UN operation. Rice's retort was sharp. "Mr. Blix," she announced, "the UN Charter is based on the primary role and responsibility of the five permanent members of the Security Council. As you are aware, the security of the United States is threatened, and it is therefore free to take whatever measures necessary to protect its security." I found myself feeling grateful that she had stopped short of saying that the United Nations *is* the Security Council, and the Security Council *is* the United States.[4]

Wolfowitz appeared indignant that he even had to be present. He was stiff and disinterested; his body language indicated that the meeting— and perhaps the whole notion of involving the United Nations—was a waste of time. When he finally spoke up, his tone was condescending. "Mr. Blix," he announced, leaning across the table, "you do know that these Iraqis have weapons of mass destruction?"

The group discussion stuttered on but proved inconclusive. Frustrated, Powell and Rice took Blix and me aside to an antechamber. "You should not feel the burden of the implications of your inspection reports," Powell told us, "because any decision to use force will be made by heads of state, and not by you." Powell may have meant to be reassuring, but in the context it came across as patronizing.

In the end, we managed to dissuade them from some of the more belligerent proposals. But they were insistent on one measure: the need to interview Iraqi scientists outside of Iraq, taking their families with them to avoid retribution by Saddam Hussein's regime. We tried to spell out the problems with this clause. I tried to explain the cultural nuances of "extended family" in the Middle East. Why, I asked, were they so certain that an Iraqi scientist would want to leave his or her country and

---

4 An underlying viewpoint was reappearing here: certain political factions in the United States have often viewed the United Nations as merely a tool, to be used when convenient, as a way to make U.S.-driven actions more palatable to other countries, but to be discarded or circumvented when UN objectives are not in U.S. interests. These individuals or groups tend not to view the United States as one UN member among many—nor really as a member of the community of nations—but rather as a sort of patron or custodian of the UN, exempt from the rules it helps set for others. This viewpoint was perhaps most strongly in evidence during the George W. Bush administration.

never return, in order to benefit the United States or the West? How could the United Nations ensure that scientists who agreed to leave would not be threatened or even killed before their departure? What could we do to prevent the scientists' extended families from being harmed as a result?

Nothing we said made a difference. The Americans didn't really listen to these human rights considerations. They were convinced that interviewing scientists outside Iraq was a great idea; they said they could not change the measure anyway, because it had been approved "at the highest level" of the U.S. government. The clause stayed in the resolution (although, in the months that followed, not once was this provision put to use).

A few weeks later, with negotiations on the resolution still under way, Blix and I were called to a short courtesy meeting at the White House. On our way to meet President Bush, we had our first encounter with Vice President Dick Cheney. It was brief; Cheney was sitting behind his desk. Cheney wasted no time on small talk; he had a direct, simple message to convey. "The U.S. is ready to work with the United Nations inspectors," he told us, "but we are also ready to discredit the inspections in order to disarm Iraq."

Having received this warning, we proceeded to our meeting with Bush. Other than Condoleezza Rice and Bush's chief of staff, Blix and I were the only audience. In what was more or less a monologue, Bush got right to the point. He asserted that he was in favor of using inspections to address Iraq's WMD issues, that he would prefer a peaceful resolution of the international concerns about Saddam Hussein's regime. "I'm not a trigger-happy Texas cowboy, with six-guns," he quipped, sliding forward on his armchair, hands on his hips, to show us how a cowboy would pull out his pistols. On the other hand, he countered, if peaceful approaches were unsuccessful, he would not hesitate to lead a "coalition of the willing," using military force. It was an odd interaction: Bush kept repeating that it was an "honor" for him to meet with us, but he was not the least bit interested in anything we might have had to say. Together with our exchange with Cheney, the encounter told us clearly that the U.S. administration viewed us as bit players in an operation they intended to control.

Still, when Resolution 1441 was adopted, one week later, the United States made one last concession. The Americans had wanted the resolution to authorize the automatic use of force if Iraq were considered to be in material breach of its obligations. To many members of the Security Council, this was unacceptable. The P-5—primarily the French, Russians, and Americans—worked out a compromise. The final version merely said that if Iraq was found in material breach, the council would "look into" the next steps to be taken.

And so, after four years of the Agency's absence, the door to Iraq inspections was reopened.

For the IAEA, the starting point for reentering Iraq was our December 1998 baseline: our existing store of knowledge of Iraq's past nuclear capabilities and facilities. Any fuel cycle or weapons-related facilities from the early 1990s had been completely dismantled; all weapons-usable material had been removed as early as February 1994; what remained was low-grade nuclear material and certain dual-use facilities and materials—and, of course, the knowledge of certain nuclear processes: no inspection program can erase knowledge already learned. At the time of the first Gulf War, Saddam Hussein's nuclear scientists had still been some distance away from constructing a nuclear weapon, but they had achieved laboratory-scale mastery of some uranium enrichment processes and weaponization techniques.

The task before us was to determine what had changed and what nuclear activities, if any, had been revived during the intervening four years. To arrive at an answer, we would rely on inspections of known facilities, visits to new sites, the restart of surveillance systems, extensive environmental monitoring, and an exhaustive program of interviews with Iraqi nuclear scientists and other relevant persons.

At this point, the IAEA was an experienced, mature organization staffed by long-term career inspectors whose loyalties to the Agency were clear. They were a functional group, well versed in dealing with nuclear safeguards challenges; for many, Iraq was familiar ground, in terms of both the culture and the nuclear facilities. The Iraq team included dozens of nationalities and views from across the political spectrum. Inevitably, some inspectors felt sympathetic to the country under investigation, and others hostile. I encouraged a focus on technical objectivity and legal accuracy, but I also understood that technical judgments might sometimes be clouded by preconceived biases, so we tried to ensure the thorough airing of all opinions, including dissenting views.

I relied in particular on Jacques Baute, a brilliant French physicist who headed the IAEA's Iraq Nuclear Verification Office and whose prior experience with the French nuclear weapons program gave him strong technical judgment. An excellent administrator well liked by everybody, Jacques was the primary architect of our work plan in Iraq, and he managed the operations smoothly with the keen understanding of the need for cultural sensitivity and the respect that made our interactions effective. Also with us was Laura Rockwood, an extroverted and independent-minded senior American legal officer who had worked with me since the mid-eighties and remained thoroughly versed in the legal intricacies of the Iraq mission since the inspections of the early 1990s. In the highly charged political atmosphere in which we were working, the ability to rely on such trusted colleagues was an enormous asset.

The inspections formally began on November 13, 2002. The central feature of the new Iraq mission was urgency, based on the imminent threat of military action if Iraq failed to show maximum cooperation to enable us to prove that it had given up its alleged weapons of mass destruction. This threat, particularly as it appeared in mainstream press accounts, in actions behind the scenes, and in the rhetoric of Western officials—primarily from the United States and the United Kingdom—dominated the landscape throughout the months of inspections. There was a relentless barrage. Every Iraqi action was deemed insufficient. Every delay was reported as evidence of a lack of cooperation. Every WMD-related accusation—Iraq's attempts to procure aluminum tubes, its alleged mobile laboratories, its purported purchase of uranium from Niger—was given sensational coverage as new proof of Saddam Hussein's malicious intent. But when the inspections found otherwise, the news was disputed or brushed aside as unimportant.

This rhetoric inevitably tainted the atmosphere of our high-level interactions with Iraqi officials, whether the meetings took place in Baghdad, New York, or Vienna. In one of our first meetings in New York, Dr. Jaffar Dhia Jaffar, who had in the past been in charge of Iraq's previous nuclear program, was visibly upset. Jaffar always came across as a bit arrogant and defiant of the entire verification process. But in this case he stepped over the line. He accused the IAEA of being biased— essentially, a tool of the West—in our unwillingness simply to close the nuclear file. His remarks to Jacques Baute became personal and abusive, going so far as to criticize his language skills. "Your English," he said, "only improved when you married a British woman."

I cut him off sharply. "Do not forget," I said, "that you and your colleagues were cheating the IAEA for many years, so you have no credibility."

Saddam Hussein's chief scientific adviser, General Amir al-Sa'adi, who had been designated our primary counterpart, tried to cool things down. "Well," he said, with the trace of a smile, "it was not really cheating; it was subterfuge."

As it turned out, Jaffar was in a foul mood because he had arrived in New York without his luggage, which meant he could not look his best. He was certain that this was an intimidation stunt by U.S. intelligence agents, who had been pursuing all the senior Iraqi scientists. Both al-Sa'adi and Jaffar told me that whenever they traveled outside Iraq, they were approached by Western intelligence operatives trying to recruit them.

The distrust persisted as the inspections got under way, and our interactions with Iraqi officials remained strained, in part because assessing the extent of Iraq's cooperation was never straightforward. First, it was colored by a history of deception, which made us view their declarations and actions with skepticism. On multiple occasions, Blix and I stated that we still needed to be convinced Iraq had come forward with all available information about its past WMD programs. After I made one such statement, al-Sa'adi said I had given him stomach cramps, because he could not produce information he didn't have. The IAEA, he insisted, needed to believe what the Iraqis were saying. But of course our experience prior to the 1991 Gulf War did not inspire confidence. We could not simply take them at their word.

Second, our Iraqi counterparts were hamstrung by a horribly author-itarian and overly centralized system. This naturally slowed their deci-sion making and responsiveness and made them appear less than transparent. Neither al-Sa'adi nor General Husam Amin, the head of Iraq's UN-interface group, could take any decision independently, with-out consultation. Nor could they speak candidly about Saddam Hussein or the regime. Whatever they thought privately, they knew the conse-quences of saying anything negative and knew that every conversation was bugged.

Naji Sabri, the Iraqi foreign minister, seemed to take a calculated backseat attitude when it came to the inspections. He was unfailingly pleasant but detached. He invariably invited us to dinner at the end of our visits to Baghdad. When we attempted to engage him on matters of consequence, however, his answers were always carefully noncom-mittal.[5]

Sabri's detachment contrasted sharply with the demeanor of the Iraqi vice president, Taha Yassin Ramadan, who clearly was following the inspection process closely. In our first meeting with him, at the vice presidential headquarters, on January 20, 2003, he was somber and for-mal, wearing his military uniform and carrying a sidearm. Just the three of us were present, plus an interpreter. Ramadan was aggressive from the outset. He told us that our inspectors were stirring up unnecessary trouble, adding fuel to the fire of international suspicion rather than resolving issues. He accused us of not being objective in our approach. It was more or less a rant, attacking the entire inspection process.

I answered him bluntly, shifting into Arabic so he could not mistake my tone or meaning. "We are here to help you," I said, "but frankly only if you are willing to help yourselves. You need to show cooperation, and you need to show transparency, because these issues are not going to be resolved if you are not proactive." I mentioned the way that some of the Iraqi administration had repeatedly attacked the UN inspectors as

---

5 It was later claimed (by *NBC Nightly News* and *60 Minutes*) that Sabri was an intelligence source for the CIA. In any case, when the war began, Sabri was not on the list of the fifty-five most-wanted Iraqis, and as soon as possible he quietly left Iraq to resettle in Qatar.

undercover agents. "Just to label UN inspectors as spies," I told him, "is not in any way helping your case."

To my surprise, Ramadan began to cool down. I believe he grasped the essence of what I was saying: first, that our role, and that of our inspectors, was not driven by a personal vendetta, but by the responsibility for carrying out an international mandate; and second, that cooperation on their part was the only way out of the mess they were in.[6]

This remained my stance throughout the process, although my nationality and heritage created expectations of a different kind of posture. Early on, I often got the feeling that the Arab world—and many Westerners—expected me, as an Egyptian Arab and a Muslim, to show bias in favor of Iraq. Of course, I also heard that I was being tough on Iraq to prove my lack of bias. My only bias was that of an international civil servant: an insistence on independence, professionalism, and treating all parties with equal respect. The Iraqis soon learned that I was not going to perform any special favors for them, nor was I biased against them. Although I ultimately received grudging acknowledgment of my objectivity from most quarters, my name and ethnicity were nonetheless used repeatedly as a means of insinuating that I was prejudiced in my judgments.

And worse. My staunch impartiality might have been the prompt for a number of curious encounters. On our first visit to Baghdad after the resumption of inspections, in November 2002, a man called me at the hotel, on my room phone. He told me he was a lawyer and said he wanted to leave the country. He wanted to know whether Blix or I could help him. I told him that this was not our business, that we were there to focus on the inspections. He thanked me and hung up.

On my next visit, the phone rang again. This time it was a woman. She said she was a Kurd working with the United Nations in Kurdistan and claimed she had a problem with her contract. "I'm sitting down by the hotel pool now," she said. "I think you could help me if I could explain more. Could you meet me?" I told her that I could not see her,

---

6 Ramadan was later placed on the U.S. list of most-wanted Iraqis. He was captured in August 2003 and executed in March 2007.

but that she could write to me. Not surprisingly, I never heard from her again.

On still another occasion, I was approached by Foreign Minister Sabri himself. He drew me aside to ask whether I had family or friends who might be interested in commercial transactions in the Iraqi oil sector. If so, he said, I should let him know. The offer was later repeated to me by Iraq's ambassador in New York, who said he was asking on behalf of the foreign minister. I made clear I wanted nothing to do with such an "opportunity."

I believe these cases were setups, instigated by the Iraqi government, perhaps intended to try to blackmail or "gently persuade" me. Nobody else would have dared call me at the hotel; any local would have presumed, with good reason, that the rooms and the telephones were bugged.

Over the first two months of inspections, the IAEA made solid progress reestablishing its understanding of Iraq's nuclear capabilities. The bulk of our inspections were at state-run or private industrial facilities, research centers, and universities—focusing on locations where we knew Iraq had maintained significant technical capabilities in the past, or on new locations suggested by the analysis of open-source information, or on facilities that were identified through satellite imagery as having been modified or constructed since 1998. The inspections were carried out without prior notification to Iraq.

Agency inspectors also combed the country in more general ways, using a variety of tools. Tracking the environmental "signature" of radioactive materials, we resumed monitoring Iraq's rivers, canals, and lakes to detect the presence of key radioisotopes. We collected samples from locations across Iraq, which were taken to IAEA laboratories for analysis. We conducted extensive radiation surveys using sensitive car-borne and handheld instruments, scanning industrial sites and additional areas for nuclear and other radioactive material. We interviewed many Iraqi scientists, managers, and technicians—primarily in their places of work during unannounced inspections—to glean any information about past and present programs.

In parallel with these on-site inspections, analysts at IAEA headquarters in Vienna were poring over new information submitted by Iraq, comparing it to the records we had accumulated between 1991 and 1998 and further data we had compiled through remote monitoring during our four years of absence from the country. The Iraqi declaration was consistent with our existing understanding of Iraq's pre-1991 nuclear program, but we continued to seek clarification where there were gaps.

After 139 inspections of 106 locations over those first sixty days, we had uncovered no evidence of efforts on the part of Iraq or its scientists to revive the country's nuclear weapons program. The inspections continued unabated. But two specific technical issues dominated the nuclear debate with the aim of accelerating the march to war: Iraq's attempts to procure high-strength aluminum tubes from abroad and the alleged purchase of uranium from Niger.

The aluminum tubes were cited on numerous occasions by Western officials as irrefutable proof of Iraq's renewed nuclear ambitions. As evidence, the officials referred to the June 2001 seizure, in Jordan, of a shipment of tubes bound for Iraq. Shortly before the readmission of inspectors to Iraq, Condoleezza Rice, for example, had gone on CNN to declare that these tubes were "only really suited for nuclear weapons programs."[7] Rice's statement was misleading: experts at the U.S. Department of Energy had long been on record saying they believed these tubes were best suited for artillery rockets.

Our inspectors made it a high priority to visit the Nasser metal fabrication facility, where we knew Iraq made conventional artillery rockets of similar dimensions. The Iraqi engineers there showed the inspectors thousands of completed rockets, fabricated from tubes of precisely the same aluminum alloy and with the same tolerances as those of the tubes intercepted in Jordan. The engineers gave a simple reason for their procurement attempts: they were short on supplies. As for why they had sought those particular specifications, their reasons were equally

---

7 September 8, 2002. This was the same appearance in which Rice, with a first-rate bit of melodrama, coined the phrase "We don't want the smoking gun to be a mushroom cloud."

straightforward: they wanted accurate rockets, they wanted to minimize design changes, and they wanted the tubes to be anodized to keep them from rusting.

Nowhere did we find evidence of a revived centrifuge enrichment program. On January 27, 2003, when I made an interim report to the Security Council, I gave our conclusion regarding these tubes: "From our analysis to date, it appears that the aluminum tubes would be consistent with the purpose stated by Iraq and, unless modified, would not be suitable for manufacturing centrifuges."

The U.S. response—or lack of one—was remarkable. President Bush delivered his State of the Union address the next day. In one of the most watched speeches of the year, he again claimed that Iraq was trying to purchase aluminum tubes "suitable for nuclear weapons production." There was no mention of the IAEA's contradictory conclusion based on direct verification of the facts in Iraq. Nor did Bush note the differing analysis of the U.S. Department of Energy.

Colin Powell's dramatic address to the UN Security Council came one week later, on February 5. Listeners expected a definitive presentation of the intelligence on Iraq's WMD programs. With characteristic charisma and force of presence, Powell reassured his audience, "My colleagues, every statement I make today is backed up by sources, solid sources. These are not assertions." When it came to discussing the aluminum tubes, he acknowledged existing "differences of opinion," but declared, "Most U.S. experts think they are intended to serve as rotors in centrifuges used to enrich uranium."

Powell later told me he had spent a week at CIA headquarters, drilling their people on every piece of "evidence" and asking questions to ensure the veracity of the information. He added jokingly that if he had gone along with all their evidence his presentation to the council would have been a few hours long.

At the secretary-general's private luncheon that followed Powell's UN statement, Dominique de Villepin, the French foreign minister—an accomplished diplomat and historian, with a presence that rivaled Powell's own—addressed Powell with what seems, in retrospect, like a prophecy: "You Americans," he said, "do not understand Iraq. This is the land of Haroun al-Rashid.[8] You may be able to destroy it in a month, but it will take you a generation to build peace."

Powell was visibly irritated. "Who is speaking about use of force?" he retorted—something of a bizarre comment, since the speech he had just delivered pointed in only one direction.

Ultimately, a painstaking analysis of the aluminum tubes issue in the *New York Times*, published when the war was in its second year, pointed out that two days before his Security Council speech, Powell's intelligence experts had sent him a memo confirming that the United States used a seventy-millimeter tactical rocket that employed the same high-grade aluminum, with similar specifications.[9] Yet Powell declared that the tubes Iraq sought required a tolerance "that far exceeds U.S. requirements for comparable rockets."

Another centerpiece of the case against the Iraqi regime was the allegation that Saddam Hussein had tried to purchase uranium from Niger. President George Bush had emphasized this point in his January 2003 State of the Union address: "The British government has learned that Saddam Hussein recently sought significant quantities of uranium from Africa." Allegedly, between 1999 and 2001, Hussein's representatives had tried to purchase five hundred tons of uranium oxide, yellowcake, from Niger. In late September 2002, the Blair administration in the United Kingdom revealed an intelligence dossier that included this assertion. The IAEA had been pressing for the relevant documentation ever since, in order to investigate, and after months of asking intelligence agencies for evidence of this illicit transaction, we were finally provided with copies of the papers on February 5, the same day as Colin Powell's Security Council address.

Although the United Kingdom and the United States had taken more than three months to supply the "evidence"—a small sheaf of letters and

---

8 Haroun al-Rashid, who ruled the Arab empire from Baghdad in the late eighth century, is a historical figure of mythic stature, considered the greatest of the Abbasid caliphs. Al-Rashid's reign was marked by extraordinary cultural, scientific, and political prosperity.
9 David Barstow, William J. Broad, and Jeff Gerth, "How the White House Embraced Disputed Arms Intelligence," *New York Times*, October 3, 2004.

communiqués between officials from Niger and Iraq—it took Jacques Baute and his team only a matter of hours to figure out that the documents were fake. One letter, alleged to be from the president of Niger, Mamadou Tandja, was full of inaccuracies and had an obviously falsified signature. Another letter from October 2000, supposedly from the Niger minister of foreign affairs and cooperation, bore the "signature" of Allele Habibou; but Minister Habibou had not held office since 1989.

Nor was the purported sale logically plausible. Niger is one of the world's largest uranium producers. The output of the two uranium mines in question is a valuable commodity, an important supply line for Japanese, Spanish, and French nuclear power companies. Sales and production are under constant supervision, not just by Niger but also by foreign entities. The notion that five hundred tons of yellowcake—enough to produce roughly one hundred nuclear bombs—could be shipped out to Iraq undetected was absurd.

Even more puzzling was the fact that a forgery that had escaped detection through months of examination by the world's top intelligence agencies was immediately exposed by an IAEA physicist using Google searches and common sense. Equipped with his conclusions about the Niger documents, Jacques consulted with a number of Western officials. They had nothing to say. Not once in the days that followed did a single American or British official dispute the logic of the IAEA analysis.

I deliberated on how to break the news to the Security Council without overly embarrassing Washington or London. On the flight to New York, consulting with Jacques Baute and Laura Rockwood, I finally decided to use less sensational terminology, describing the documents as "not authentic." But of course the message was clear: the Niger uranium sales allegation, a keystone of the U.S. and U.K. case insisting that Iraq had reconstituted its nuclear weapons program, was based on a fraud.

The United States was clearly unhappy when I reported this conclusion to the Security Council. It compounded our earlier debunking of the aluminum tubes issue. Colin Powell, who always kept his cool and was unfailingly courteous to me, reacted at the council meeting somewhat peevishly, pointing out that the Agency had "missed Iraq" in 1991.

The reaction in the media was disheartening. The major media organizations at the time had completely bought into the WMD claims by the U.S. administration. Yet our findings were discounted on the grounds that they were unimportant. The *Washington Post*, on March 1, referred to the Niger documents as "one secondary bit of evidence," declaring that it was "not central to the case against Saddam Hussein." Not to be outdone, the *Wall Street Journal* on March 13 published an editorial pointedly titled "Bush in Lilliput." "Mr. ElBaradei," they wrote, "made a public fuss last week about one British-U.S. claim that turns out to have been false, but which was in any case peripheral to Iraq's weapons of mass destruction." Neither newspaper bothered to mention that, less than two months earlier, the Niger uranium sale had been significant enough for the president of the United States to feature it in his State of the Union address. The coverage in the *New York Times* was similarly dismissive. On March 8, the Niger issue was mentioned in passing in a cover story focused on the "UN Split." The next day, the story was covered more fully ("Forensic Experts Uncovered Forgery on Iraq, an Inspector Says")—but relegated to page 13.

Efforts on the diplomatic front seemed equally ill-fated. When the Arab states met at an emergency summit before the war, on March 2, in Sharm el-Sheikh, it erupted into a circus of petty disagreements and name-calling. There were serious proposals on the table about sending a delegation to Iraq to offer possible solutions that could avoid a war. Some wanted to urge Saddam Hussein to resign. The ruler of the United Arab Emirates at that time, Sheikh Zayed bin Sultan al-Nahyan, wanted to offer Saddam Hussein asylum as a face-saving way out.

Other Arab leaders, however, appeared to be supportive of the war. They clearly loathed Saddam Hussein and hoped an invasion of Iraq would get rid of him altogether. Early in the inspections process I had met with the president of Egypt, Hosni Mubarak, who obviously had a personal grudge against Saddam Hussein; he kept saying that Saddam had double-crossed him during the first Gulf War, when he invaded Kuwait after giving Mubarak assurances to the contrary. I briefed

Mubarak about our activities in Iraq but also tried to direct the conversation to a relevant broader theme, urging him to lead a movement of modernization and moderation in the Arab world. "If that were to happen," I said, "Egypt would get support pouring in from every front, both politically and economically."

Mubarak and I spoke again about Iraq when I asked him to intervene with Saddam Hussein to improve his cooperation with the United Nations. Mubarak mentioned that he had received a letter from Saddam saying, "Do not worry; everything is okay." He also passed on a bit of information. "I know that Saddam has biological weapons," Mubarak told me, "and he is hiding them in the cemeteries." It was the first and last time I heard that rumor.[10]

With such sentiments at work, inevitably the Arab Summit devolved into a series of virulent arguments. Sheikh Zayed's asylum proposal somehow did not get put on the agenda. For this reason the sheikh and his delegation were furious with the secretary-general of the Arab League, Amr Moussa. The idea of sending a delegation to Iraq was aborted altogether. Without a united position, the leaders of the Arab world in the end had almost no say or influence in a war launched at the heart of their region—other than, in some cases, to provide bases and facilities for U.S. troops.

Even the most experienced and pragmatic politicians seemed unable to leverage diplomatic influence. French president Jacques Chirac had voiced strong disagreement with the Bush doctrine of "you're either with us or against us." His candor was in evidence when Blix and I met with him in mid-January at the Elysée Palace and complained that we were not getting much information from Western intelligence agencies regarding Iraq's alleged WMD programs. Chirac was astonishingly

---

10 In President Bush's memoir, *Decision Points,* he writes that Mubarak had told U.S. general Tommy Franks that "Iraq had biological weapons and was certain to use them on our troops." This information, Bush writes, influenced his thinking on Iraq's WMD status and the need for military action. Quoted in Diaa Bekheet, "Bush: Mubarak Informed U.S. that Iraq Had Biological Weapons," *Voice of America,* November 11, 2010. Retrieved from *VoANews.com,* at www.voanews.com/english/news/Bush-Says-Egypts-Mubarak-Informed-US-that-Iraq-Had-Biological-Weapons-107247693.html.

candid. "You know why you don't get the information," he declared. "It is because they don't have any."

In fact, French intelligence experts had been telling Blix and me they were sure that Iraq was continuing to keep "small quantities" of chemical and biological weapons. The head of the French intelligence agency happened to be present at our meeting, and his face dropped at Chirac's casual remark. Chirac paid no attention, taking his bluntness one step further: intelligence agencies, he said, were in the habit of first reaching their conclusions and then building the supporting arguments. By this time, his intelligence chief was studying the carpet intently, avoiding eye contact.

To my ears, it was refreshing to hear a leader of Chirac's stature speak so openly what we at the Agency were thinking. He said the threat Bush had made to the Security Council—that the United Nations would become irrelevant if they did not adopt a resolution to use force—was complete nonsense. If the United States decided to move on its own, Chirac said, "It will be the U.S. that will be regarded as an outlaw, and not the UN." Unfortunately, in the United States at the time, Chirac's stance on Iraq was marginalized, even derided.[11]

Soon after that encounter, in early February Blix and I met with British prime minister Tony Blair at his modest office at Downing Street. He saw each of us separately: Blix first, then me. This was unusual; most of our interactions at that level were conducted jointly. Blair was relaxed and informal, with his jacket off. When he came out after seeing Blix, he jokingly called out, "Next!" as if I were at the dentist.

The tone of the meeting was positive. I voiced to Blair my concern that going to war with Iraq over WMD would ignite regional tensions. "The perception in the Middle East," I explained, "is that the focus on Iraq is not because of weapons of mass destruction per se, but because Iraq is a Muslim and Arab country, and therefore is not allowed, like Israel, to have such weapons." I echoed something Chirac had said: that

---

11 Many U.S. leaders characterized the French position on the Iraq war as disloyalty; members of Congress went so far as to demand that French fries and French toast on the House cafeteria menu be renamed "freedom fries" and "freedom toast."

the eagerness to take action on Iraq would not sell well in the face of doing nothing about the Israeli-Palestinian conflict. I also mentioned the criticisms I had been hearing about the disparity in treatment between Iraq and North Korea.

Blair expressed understanding of my points and shared my concerns about inaction on the Palestinian issue. He recounted that Bush had promised he would address the Palestinian situation once the "matter of Iraq" was settled.

It was Jack Straw, the British foreign minister, who explained the British rationale: they were trying to give full support to the Americans in public, he said, in order to be able to influence U.S. decisions privately. This view remained consistent: it would be much more dangerous to have the United States act on its own, and by "hugging" the Americans, Britain had a better shot at controlling their actions. Frankly, I did not notice a whiff of British influence over U.S. policy during the Blair administration. It always seemed to be a one-way street, with the British acting as spokespersons or apologists for U.S. behavior.

With so little to make their case on the nuclear front—other than the aluminum tubes allegations and the Niger yellowcake fiasco—many U.S. officials nonetheless remained certain that Iraq had at least some chemical and biological weapons squirreled away. Regarding nuclear weapons, the suggestions became, on occasion, outlandish: I recall a meeting at the U.S. State Department with Assistant Secretary John Wolf in which he kept repeating that our inspectors needed to seize all the hard drives of the Iraqi scientists' computers, to get access to what was going on. At another point I met with the House Foreign Relations Committee, chaired by Henry Hyde. We were explaining the progress of our inspections when Congressman Tom Lantos, the ranking Democrat, broke in: "I have a solution for you," he said. "Take all the Iraqi scientists on a two-week cruise, and that will give you all the information you need about the Iraq program." I hoped he was joking. I did not reply.

Clearly, what Chirac had said was true: neither the United States nor other countries had much in the way of intelligence information to back their convictions about Iraq's development of WMD. At the IAEA, during this period, we received very few leads from the Americans or other intelligence agencies, in sharp contrast to the extensive information received by the IAEA and UNSCOM in the early 1990s.

In the absence of such intelligence, the Americans pinned their best hopes on the defection of Iraqi scientists, who, they were sure, would reveal insider information about the weapons locations and programs the United States was so sure existed. This was the motivation behind the strategy of taking scientists and their families abroad for interviews. However, most of Iraq's nuclear experts did not even want to be interviewed in the absence of a representative of the Iraqi authorities or without a tape recorder. They were intent on avoiding misunderstandings—with the Iraqi authorities or with the inspectors. We could not force them to leave the country, nor were we keen to do so, given the potential repercussions for their extended families and friends.

Moreover, we felt we had sufficient means to facilitate our inspections without this additional measure; we had confidence that, given a reasonable timeline, we would uncover whatever illicit WMD activities existed. IAEA inspectors were well acquainted with the scientific and technological capacities of Iraq, and with the physical lay of the land. Even after a four-year hiatus, it had not taken long for the returning IAEA inspectors to recover a basic sense of Iraq's nuclear capacity.

Yet this credibility was being dismissed; the self-appointed "coalition of the willing" had decided to ignore our expertise. Despite the on-the-ground knowledge of the UN inspectorate, we were losing the battle of information, in the Western press, and to some extent in the public eye. IAEA and UNMOVIC statements were being discounted, or quoted selectively, even though we were the ones with the best access to the truth, the eyes and ears of the international community.

War was beginning to seem inevitable—regardless of the facts. Troops were massing in the Persian Gulf. We were running out of time.

On March 12, Tony Blair and Jack Straw put forward a draft UN resolution in a seeming effort to prevent war. It proposed six "tests" for disarmament. If Iraq could pass these tests by March 17, Saddam Hussein would be allowed to remain in power, and no military action would take place.

The six tests were essentially intended to be commitments by Iraq to:

1. Broadcast a public statement by Saddam Hussein, on air in Iraq, admitting to the possession of weapons of mass destruction and pledging to give them up;
2. Allow Iraqi scientists to be interviewed by UN inspectors outside Iraq;
3. Surrender ten thousand liters of anthrax that the British believed Iraq was still holding;
4. Destroy all proscribed missiles;
5. Provide an account of Iraq's unmanned aerial vehicles, or drones; and
6. Surrender all mobile bioproduction laboratories for destruction.

The draft resolution did not pass. Even if it had, at least three conditions would have been impossible to meet, since neither the anthrax nor the mobile laboratories existed, and Saddam Hussein could not admit to weapons he did not have. Even more curious is that the British would have allowed Saddam Hussein to remain in power. This flies in the face of later claims that regime change in Iraq, by itself, was sufficient justification for the invasion.

As the weekend of March 14–16 approached, the British appeared desperate to find a diplomatic solution. As a last-ditch effort, they proposed the idea of a "benchmark": that is, a list of certain activities for Iraq to perform within a specified time period to prove its willingness to cooperate. I suggested that Blix and I could go to Baghdad with this benchmark list, to work through the concept with the Iraqi principals. The British seemed pleased with this suggestion.

In parallel, I had been pressing al-Sa'adi for an invitation for Blix and me to meet directly with Saddam Hussein. That letter of invitation arrived on Saturday, March 15. I spoke to the British and the French, to see whether they would support this visit as a diplomatic channel. The British said they thought the French should take the initiative.

But the French and the Germans were unenthusiastic. They sensed that the decision to go to war had already been taken in Washington. If they supported a diplomatic mission to meet with Saddam Hussein, and the mission failed, the failure itself might provide a further pretext or justification for military aggression—a pretext they did not wish to supply. They declined to support the mission. As it turned out, Blix himself was not willing to visit Baghdad again; he said he felt it was "too late."

Blix and I were a good team, but we did not always see eye to eye. While our differences rarely surfaced in public, we sometimes disagreed pointedly behind closed doors. In particular, I had wanted him to join me in requesting more time for the inspections to run their course, considering we had not found evidence of the existence of WMDs or any imminent threat, but he was unwilling to do so. This reluctance may have been rooted in part in the contrasts between the inspectorates we headed. UNMOVIC was a young organization; its inspectors, while technically skilled, were mostly new—new to Iraq, new to UNMOVIC, new to the inspection process, and new to Blix. Also, Blix did not have seasoned technical advisers in chemical and biological issues or missile technology. Demetrius Perricos, Blix's primary technical adviser, was a high-level, thoroughly experienced former IAEA official, and a longtime confidant, but his expertise was nuclear. Because many of the IAEA inspectors were returning to well-trodden ground and familiar faces, the Agency was correspondingly more confident in its judgments.

Blix also clearly felt that he had been betrayed by Iraq in the early 1990s—lied to outright by everyone from the head of Iraq's Atomic Energy Organization on down. He also had suffered through a hostile media campaign that described him unfairly as spineless because the IAEA had not discovered the Iraq nuclear program before the first Gulf War, the press having failed to understand the limitations on the Agency's authority at that time. Now, as the head of UNMOVIC, Blix could afford to be tough in his dealings with the Iraqis.

Very early on, prior to the return of the inspectors, the Iraqis had requested "technical discussions" with UNMOVIC and the IAEA to identify clearly what disarmament issues were viewed as outstanding and what Iraq could do to bring the issues satisfactorily to closure. Blix refused. He told me he suspected Iraq wanted to manipulate these discussions to "write off" valid issues. No such discussions would take place, he declared, before the UNMOVIC inspectors had physically returned to Iraq.

The IAEA was already engaged in similar discussions with our Iraqi counterparts with useful results. The interaction was helping our preparation and would make our inspectors more efficient when the door finally opened for our return to Iraq. And of course the IAEA was not allowing any issues to be written off. "You are the head of UNMOVIC," I told Blix. "No one can close out UNMOVIC issues without your authority."

At one point during these preliminary discussions, in a meeting at the Hotel Sacher in Vienna, in the presence of UN secretary-general Kofi Annan, Blix accused me of taking the Iraqi side. "This is unfair," Annan said to Blix. "Why are we having these meetings at all with the Iraqis if you are not willing to discuss with them what the remaining disarmament issues are?" But Blix would not relent.

In fairness to him and to UNMOVIC, it was not easy for them, throughout the inspections, to reach clear verification conclusions because, despite past intelligence assertions to the contrary, the Iraqis had not kept accurate records of the chemical and biological weapons they had destroyed in the 1990s. Furthermore, Blix was not always supported with accurate data. At one meeting in Baghdad, for example, he told the Iraqis that the list of scientists in their declaration was not complete and put forward the names of four or five additional individuals. General al-Sa'adi conferred with his team, then explained that the scientists named either were dead or had left the country or were in the report with slight Arabic-to-English spelling variations.

Blix also included in one report to the Security Council a statement that was subsequently misused by the United States and the United Kingdom to push for war. We would customarily exchange drafts of our reports the night before the meetings; on this one occasion, we did not do so. "Iraq," Blix said in this report, "has not taken the strategic decision to disarm, even now." I thought I understood the genesis of this remark. In one of the letters from the Iraqis, they had referred to inspections as being about "so-called" disarmament issues. Blix had read this phrase as a sign of arrogance, an indication that the Iraqis were not taking their obligation to disarm seriously. In the same statement to the Security Council, Blix also stated, "I have no evidence that they have any weapons left." But this part of the report was not given the same exposure. The irony was, of course, that as it turned out, there were no disarmament issues in Iraq.

When in the weeks leading up to the war I pressed Blix to join me in asking the Security Council for more time, he declined. He said this might be interpreted to imply that he would be able to achieve results by a particular date, and he was not sure if UNMOVIC could follow through. "But," he said, "if they ask me whether we need more time, I will say yes."

On March 16, four days before the war began, President Bush and Prime Minister Blair met with the Spanish prime minister, José María Aznar, on the Azores Islands. They were hosted by the prime minister of Portugal, José Manuel Barroso. From what I learned of this meeting, the British benchmark proposal received only marginal attention. The talks centered on a different topic: whether the so-called moment of truth had arrived. Blair and Aznar made clear they still wanted to give diplomacy a chance. Bush was unwilling to wait: the course of action that would determine Iraq's fate, he insisted, would be decided that day.

Indeed, that morning in the United States, Dick Cheney gave an interview on *Meet the Press*. The host, Tim Russert, asked him what he thought about the IAEA's conclusion that Iraq had not resumed its nuclear weapons program. "We believe [Saddam Hussein] has, in fact, reconstituted nuclear weapons," Cheney said. "I think Mr. ElBaradei, frankly, is wrong."

I thought back to Cheney's warning, given before the start of the inspections, that he would willingly discredit their outcome. Now, on the brink of war, he was attempting to do exactly that. "If you look at the track record of the International Atomic Energy Agency and this kind of issue, especially where Iraq is concerned," Cheney told Russert, "they have consistently underestimated or missed what it was Saddam

Hussein was doing. I don't have any reason to believe they're any more valid this time than they've been in the past."

Of course I cannot divine—nor could I then—what Cheney knew or believed about Iraq's WMD programs. But he knew exactly why the IAEA's conclusions about Iraq in 2003 should be granted a much higher degree of validity than those of 1991. He knew as well as anyone that in the 1990s we had been authorized to verify only what Hussein's government reported to us. We had no authority to travel elsewhere in the country, nor to look for clandestine nuclear facilities, nor to ferret out illicit nuclear material transactions.

He was also acutely aware that times had changed. The IAEA had since spent years in Iraq with sweeping "anytime, anywhere" authority. We had crisscrossed the country. We had interviewed every nuclear scientist available. We had destroyed equipment, confiscated records, put the remaining nuclear material under IAEA seal, and blown up the nuclear production facilities at Al Atheer. To liken 2003 to 1991 was an act of deliberate distortion. The die, it seemed, had been cast.

The phone call came very late that night, at around one o'clock in the morning Vienna time, on Monday, March 17. It was Ken Brill, the U.S. ambassador to the IAEA, calling to say that his government was advising us to move out of Baghdad. As Brill transmitted the message, the intent from Washington was to give us advance notice so that we could protect our people on the ground.

I immediately phoned Hans Blix, who had received a similar call, and Kofi Annan. He had clearly wanted to avoid a war and find a diplomatic solution. Annan had struggled to maintain the legitimacy of the United Nations and to keep the Security Council from being manipulated in the interests of a few countries. In a speech given a month earlier, at William and Mary College, he declared, "This is an issue not for any one state alone, but for the international community as a whole." Later, he added, "When states decide to use force, not in self-defense, but to deal with broader threats to international peace and security, there is no substitute for the unique legitimacy provided by the Security Council."

Kofi Annan had been heavily criticized for a stance he had taken in 1998, after successfully pressing for Saddam Hussein to allow access to eight sites—presidential palaces—that were previously off limits. At the time, he had said, "Can I trust Saddam Hussein? I think I can do business with him. . . . I'm not, I think, perhaps not as pessimistic as some of you are." In response, some had ridiculed the secretary-general as naïve.

Now, at this critical hour, I found myself wishing that the soft-spoken Annan had raised the pitch on Iraq, particularly in the face of accusations made by Bush back in November that the United Nations had no spine and that it would become irrelevant. I had been quite impressed by Annan's determined efforts to engage civil society to explain the role of the United Nations, pressing for global action to address poverty and HIV/AIDS. Although Annan had no mandate in the inspection process, he would have reflected the views of the over-whelming majority of the public, globally, had he been more vocal in defense of the principles of world order spelled out in the UN Charter. But at the time, he was focused on resolving the question of divided Cyprus.

In the desperate early hours of Monday, March 17, as we spoke on the phone, Annan wanted to delay making a decision on pulling UN personnel out of Iraq until the following morning, New York time, to discuss the matter with the president of the Security Council and to talk to Secretary Powell. I also called the president of the Security Council to inform him about the message we had received. He, too, decided to discuss the issue with his colleagues in the morning. Blix wanted to pull out of Baghdad immediately because of safety concerns for the UN staff. I was of the view that we should wait—that we should not leave simply because the United States had told us to do so.

I hung up the phone. Sleep would be a long time coming. Well into the dawn, I spoke with my wife, Aida, my favorite source of good counsel. Together we speculated on how this was going to unfold. How long would the war last? What would be the extent of casualties? There was nothing more I could do. My feelings vacillated from anger to a sense of helplessness to grief for the coming loss of life. Where was the justification?

It is true that, throughout the inspections, I believed the Iraqis could have acted faster and shown more transparency. I was never completely certain as to why they did not. In part, I believe they wanted to preserve their dignity: respect is the most valuable currency in Middle Eastern negotiations, and it would have been unacceptable for the Iraqis to appear intimidated or humiliated by the inspections. It may have been the persistent suspicion that the UN inspections were an instrument for intelligence gathering, in preparation for war. Or perhaps they simply believed that because there were no WMDs to be discovered, the truth would eventually prevail.

The Iraqis also understood that the United States did not intend to let Saddam Hussein off the hook. In this context, perhaps transparency and full support for the inspections might not have seemed like the pathway to a solution. And of course many believed that the war was inevitable, that there was no light at the end of the tunnel.

Hans Blix, Kofi Annan, and I reconvened by conference call later that Monday morning. We were numb, yielding to a course of action in which none of us believed. Annan had decided to recommend to the Security Council that, out of concerns for safety, we suspend all UN operations in Iraq. The council's response was to "take note" of the decision. Some members, such as the Russians and the Syrians, were not pleased; but of course the council as a whole understood the futility of jeopardizing the safety of UN personnel in order to protest the action of the coalition. Given that the IAEA depended on UNMOVIC for logistics, we had no choice but to join the action. I issued the order for our inspectors to come home.

By coincidence, that same day was also the start of a meeting of the IAEA Board of Governors, one of five such regular meetings that occur throughout the year. There were multiple accolades delivered by Board members that morning. Countries as varied as South Africa, Japan, France, Germany, and Brazil commended the Agency for its professionalism and integrity in carrying out the Iraq inspections.

The words of the South African ambassador to the IAEA, Abdul

Minty, were especially foreboding. Not only was the world facing the regrettable prospect of a war with far-reaching consequences, he said, but the disregard shown for the role of the United Nations would have a profound impact on future international relations.

The statement of the U.S. ambassador made a sharp contrast; he did not even mention Iraq. The British were also silent on the topic. Most of the diplomats in the room were engrossed in following the evolving preparations for war.

I was not in the mood for conversation. When it was my turn to address the Board, I closed my speech with a quote. "In regard to all of our activities," I said, "I am reminded of the words of Adlai Stevenson in 1952: 'There is no evil in the atom; only in men's souls.'"

The IAEA's role in the Iraq narrative did not conclude with the onset of the war in March 2003. Our verification mandate from the Security Council remained in force. We were concerned about the integrity of nuclear material that had been stored under international seal. We also were hearing rumors, from our Iraqi contacts, of safety and security concerns related to uncontrolled looting at sites formerly under strict controls.

From the Tuwaitha Nuclear Research Center, for example, there were reports that metal drums containing radioactive material were being emptied and used by civilians to store and transport drinking water, milk, and other consumables, and to wash clothes. The safety implications of this were horrendous. We were also told that nonirradiated screwworm flies, which could pose health hazards to humans and livestock, had been released from laboratories.[12] It was hard to know what

---

12 Screwworms are flesh-eating pests that have largely been eliminated from North America and other regions using the "sterile insect technique," in which healthy male flies are irradiated, making them sterile, and then released into the environment to mate. Since the females can breed only once in their lifespan, this rapidly cuts down on the screwworm population. The IAEA has helped many countries develop the capacity to use this technique for screwworms and other pests. Iraq had an inventory of screwworms in storage for this purpose.

to believe. Tuwaitha was a vast site, with hundreds of structures; many tons of yellowcake uranium oxide were stored there, along with much smaller quantities of low-enriched uranium, various radioactive isotopes, and other hazardous materials. The prospect of Tuwaitha and other nuclear sites being left unsecured, accessible to untrained civilians—or, for that matter, to militants who might want to incorporate the radioactive material into a "dirty bomb" or sell it on the international black market—was appalling.[13]

In media interviews and editorials, I began to press for the return of Agency inspectors to Iraq. I issued a press release on April 11, noting that I had written to the Americans regarding the security and physical protection of Tuwaitha and that I had gotten some verbal assurances from them.

Further, I made clear to anyone who would listen that the situation required IAEA expertise. According to the Associated Press, a group of U.S. Marines entering Tuwaitha believed they had discovered evidence of Saddam Hussein's clandestine nuclear program in "an underground network of laboratories, warehouses, and bombproof offices." The truth was that the marines had not discovered anything new. They had broken through IAEA seals. The material was controlled; they simply did not know what they were looking at.[14]

As I told Wolf Blitzer on CNN on April 27, only the IAEA had the legal authority and the relevant field experience to perform such searches. "We have been in Iraq for over ten years. We know the people; we know the infrastructure; we know the documents; we know where to go. Why should we reinvent the wheel?" As international civil servants, we also had greater credibility.

The U.S. ambassador to the IAEA, Ken Brill, called David Waller,

---

13 A dirty bomb, otherwise known as a "radiological dispersal device," is a low-tech device that could be used by extremist groups. Essentially, it consists of conventional explosives wrapped around nuclear or radioactive material. The result would not be a nuclear detonation, but still could effectively disperse the material across, for example, several city blocks, contaminating the area and causing widespread panic and economic disruption.

14 William J. Kole, "Experts Say U.S. 'Discovery' of Nuclear Materials in Iraq Was Breach of UN-Monitored Site," Associated Press, April 10, 2003.

my deputy director general for management and the highest-ranking American in the Agency, to say that Washington was unhappy that I was "speaking outside of the technical box." The next time I saw Brill, I expressed my dismay about this criticism. He said I should not give the United States or the coalition advice on policy and on what to do. I replied, "As long as I believe this policy aspect to be part of my job, and as long as I am doing this job, I will continue to tell them my views."

In late April, I had breakfast with John Wolf, the U.S. assistant secretary of state for nonproliferation. Ken Brill was also present. They told me the State Department was no longer in the loop regarding Iraq; the Defense Department was now in control. However, they urged me not to push for the IAEA inspectors' return. If I did, they said, "you will get an answer you will not like."

"You have a political agenda," I told them, "but as the head of the IAEA, I have a different agenda: to provide the international community with the facts and to make a technical assessment, without political spin." I promised that the Agency, if allowed to return, would be as fully transparent and objective as always.

Soon after that conversation, I wrote a letter to the United States, saying that we needed to go back into Iraq to inspect. I received no response. When I met with Jack Straw in London on May 12, I again pressed my point. By this time press reports were beginning to draw attention to the humanitarian and other risks of unsecured nuclear material.[15] I told Straw that, given the safety hazards, inaction on the part of the coalition was basically sending the message that the lives of Iraqis were expendable.

Straw said he understood and agreed with my request that we should go back, particularly to Tuwaitha. But Washington, he said, was split on the issue. Straw intended to call Colin Powell the same day to make that point. He also asked one of his assistants to ask Blair to bring it up with Bush when they spoke later that day. A draft Security Council resolution aimed at, among other things, lifting some of the sanctions on Iraq,

15 For example, two articles in the *Washington Post*, by Barton Gellman, on April 25 and May 4, detailed the haphazard efforts to control known nuclear sites in Iraq.

terminating the Oil-for-Food program, and giving the coalition legal standing as a peace-keeping force was also in the works; however, I was later told that since the British could not get the Americans to agree, the resolution did not include the return of IAEA inspectors.[16]

After extensive wrangling, the coalition made one concession, agreeing to provide logistical support for IAEA inspectors to carry out a "physical inventory inspection" at Tuwaitha. The inspection took place in mid-June. It was limited in scope. We were not able to investigate the potential civilian health effects resulting from the looting. Nor could we resume our larger mandate of inspection in Iraq, to bring it to closure. But by that time, the United States and its allies had created a separate entity to search for Iraq's "missing" WMD: the Iraq Survey Group.

The IAEA's broadest prewar conclusion about Iraq—that there was no evidence that Saddam Hussein's regime had reconstituted its nuclear weapons program—had been roundly criticized. UNMOVIC's failure to turn up biological and chemical weapons was also regarded with suspicion. The coalition was determined to prove, at least after the fact, that Iraq's WMD stockpiles and associated infrastructure—the raison d'être for the war—really did exist. The Iraq Survey Group, a group of more than a thousand American, British, and Australian experts and support staff, was given that mission. They were to report directly to U.S. secretary of defense Donald Rumsfeld.

David Kay reemerged to lead the Iraq Survey Group. Kay had left the IAEA after his Iraq missions in the early 1990s, reportedly unhappy that he had not been offered a senior post in the Agency. He had taken a position with the Uranium Institute,[17] a nuclear industry advocacy group, but he left when individuals close to the organization reportedly

---

16 The last of the sanctions on Iraq were not lifted until December 15, 2010, no longer barring the country, for example, from pursuing a civilian nuclear program, and returning control of oil and natural gas revenues to the Iraqi government as of June 30, 2011. "UN Lifts Nuclear Weapons Sanctions on Iraq," Associated Press, December 15, 2010.

17 Later renamed the World Nuclear Association.

were displeased with his statements criticizing the IAEA and, by implication, undermining the Uranium Institute's business of promoting
nuclear energy. In the months leading up to the war, Kay had been interviewed as an expert on Iraq's WMD programs and had not hesitated to
offer his opinion: "Iraq," he declared, "stands in clear violation of international orders to rid itself of these weapons."

But of course, the Iraq Survey Group found no evidence to support
such a claim. Kay resigned in January 2004 and was honest enough to
tell the U.S. Senate Armed Services Committee, "It turns out we were
all wrong." He was succeeded by Charles Duelfer, a past deputy executive chairman of UNSCOM, and the search pressed doggedly onward.
Finally, in early 2005, after two and a half years of Iraq inspections, at a
cost of $3 billion, the Iraq Survey Group was disbanded. Nothing had
been found to contradict the findings of the IAEA or UNMOVIC. To
put this in perspective, $3 billion is roughly the equivalent of the
IAEA's verification budget for inspections worldwide for twenty-five
years.

As the months passed, the tragedies and ironies of the war continued to
mount. On August 14, 2003, the UN Assistance Mission for Iraq, established to coordinate humanitarian assistance and other affairs, took up
residence in the Canal Hotel in Baghdad, where the IAEA and UNSCOM
had previously been headquartered. Five days later, a suicide bomber
struck the Canal Hotel with a massive truck bomb. More than twenty
people were killed, including Sergio Vieira de Mello, the UN high com-
missioner for human rights, who had been appointed UN special representative in Iraq. Vieira de Mello was a star: charismatic and bright as
well as pragmatic and results-focused. Many regarded him as a possible
successor to Kofi Annan.

The bombing was naturally a shock. We lost valued colleagues; I
knew many of the people who lost their lives, including Vieira de Mello.
But of equal significance was that the incident symbolized a turning
point in the image of the United Nations. For decades the iconic UN
blue helmet had signaled impartiality—and with it, immunity. We now

were being treated as the adjunct of an occupying force, playing into the hands of the major powers.

A month later, another car bomb was detonated outside the Canal Hotel, killing an Iraqi policeman and wounding still more UN workers. The roughly six hundred UN international staff in Baghdad were withdrawn; other aid agencies withdrew their employees, too. At the following meeting of the heads of UN agencies in New York, I stressed to my colleagues the urgency of restoring the perception of the United Nations and its agencies as politically independent entities.

Late in October 2004, on the eve of the U.S. presidential election, another controversy erupted. The Iraqi Ministry of Science and Technology had written to the IAEA on October 10 to say that massive amounts of HMX and RDX explosives—enough for seven hundred thousand car bombs—had been looted from an unguarded munitions site at Al-Qa'qaa, previously under IAEA seal.[18] I decided to inform the United States first, before informing the Security Council. Then the news was leaked to the media from Baghdad, resulting in major stories in the *New York Times* and on *60 Minutes*.[19] At that point, I sent a letter to the Security Council, as required by IAEA mandate, explaining what the Agency knew about the issue.

A political uproar followed: I was accused of trying to manipulate the U.S. presidential election, as if I had somehow influenced the timing of the revelation. William Safire weighed in, putting me in essentially the same category as Osama Bin Laden, and accusing me of casting my vote for John Kerry, by virtue of having relayed the Al-Qa'qaa report to the Security Council.[20] This below-the-belt punch was especially tough. Safire was merciless: "Bin Laden was the second outsider to try to influence our election in an 'October surprise.' I suspect the first was Mohamed ElBaradei, the chief U.N. arms inspector."

---

18 HMX and RDX are powerful chemical explosives. Both were controlled by the IAEA because, while they have many nonnuclear applications, they can be used as detonating material for a nuclear weapon.

19 "Huge Cache of Explosives Vanished from Site in Iraq," *New York Times*, October 25, 2004.

20 From "Osama Casts His Vote," *New York Times*, November 1, 2004.

Colin Powell rang me up in New York, where I was attending the UN General Assembly. He made no accusations about leaking information, but he said, as one friend to another, that I should be cautious during the election season if asked about this issue by the media.

I explained to Powell how the events had transpired. I pointed out that, after receiving Iraq's letter, I had informed the United States first, via the U.S. mission in Vienna. I hoped there might be some chance that coalition troops could still retrieve some of the explosives, before the news went public. Naturally I was aware of the sensitivity of the timing. But once the story leaked from Iraq and hit the media, I had little choice as to what action to take. The British ambassador to the United Nations, Sir Emyr Jones-Parry, had called our offices in New York to get the facts. Legally, the explosives at Al-Qa'qaa were under our custody. It had become imperative that we report their disappearance to the Security Council.

I told Powell that in my view the interesting question was why the Iraqis had chosen this timing to report the missing explosives. The central problem, of course, was the lack of control in Iraq overall; this was only one of many critical facilities that had been left unsecured by the coalition. I was reminded of Powell's long-standing doctrine that if you decide to go to war, you have to ensure an adequate number of troops.

Iraq's chargé d'affaires in Vienna later told me that the question of whether to report the missing explosives to the IAEA had been discussed at length in Baghdad. The political counselor at the American embassy in Baghdad had advised the Iraqis not to inform us, because, in his view, our Security Council mandate was suspended. However, after discussing it with their minister of science and technology, Dr. Rashad Omar, they decided they had to make the report. Why they timed the letter a few weeks before the election and whether they were aware of the possible implications of it remain interesting questions.

David Sanger of the *New York Times* informed me that Karl Rove, Bush's senior adviser, believed strongly that I had engineered the leak of the Al-Qa'qaa explosives story to the media. Rove also was said to have been incensed by my candor in a lecture at Stanford University on

November 4, just a few days after the U.S. election. The speech was intended to draw lessons from the Iraq debacle and to emphasize the importance of working through multinational institutions and collective actions. I said I believed the inspections had been working and I questioned whether preemptive military action had been justified according to the principles outlined in the UN Charter. I also suggested that all parties lose when the international community is divided on critical issues of peace and security:

> The Coalition lost in credibility in some people's eyes by proceeding to use force without the endorsement of the Security Council. The United Nations lost in credibility as the body driving the action against Iraq on behalf of international legitimacy, and as a result has come to be perceived in some quarters—particularly by many in Iraq—as an adjunct of the Coalition force, and not as an independent and impartial institution. And perhaps it is the Iraqi people who have lost the most: after years of suffering under a brutal dictatorship, and after enduring the hardships brought on through an extended period of sanctions, they have had still more misery brought on by the ravages of war and the unforeseen and extended period of insurgency and civil disorder.

Given what has been said by a multitude of political analysts since then, there was nothing egregious in these remarks. The problem was that, at that time, almost no one from any prominent diplomatic quarter was willing to question publicly the actions of the U.S. government. The headline in the next day's *San Francisco Chronicle* didn't help matters: "UN Arms Inspector Slams Bush Administration."

The harshest reality of the Iraq War and its extended aftermath—an aspect that has been disturbingly minimized in Western media reports—is the Iraqi civilian loss of life. Estimates have ranged as high as eight hundred thousand Iraqi deaths during the first three years of the war. This does not count the millions maimed or wounded, or the millions displaced from their homes and stripped of their livelihoods.

The United States and the West in general have maintained a tight tally of the numbers of their soldiers killed. Yet the Iraqi civilian population remains largely faceless and nameless in media reports. The same has been true, on a somewhat smaller scale, in Afghanistan.

How can Western leaders fail to understand the outrage—the feelings of injustice, humiliation, and bitterness—that this tragedy has provoked or the cultural scars that are likely to be with us for at least a generation?

In January 2005, I met Muwafaq al-Rubaie, the Iraqi national security adviser, at a meeting of the World Economic Forum in Davos. He was working in close cooperation with the U.S. government, yet he told me that the way the Americans were managing Iraq was "criminal." Al-Rubaie said that when the U.S. forces went into Fallujah and killed hundreds of civilians, he protested to Gen. George Casey, the top U.S. commander in Iraq at the time, telling him this was not a humane way to conduct the war. Casey's response, as al-Rubaie relayed it, was devoid of sympathy, to put it mildly: "I am a marine, and that is how I do things."

The U.S. and coalition actions in Iraq, and more broadly in the so-called war on terror, were mooted by many as a precursor to a clash of civilizations and as superb tools for extremists to use in recruitment. The most extreme examples included the CIA renditions,[21] the prison at Guantánamo Bay, and the Abu Ghraib prison abuses. These and other events and images—an almost daily diet of violence inflicted on civilians, filmed in Iraq and Afghanistan and broadcast on Arab television— suggested a basic disdain for human rights, blatant cultural discrimination, and disregard for international norms regarding the conduct of war (such as the protection of civilians and the indiscriminate use of force).

---

21 "Rendition," sometimes referred to as "extraordinary rendition," is the process of transferring prisoners from country to country outside of judicial proceedings. CIA renditions during this period were rumored to be for the purpose of sending prisoners to countries where torture was practiced. These renditions have been the subject of multiple investigations and reports. An example is the June 2007 report from the Committee on Legal Affairs and Human Rights of the Council of Europe; that report is entitled "Secret detentions and illegal transfers of detainees involving Council of Europe member states: second report." Retrieved at: http://news.bbc.co.uk/2/shared/bsp/hi/pdfs/marty_08_06_07.pdf.

Tragically, these actions also sullied the perception of democracy across the Arab and Muslim world. Far from promoting the American values of freedom and respect for human dignity—values I had come to cherish and strongly believe in as a student in New York—the United States and its allies promoted an ethos of violence and cultural division that harkened back to an earlier era of human history.

As the head of the IAEA, I became deeply concerned that the reputation of international institutions, including the Agency, would be severely damaged by association—that we would be perceived as agents of the United States and its Western allies. Perhaps the most difficult thing for me to accept about the Iraq inspections was that they had been, in essence, a farcical exercise: that is, the United States and its closest allies had never intended to take the inspection results seriously, except insofar as they could be used to bolster the case for regime change by military force.

Since the early 1990s, I had been aware that the nuclear nonproliferation regime had entered a new era, one characterized by clandestine activity and the willingness of some countries to blatantly deceive, on a grand scale, in order to achieve political and security goals, in an environment that was sometimes conducive to such deception. What the Iraq War taught me was that this deliberate deception was not limited to small countries ruled by ruthless dictators. More than ever, the core Agency principles of maintaining independence and objectivity—or, as the inspectors liked to put it, "Verify, verify, verify"—had become an ethical code that defined our organization's integrity.

Ultimately, the story of the Iraq War may come down to a series of hard-hitting questions. If the community of nations seeks to live by the rule of law, then what steps should be taken when violations of international law result in massive civilian casualties? Who should be held accountable when military action has been taken in contravention of the law as codified in the UN Charter; or, worse still, when military action is found to have been based on faulty information, the deliberately selective treatment of information, or the promulgation of misinformation?

The United Nations Charter prohibits the unilateral use of military force by one state against another except in cases of self-defense against an armed attack. When an imminent threat is involved, the argument has been made that "preemptive self-defense" is also justified, particularly in the nuclear era. Regime change, however, is not a legal cause for war. Nor is it legal to invent a case for war when regime change is the underlying motivation. And when a war is launched, the Fourth Geneva Convention is crystal clear about the need to protect civilians, just as international humanitarian law plainly prohibits the indiscriminate use of force.[22]

In a *Newsweek* article entitled "The Dilemma of Dissent," and in his recent book *War of Necessity, War of Choice*, Richard Haass writes that, already in July 2002, he had discussed with Rice his concern about what he saw as preparation for war in Iraq. According to Haass, before he got very far, Rice stopped him. "You can save your breath, Richard. The President has already made up his mind on Iraq." Haass adds that "the way she said it made clear [Bush] had decided to go to war."[23]

The same has been implied by other insider sources of information. The British ambassador to Washington, Sir Christopher Meyer, has alleged that the decision to go to war was made in 2002, at Camp David, in a meeting between Blair and Bush. Multiple other reports have suggested that, in the wake of the September 2001 terrorist attacks in the United States, the neoconservative obsession was to penalize a Muslim, and preferably an Arab, country, with Iraq the chosen target. In these renderings, the Iraq War was a war of ideology, motivated by the fantasy

---

22 The four Geneva Conventions of 1949 and their Additional Protocols are at the core of international humanitarian law, the body of international law that regulates the conduct of armed conflict and seeks to limit its effects. They specifically protect people who are not taking part in the hostilities (civilians, health workers, and aid workers) and those who are no longer participating in the hostilities, such as wounded, sick, and shipwrecked soldiers and prisoners of war. The UN Security Council concluded in 1993 that the conventions had become part of customary international law, making them binding on all countries, including nonsignatories.

23 Richard Haass is the current president of the Council on Foreign Relations and, at the time of the Iraq invasion, was a close adviser to Colin Powell. His article appeared in *Newsweek* on May 2, 2009. His book, *War of Necessity, War of Choice: A Memoir of Two Iraq Wars*, was published by Simon and Schuster in 2009.

of establishing Iraq as an oasis of democracy that would, in turn, transform the geopolitical landscape of the Middle East.

Both Blair and Bush have indicated that regime change was at the heart of the motivation to go to war, regardless of the justification cited. Together with a number of their key associates, they significantly inflated the imminence of the threat posed by Saddam Hussein's weapons of mass destruction, weapons which in fact did not exist.[24] In September 2003, Dick Cheney gave an interview on MSNBC's *Meet the Press* in which, in response to pointed questions, he acknowledged that he had "misspoken" before the war. "We never had any evidence that [Saddam Hussein] had acquired a nuclear weapon."

Bush and Blair similarly promoted statements that proved to have little basis in fact, such as touting Iraq's import of uranium from Niger based on a transparent forgery (Bush), or declaring Iraq's capability to launch a chemical weapons attack in forty-five minutes (Blair). Both were deliberately selective in their use of the available facts. And both presided over a war in which, time after time, bombing campaigns and armored assaults made little attempt to protect the civilian population against the indiscriminate use of force, referring euphemistically to civilian deaths and injuries as "collateral damage."

What should be done about this troubling litany? Should the United Nations request an opinion from the International Court of Justice as to the legality of the Iraq War? If the answer is that the war was in fact illegal—and moreover, if consideration is given to the massive civilian casualties incurred—should not the International Criminal Court investigate whether this constitutes a "war crime" and determine who is

---

24 In testimony to the Chilcot inquiry, Blair said that his support for the U.S. action was prompted by the fear of "disastrous consequences for a tough stance on WMD and its proliferation—and for [the UK's] relationship with the U.S." Blair also described telling Bush in late 2001 that "if [regime change] became the only way of dealing with this issue, we were going to be up for that." In mid-2002, when Colin Powell wrote in a memo that "We need to make the case. . . . We need to have the sort of Rolls-Royce information campaign we had at the end of Afghanistan before we start in Iraq," Blair added in the margin, "I agree with this entirely." Richard Norton-Taylor, "Tony Blair's Promise to George Bush," *Guardian*, January 21, 2011, retrieved at www.guardian.co.uk/politics/2011/jan/21/tony-blair-george-bush-iraq/.

accountable?[25] Should Iraq request reparations at the International Court of Justice, or another forum, for the damages incurred during a war launched in violation of international law and on the basis of falsehoods?

If we are to live by the rule of law, then the prosecution of war crimes should not be limited to those who lose—the Slobodan Miloševićs of the world—or to the Omar al-Bashirs, who originate from poor and long-oppressed regions. Legal norms, to retain legitimacy, must be uniform in their application. Otherwise, as an international community, we are guilty of applying double standards.

Do we, as a community of nations, have the wisdom and courage to take the corrective measures needed, to ensure that such a tragedy will never happen again?

---

25 If the prosecutor of the International Criminal Court were to issue an indictment against specific individuals, then any country party to the convention could legally arrest them if they traveled to that country.

4

NORTH KOREA, 2003 AND AFTER

The Nuclear Weapons Club Adds a Member

Near the end of 2002, less than a month after UN inspectors had gained reentry into Iraq, the North Korean saga took its own dramatic twist. Over the next few years, we would see the two lead actors in this drama— North Korea and the United States—play out a strikingly familiar script of provocation and counterprovocation, brinksmanship and pacification, on-again, off-again negotiations, with the rest of the international community bereft of the tools to change the dynamic.

The nuclear torch had long since been passed to Kim Jong Il, the son of Kim Il Sung, with little change. The Agreed Framework, an agreement with the United States that specified steps to resolve tensions over North Korea's nuclear program, was still in place. But both sides were frustrated: the North Koreans, because of U.S. delays in delivering the two light water reactors promised in exchange for a freeze of North Korea's known nuclear operations; the Americans, because the regime had neither collapsed nor provided any greater insight into its past nuclear activities. Caught in between, the IAEA was maintaining a presence at Yongbyon, monitoring the freeze of the nuclear facilities but unable to conduct meaningful safeguards verification elsewhere in the country.[1]

---

1 IAEA inspectors were there to verify that North Korea was not reprocessing its spent fuel into plutonium, but the Agency's verification activities were limited in scope to the declared facilities subject to the freeze.

There had been hints of a thaw in the U.S.–North Korea relationship in the final months of 2000. The outgoing secretary of state, Madeleine Albright, had fêted Kim Jong Il's emissary[2] in Washington. Pyongyang had issued an invitation to the American president for a visit. Albright herself had been warmly received by Kim Jong Il. Not long thereafter, the new secretary of state, Colin Powell, had signaled the intent to continue the dialogue. "We do plan to engage with North Korea, to pick up where President Clinton and his administration left off," Powell said. "Some promising elements were left on the table, and we'll be examining those elements."[3]

But President Bush had a different perspective. In a meeting that same month with Kim Dae Jung, the South Korean president who had won the 2000 Nobel Peace Prize for his "Sunshine Policy" of détente with his northern neighbor, Bush made clear his aversion to dealing with the North Korean regime. By January 2002, North Korea had been lumped into the "axis of evil," along with Iran and Iraq. Bush was quoted referring to Kim Jong Il as a "spoiled child" and a "pygmy."[4]

The last feeble signs of progress appeared late that summer when—many years behind schedule—the first concrete was finally poured at the site of the promised light water nuclear power reactor plants, intended to become the cornerstone of a peaceful North Korean nuclear energy program. In September, Japanese prime minister Junichiro Koizumi was received by Kim Jong Il in Pyongyang—a diplomatic breakthrough—and the two countries announced their intention to normalize relations.[5]

Then everything changed. The trigger was a report to Washington by U.S. assistant secretary of state for East Asian and Pacific affairs James Kelly regarding a recent meeting with North Korean officials. To this day, the details of that meeting are murky, but it appears that Kelly accused the North Koreans of running a secret uranium enrichment program.

---

2 Vice Marshal Cho Myong Rok, regarded as Kim Jong Il's second in command.

3 Jake Tapper, "Did Bush Bungle Relations with North Korea?" Salon, March 15, 2001.

4 Howard Fineman, "I Sniff Some Politics," Newsweek, May 27, 2002.

5 Japan-DPRK Pyongyang Declaration, September 17, 2002.

What Kelly reported was that his North Korean counterpart had admitted to the program's existence; however, no details were given at the time regarding its nature or scope.

The United States called for inspections of this alleged enrichment program. The news was leaked to the press: immediately, media accounts appeared declaring that North Korea had cheated on the Agreed Framework. Rather than continuing the dialogue to get to the bottom of these "revelations" and address them within the Agreed Framework, the United States persuaded the executive board of the Korean Peninsula Energy Development Organization, or KEDO, the organization formed to implement the provisions of the Agreed Framework, to suspend its deliveries of heavy fuel oil to North Korea.[6] The oil shipments, North Korea's energy lifeline, were brought to an abrupt halt.

Pyongyang responded forcefully, declaring the Agreed Framework dead—because of the U.S. interruption of oil supplies—and announcing that it would restart the Yongbyon reactor. North Korea threatened to expel the IAEA inspectors, resume operations to reprocess its spent fuel, and withdraw from the NPT.

This was no bluff. The next day, Pyongyang officially asked the IAEA to remove its seals and surveillance equipment from the Yongbyon facilities. For a few days, we exchanged messages with our North Korean counterparts. It was Christmastime, and I was operating from a beach resort in Colombo, Sri Lanka, where my family was on holiday. I gave phone interviews to CNN from our hotel room, using my son, Mostafa, as an assistant. I kept the IAEA Board of Governors informed of the deteriorating situation. Coordinating with my team in Vienna, we tried every argument we could think of to dissuade Pyongyang from rash action.

---

6 KEDO was founded in 1995 by the United States, South Korea, and Japan, to implement the principal energy provisions of the Agreed Framework, including the construction of the two promised light water nuclear power reactors. Until the reactors were completed, North Korea was to be provided with five hundred thousand metric tons of heavy fuel oil annually. As I have noted, North Korea was already complaining of a lack of good faith on the part of the United States and KEDO, because of delays in the light water reactor construction. The suspension of fuel oil shipments was the proverbial last straw.

On December 26, I made a statement condemning these actions because of the "serious proliferation concerns" they raised and criticizing North Korea for its "nuclear brinksmanship." But no one was backing down. The director general of North Korea's General Department of Atomic Energy, Ri Je Son, requested formally that we remove our inspectors immediately. We had no choice but to bring them back to Vienna.

In an emergency session, the IAEA Board adopted a resolution deploring North Korea's unilateral actions and calling for reinstatement of IAEA measures. Four days later, on January 10, 2003, North Korea announced its withdrawal from the NPT. Within weeks, North Korean technicians began removing and disabling the IAEA monitoring equipment. They initiated repairs to restart the reactor, began moving fuel rods, and took steps to resume reprocessing spent fuel.

I publicly urged Pyongyang to reverse its decision, saying it was counterproductive to the efforts to achieve peace and stability in the Korean Peninsula. In fact, cabinet-level officials from North and South Korea met later in the month, looking for some sort of diplomatic way out. But it was clear that the damage had been done, at least for the time being

The hard-liners in the United States were clearly pleased that rapprochement with North Korea was brought to a halt. To them, the very idea of engaging with Kim Jong Il's regime was repugnant. Nor were they fond of the Agreed Framework, which they characterized as rewarding North Korea for its violation of the NPT. While the Agreed Framework was indeed a flawed arrangement, the alternative would turn out to be much worse.

Of course, the IAEA Board referred the situation to the Security Council, but the council took no action. Granted, its attention, like that of the rest of the world, was strongly focused on the catastrophe taking shape a continent away in Iraq. But the real reason was China, a veto-wielding member of the P-5, whose view held sway. China stuck to its customary, and justifiable, belief that the only way to resolve the North Korean crisis or similar issues was through negotiations and dialogue. Thus, in April 2003, Beijing hosted direct talks between the United States and North Korea, but the parties made little progress, attempts at closed-door diplomacy giving way to demands, public accusations, and rejected offers.

Soon after, North Korea announced the end of its last remaining non-proliferation pact: a 1992 bilateral agreement with South Korea to keep the peninsula free of nuclear weapons. Undeterred, China continued to press for a diplomatic resolution, hosting the first of what would be dubbed the "six-nation" or "six-party" talks: a long-running series of negotiations that, in addition to North Korea and the United States, would include Japan, Russia, and South Korea.

The IAEA was given no role in the six-party talks. Indeed, in every practical sense, the years that followed North Korea's 2003 exit from the NPT were, from the IAEA's perspective, a black box. We were kept in the dark. We had no inspection presence in North Korea. While I supported the efforts to engage the North Koreans in dialogue through the six-party talks, the lack of a unified and consistent international response to the North Korean escalation was, in my view, setting a dangerous precedent. On the one hand, in the case of Iraq, the government had invited in the international weapons inspectors who had found no evidence of continuing WMD programs, yet the inspection findings had been put to one side in favor of an invasion (allegedly based on a "threat to international peace and security"). On the other hand, North Korea's government had failed to answer questions about concealed plutonium, secret facilities, and its alleged undeclared enrichment program; Agency inspectors had been sent out of the country; and the North Koreans had withdrawn from the NPT—sending a strong signal regarding their intentions—yet there was no collective condemnation by the Security Council, and the IAEA, the body charged with preventing nuclear proliferation, was not even part of ongoing talks.[7]

---

7 Since withdrawal from the NPT takes three months to go into effect, North Korea's decision became official on April 10, 2003. Although the IAEA Board had referred the matter to the Security Council for action, the council did not issue a resolution on the matter; following its closed-door meeting on April 9, council president Adolfo Aguilar Zinser of Mexico merely told reporters that council members had "expressed their concern" and would continue to follow up on developments.

At each meeting of the IAEA Board, I expressed my concern and our willingness to work with all parties toward a comprehensive solution that would address both North Korea's security interests and the non-proliferation priorities of the international community. Behind the scenes, I asked various members of the six-party talks for information, but there seemed to be little to report.

I also used public forums to express my dissatisfaction. During an open discussion at the Council on Foreign Relations, I told the group: "What I worry about with North Korea is that it sends the worst signals to would-be proliferators: that if you want to protect yourself, you should accelerate your [nuclear] program—because then you are immune in a way. Then people will sit around the table with you. And if you do not do that fast enough, you might be subject to preemption"—referring, of course, to the military action in Iraq.[8]

I met with Colin Powell in Washington in June 2004. By that time, the six parties were finishing their third round of talks, with no break-throughs in sight. Powell told me that he was open to taking a more flexible approach on North Korea. He speculated, however, that the North Koreans might be stalling until November. "If I were the North Koreans," he said, "I would wait for the result of the elections—because if the Democrats were to win the White House, they most likely would adopt a more flexible approach."

From what I could glean, in addition to the construction of the two power reactors, North Korea was pushing for more aid, as well as for security guarantees and eventual normalization of relations with the United States in exchange for giving up its nuclear program. The United States, and to some extent Japan, were pushing back. They wanted North Korea to completely dismantle its nuclear facilities and to do so in a way that would prevent any restart of fuel cycle operations; the United States also urged withholding international aid until North Korea had taken

---

8 May 14, 2004. The discussion was moderated by Graham Allison, director of the Belfer Center for Science and International Affairs, John F. Kennedy School of Government, Harvard University.

major, verifiable steps. China, Russia, and South Korea favored a more moderate, action-for-action approach.

No one was budging.

The diplomatic outlook grew progressively more gloomy. When the time came for the fourth round of talks, North Korea refused to attend, blaming the "hostile" stance of the United States. When I visited South Korea and Japan that fall, I realized that other members of the six-party talks were also unhappy with the Americans' hard-line approach. South Korea's vice foreign minister attributed the problem to a difference in perspective: for the United States, he said, North Korea is just another case of WMD; whereas "for us, the North Koreans are our enemies, but also our brothers." Japan, I was told, would prefer to start focusing on North Korea's plutonium separation, a proliferation risk that was undisputed, and defer the issue of alleged uranium enrichment. With the IAEA out of the country, there was no "freeze" in place to prevent North Korea from reprocessing its spent fuel, separating the plutonium, and building nuclear weapons.

Toward the end of that year, I was contacted confidentially by Bill Richardson, the governor of New Mexico. I had known Richardson since his stint as U.S. ambassador to the UN in 1997–98, and after that when he was secretary of energy. He wanted to see whether he could mediate the situation and was interested in going to North Korea as my envoy, an unusual but acceptable proposal. He added that he would like to keep his hand in foreign policy issues, which he obviously was missing in his role as governor.

Richardson had experience with North Korean diplomacy: as a U.S. congressional representative in 1996, he had successfully secured the release of Evan Hunziker, an American citizen held in North Korean custody; and in early January 2003, when the North Korean situation was falling apart, Pyongyang had sent its own envoys to meet with Richardson in New Mexico, presumably hoping to use him as an intermediary. He had also been sent to Baghdad to secure the release of two U.S. aerospace workers during Bill Clinton's presidency and had traveled to Bangladesh in 1996 to secure a pardon for an American woman accused of heroin smuggling. So he had a record of mediation successes in problem areas, which often gained significant media coverage.

I agreed to support Richardson's mission. He also set out to obtain State Department approval, which came in the form of a promise of military air transport, with the caveat that he would not be speaking on behalf of the U.S. government. Shortly thereafter, Richardson sent me a fax: the North Koreans, who had earlier been open to the visit, had changed their minds.

In another curious turn, I was asked by a divisional director of the IAEA to see a Swedish banker by the name of Peter Castenfelt who had connections to high-level officials in North Korea. Although I felt quite skeptical, I agreed to the meeting. Castenfelt's appearance, when he showed up at the IAEA offices in Vienna, did nothing to reassure me: his clothes were mussed, as was his hair. He grinned as he shook my hand, eyeing me through oversized spectacles.

When we sat down, Castenfelt got right to his message. Kim Jong Il, he said, had a dilemma. He wanted to open up the country, to lead North Korea out of its isolated state. Many young North Korean entrepreneurs supported him. The problem was the old army generals of his father's generation, who opposed Kim Jong Il's every step toward rapprochement with the international community. Castenfelt said the North Koreans recognized that restoring a relationship with the IAEA was important. In fact, he revealed that the North Koreans had prepared a letter inviting me to visit, but then had decided to postpone sending it because I had made a statement about them they did not like.

Peter Castenfelt was an enigmatic figure. From what I could gather, he had been involved with Russia during Boris Yeltsin's time, interceding to get loans for Russia from the International Monetary Fund. Germany and Russia later sent him to persuade Slobodan Milošević to stop bombing Kosovo. He seemed to have high-level connections everywhere, including in the United States and Iran. I was never sure what he sought from his role, and he exited the North Korean stage as suddenly as he had entered it.

Abruptly, the clouds broke. The fourth round of six-party talks were deadlocked in August 2005 but then resumed in September, with all parties reaching agreement on a Joint Statement that laid out the principles for addressing the North Korean situation. The statement included North Korea's agreement to abandon its nuclear weapons program and to return to the NPT and to IAEA safeguards.

What had changed? In my view, the primary difference was Condoleezza Rice, now U.S. secretary of state, who was able to convince Bush (against the opposition of her colleagues, particularly Dick Cheney and his faction) that a shift of course was necessary. Her influence was evident in the appointment of Ambassador Christopher Hill as the head of the U.S. delegation to the six-party talks, and a few months later as assistant secretary of state for East Asian and Pacific affairs. Hill, a pragmatist who believed in step-by-step building of trust through dialogue, broke with precedent and began to engage directly with his counterparts in Pyongyang. I found Hill to be a rare commodity, a high-level Bush administration appointee with a nonideological, commonsense approach to handling geopolitical crises. Hill was remarkably adept at diplomacy with the North Koreans; there were rumors that the Japanese had started privately calling him "Chris Jong-Hill."

It was evident that Hill had little patience for the hard-liners in Washington; at one point, when we were speaking one-on-one, he told me, "John Bolton's body may be out, but his hands are still there," referring to Bolton's continuing influence in Washington. Hill and I were generally in agreement on issues of common concern: the value of dialogue, the shortsightedness of uncompromising positions, and the importance of a pragmatic, committed, step-by-step approach on North Korea. Unfortunately, from what he eventually shared with me, all sorts of obstacles arose to block his progress on the North Korean nuclear situation. I once mentioned that I found the bench to be very thin at the State Department when it came to arms control expertise. Hill grinned and said that's why he was getting such bad counsel.

The Joint Statement, unlike the Agreed Framework, did not include a specific timetable or even a complete road map, and some in the

United States referred to it derisively as the "son of the Agreed Framework," implying that three years after trashing the Agreed Framework, the U.S. administration had merely replaced it with an inferior alternative. Still, it was an important step forward. North Korea promised concessions in return for energy assistance. The United States declared it had no intention of invading North Korea, said it would provide a security guarantee to this effect, and pledged to respect North Korea's sovereignty.

And then, yet again, the negotiations ground to a halt. The United States, citing an ongoing U.S. Treasury Department investigation, froze roughly $25 million in North Korean assets in Banco Delta Asia in Macau, claiming that they were linked to money laundering and counterfeiting. Pyongyang was incensed but offered to resume the six-party talks if the United States released the funds. The United States refused, saying the nuclear and financial issues were unrelated.

With talks once more at an impasse, North Korea announced that it would conduct its first nuclear test. And six days later, on October 9, 2006, Pyongyang kept its word. The detonation was quite small by test standards; there was much doubt in nuclear circles about the effectiveness of the North Korean technology. But there was no denying the most sobering aspect: another country—isolated, impoverished, feeling deeply threatened by the United States but nonetheless defiant—had joined the exclusive club of nuclear weapon possessor states.

If the intent of the North Korean nuclear test was to get attention, it worked. Reactions were swift. The UN Security Council issued a resolution condemning the test, adding sanctions that had little teeth and in some cases repeated what was already in place. Former U.S. secretary of defense William Perry, writing in the *Washington Post*, declared the test a demonstration of "the total failure of the Bush administration's policy" toward North Korea.[9] Ex-president Jimmy Carter was more conciliatory, pointing out that it was still possible to return to the 2005 Joint Statement: "What must be avoided," he wrote, "is to leave a beleaguered nuclear

---

9 "In Search of a North Korea Policy," October 11, 2006.

nation convinced that it is permanently excluded from the international community, its existence threatened, its people suffering horrible deprivation, and its hard-liners in total control of military and political policy."[10]

A sharply opposing perspective, but one that reflected the viewpoint of the U.S. hawks, was offered by David Frum, a Canadian who had previously served as President Bush's speechwriter and claimed credit for the "axis of evil" concept. Writing in the *New York Times* one day after the test, he advocated harsh measures: accelerating the deployment of U.S. missile defense systems; ending humanitarian aid to North Korea; bringing a number of Asian countries into NATO. Frum had one more brainstorm: the United States, he wrote, should "encourage Japan to renounce the Nuclear Nonproliferation Treaty and create its own nuclear deterrent."[11] I breathed a sigh of relief that Frum was no longer in the policy-making loop.

With a new urgency in the air, the talks between the parties quickly resumed. Condoleezza Rice, in a meeting in late October, asked me if I thought the IAEA might play a role in helping to resolve the North Korean impasse. "It is not enough," she said, "for North Korea to state its readiness to denuclearize the Korean peninsula. They should do something concrete."

Of course, we were willing to be involved in any way that could defuse the crisis. "We could start with some agreed inspection activities," I replied, "and proceed incrementally from there." Rice concurred. I could not help thinking that after all this time, we were basically reinstating the action-for-action approach of the long-discarded Agreed Framework. Even more peculiar, given what had transpired in Iraq and the ongoing U.S. behavior in relation to Iran's nuclear program, was that the United States was resuming its participation in talks with the North Koreans—and seemingly open to Pyongyang getting its way—almost immediately after they had detonated their first nuclear weapon.

---

10 "Solving the Korean Stalemate, One Step at a Time," *New York Times*, October 11, 2006.
11 "Mutually Assured Disruption," *New York Times*, October 10, 2006.

To ease the tensions, the United States began working on a way for its lawyers and policy makers to "unfreeze" the North Korean funds in the Macau bank. In February 2007, North Korea agreed to begin shutting down the Yongbyon reactor and to allow IAEA nuclear inspectors back into the country in exchange for aid—the first step in a new disarmament deal. On the twenty-third of that month, I received a letter of invitation from North Korea to visit. The invitation quoted my comment that the only way to resolve the Korean issue was through peaceful dialogue and engagement, not through pressure. This was a welcome sign. I made the invitation public, with a statement that "this is a step in the right direction."

During a phone call with Rice the next day, we joked about my upcoming visit. "Thank you very much," I told her, "for arranging for me to go to North Korea again during the winter." I told her how cold it had been during my 1992 visit, recalling how I had shivered in my hotel room.

My departure for Pyongyang was preceded by a stunning disclosure. It came in the form of an Agence France-Presse article,[12] based on congressional testimony, stating that the U.S. confidence about its intelligence on the alleged North Korean uranium enrichment program—the intelligence that had torpedoed the Agreed Framework back in 2002—was at "mid-level," meaning there was some uncertainty or conflicting information.

I was astounded. The secret uranium enrichment program was the reason the United States had given for cutting fuel assistance to North Korea, the initiator that had set in motion the entire sequence of political maneuvers over the subsequent four years—North Korea's expulsion of the IAEA, its withdrawal from the NPT, the acceleration of its weapons program, the on-again, off-again talks, the threats and sanctions, and finally the testing of a nuclear device. All this stemmed from an uncertain

---

12 "U.S. Now Uncertain About North Korea Uranium Enrichment," Agence France-Presse, March 1, 2007.

claim. The revelation was yet another blow—to the credibility and competent handling of U.S. intelligence information.

At a later point, Christopher Hill told me he had read the minutes of the original meeting, in which North Korea had "confessed" to his predecessor, James Kelly. He made a face and shrugged; it seemed obvious to me that Hill was not convinced of the nature of the confession.

As the head of the IAEA, I could not openly express my disagreement with how the issue was handled. But I didn't need to: many critics, including some who had been silent at the time of the Iraq invasion, now spoke out. The overreaction to questionable intelligence had driven a pariah nation into still greater isolation. And that isolation had given North Korea's generals and scientists the extra time and motivation to develop and detonate a nuclear weapon.

The bottom line was that Pyongyang now had a much stronger negotiating position than before. It was an unfortunate example of ideology and absolutism getting in the way of common sense and pragmatism.

My return visit to North Korea, in March 2007—the first in fifteen years—began with a glitch. I had passed along a request in advance, through the Chinese government, asking the North Koreans to arrange a meeting at the highest level. Stopping en route in Beijing, I was told that the North Koreans were unhappy I had not approached them directly, since they had, after all, issued the invitation for my visit. I pointed out that the IAEA no longer had an accredited North Korean ambassador, a direct channel for communication. But the thrust of their statement was clear: they did not want to be considered a satellite of China.

The only airline to fly between Beijing and Pyongyang was Air Koryo, the official North Korean carrier. I recalled my experience with Air Koryo in 1992, so we took a small private Chinese jet instead. The Pyongyang airport was deserted when we arrived. From what I could see, there was no other flight going or coming. We were the only passengers in the terminal. I was told that the entire Pyongyang traffic volume consisted of one flight to Beijing every other day.

The same Orwellian atmosphere I remembered from 1992 still pervaded the city: there were no private cars, motorcycles, or even many bicycles on the streets, only a few official vehicles. Most people we saw outside were walking. Patriotic music was piped through loudspeakers at various places in the city, including the area where we were staying.

The Hotel Koryo was deserted, except for the staff and a handful of foreigners, including an Australian delegation that was there to discuss humanitarian assistance. I was given a first-class room: a worn, drab-colored suite consisting of a bedroom and a salon. The furnishings were a hodgepodge of 1950s style. The bathroom fixtures were also old. There was no room service. The cost was roughly two hundred dollars per night.

The country's financial situation was obviously bleak. Even as the guests of the North Korean government, we were asked to pay for everything, including the cars that took us from place to place. The food at our hotel was adequate, but the head of the Australian team said that stunted growth due to malnutrition was evident in 60 percent of North Korean children under the age of two. The Egyptian chargé d'affaires told me that even at the diplomatic quarters they had electricity and running water for only a few hours a day.

My hope for this short visit was to lay the groundwork for reestablishing North Korea's relationship with the IAEA. I had brought a small IAEA team with me, prepared to dive into technical and policy matters if Pyongyang gave the signal. Our agenda of meetings, spanning multiple levels of the North Korean government, looked promising.

But our cool welcome was followed by a frustrating sequence of ambiguous political signals typical of Pyongyang. Our appointment with the vice minister representing North Korea at the six-party talks was canceled at the last minute. We were told he was sick, but the media widely interpreted it as an intentional slight.

Before meeting with the vice chairman of the Presidium, or Parliament, we were given a mini-tour. At the Chamber of the Deputies, we craned our necks at a fifteen-meter statue of Kim Il Sung, the "eternal" president. It reminded me of meeting the emir of Zaria, in northern Nigeria, where local people were expected to crawl on the ground to show respect. Here a godlike status was similarly conferred on a dead person. "Let's go to the meeting," I said, my irritation showing.

Over traditional ginseng tea, the vice chairman began by describing North Korea's "army-centered policy," declaring that the whole country was "of one mind." I replied that countries and governments were ultimately judged by how much their people enjoyed the right to live in freedom and dignity. No country, I said, could afford to be isolated from the rest of the international community. The translator laughed nervously at my critical comments, leaving me unsure of whether the vice chairman received my message.

The next meeting, with the vice minister for foreign affairs, also seemed to follow a rehearsed script. North Korea, he said, had an "unpleasant history" of encountering "bias" at the IAEA. I assured the vice minister that we tried to perform our responsibilities with objectivity. After nods all around, the North Koreans said they wished to look to the future. I suggested that they consider coming back as member of the Agency. The vice minister said they first would have to see how the United States would behave, but he commended me for publicly supporting a peaceful settlement of the North Korean nuclear issue and for stressing the need to take into account the country's security and economic concerns.

Our most pleasant interactions were with Ri Je Son, the director general of North Korea's General Bureau of Atomic Energy, which took place at our hotel and included tasty meals: traditional Korean dishes of meat, fish, kimchee, and vegetables, coupled with wine and a traditional rice-based liqueur. With striking honesty, Ri Je Son volunteered, in response to my question, that his people could not afford to have meat every day. From a policy standpoint, however, he, too, adhered carefully to the party line—the "bad experience" with the IAEA in the past and the desire to focus on the future.

Back in my chilly suite, I realized that, despite all the posturing and the lack of a notable breakthrough, the mere resumption of dialogue would help to facilitate our interactions in the coming months. I turned on the television to the inevitable programming: more war movies featuring the atrocities perpetrated on North Korea by the United States and Japan. I was glad it was a short visit.

On March 19, 2007, Chris Hill announced that North Korea's frozen funds in Banco Delta Asia were being "unfrozen," in response to Pyongyang's positive actions. The actual transfer was delayed until June, when the Russians intervened to physically move the funds from Macau to North Korea. South Korea also played its part, sending a sizable shipment of fuel oil to its northern neighbor in July. When I met that month with the South Korean president, Roh Moo Hyun, he spoke with regret about the inefficiency of the negotiations process and the time lost. "It has taken us five years," he said, "just to convince the Americans to talk bilaterally to Pyongyang."

The transfer of funds led to rapid progress. The North Koreans began shutting down the reactor in Yongbyon, as promised. The IAEA also responded promptly. By July 17, a team of ten Agency inspectors had verified the shutdown of all of North Korea's designated nuclear facilities, applied IAEA seals, and begun installing surveillance equipment.

The sequence of events that followed, a period that would last through most of 2008, marked the most sustained and meaningful progress on resolving concerns related to the North Korean nuclear program since late 2000. The six-party talks continued, entering the "second phase" of actions under the Joint Agreement. Shipments of fuel oil arrived as promised. Japan and North Korea resolved to renormalize their relations. The North Koreans agreed to provide a complete and accurate declaration of their nuclear facilities and materials. The dismantling of facilities proceeded on schedule. Delegations of experts from the United States, China, and Russia were allowed to visit Yongbyon. When Chris Hill traveled to Pyongyang for further consultations, he carried with him a cordial letter from President Bush to Kim Jong Il.

Western media organizations were even invited for tours of North Korea's shut-down nuclear plant. In February 2008, CNN's Christiane

Amanpour reported live from the facilities at Yongbyon, declaring that North Korea had "lifted the nuclear veil." Technicians from the U.S. Department of Energy were on site, Amanpour observed, helping to dismantle portions of North Korea's nuclear sites. "It seems a far cry from the hostility conjured by the 'axis of evil.'" The New York Philharmonic, with conductor Lorin Maazel, had landed in Pyongyang—"a small step on the long road to normality," in Amanpour's words.[13]

The IAEA's official status with North Korea, however, was in something of a limbo state. When asked by the six parties to verify the shutdown of the Yongbyon facilities, we had responded promptly. However, under the terms of the Joint Agreement, the United States had begun to disable North Korea's facilities without IAEA involvement, preferring to do things bilaterally. I was reluctant to complain too loudly, because the progress toward dismantlement, in and of itself, was encouraging. The IAEA had gotten tacit agreement from the United States that the Americans involved would "observe" the process and keep records to ensure the Agency's continuity of knowledge, but our inspectors still worried that, if not present throughout dismantlement, they would lose critical threads of information that could make it difficult later to verify the control of nuclear material.

John Rood, the acting U.S. undersecretary of state for arms control and international security, came to see me in Vienna on May 6, 2008. He said the United States hoped to have North Korea provide its nuclear declaration to the Chinese and to have the IAEA verify the declaration, to reinforce that the rapprochement with North Korea was a multilateral rather than a bilateral process. We would be happy to do so, I said, but passed on to him what we had heard from the North Koreans: the United States did not want the Agency involved.

We would agree to carry out the verification regardless, but I wanted Rood to understand the IAEA's ambiguous position. Some countries, including most of the Europeans and Japan, took the view that North Korea remained a party to the NPT—in which case the IAEA had a legal obligation to verify their declaration. Others, like the United

---

13 "North Korea Lifts Nuclear Veil," CNN, February 26, 2008.

States, believed that North Korea was no longer part of the NPT. In my opinion as a lawyer, it was clear that North Korea had served legal notice of its withdrawal from the NPT in January 2003 and was therefore no longer a party.

I pressed the IAEA Board for clarification of our situation. The parties to the NPT, I said, needed to determine whether North Korea remained a party to the treaty and to provide the Agency with corresponding guidance. For my part, I wanted to be sure that the Agency could not be blamed for not pushing to exercise its responsibilities. I received no response; in fact, the issue remains unresolved to this day.

On June 26, the North Korean authorities had handed over their declaration to China, with extensive documentation describing their country's past and current nuclear program. One day later, in a symbolic gesture, the demolition of the sixty-foot-high cooling tower from the Yongbyon reactor was witnessed by a small crowd of international journalists and diplomats. Soon after, Chris Hill came to Vienna to brief me on his negotiation with Pyongyang regarding verification modalities. The six parties wanted the Agency to play a leading role, but North Korea was adamantly refusing our involvement. North Korea's position was coming from the highest levels of government. Some of the North Koreans, it seemed, remembered the Agency inspections of 1993 as a bad experience. I had also heard that North Korea was hoping that an inspection by the six parties would be "verification lite," in comparison with the Agency's rigorous approach.

Whatever the case, Hill showed me a draft proposal that suggested that the IAEA was to act as a "consultant as relevant" to the six parties. The actual verification and the assessment of the verification results would be done by the six. The Agency was to work under their "auspices."

I rejected the terms. I told Hill I could not accept having the IAEA's verification authority and role compromised in this way. Of course I understood that the six parties wanted the credibility that would come from the Agency's involvement, but in fact the opposite would occur: the inspections would not be credible if conducted under the auspices of an ad hoc group of countries. Either we would perform verification under the auspices of the international community, as we had done for fifty years, or they could find someone else to do the job. I asked my IAEA colleagues to pass the same message to the other members of the six-party talks.

When I saw a copy of the North Korean declaration, which should have included all nuclear activity, past and present, it was immediately clear that the document was incomplete. It declared the amount of plutonium produced but gave no information about the country's past nuclear weapons program or the number of weapons—nor did it mention the alleged uranium enrichment activities.

Hill agreed: the North Koreans, he said, would likely continue to hold on to their existing nuclear weapons for as long as possible. Nevertheless, real progress had been made, because at least their weapons program had been frozen at the current level, as a result of dismantling the facilities. Achieving a final resolution would require more time and patience. Even verification of the declared plutonium would no doubt be a lengthy and complex process.

At the time, I took particular note of Hill's remark that, given Japan's perception of its own security, some observers were no longer excluding the possibility of Japan rethinking its nuclear weapons status. Hill did not elaborate, and I did not press him on the point. But I remembered that back in October 2006, both the Japanese foreign minister, Taro Aso, and the Liberal Democratic Party policy chief, Shoichi Nakagawa, had suggested opening discussions about a Japanese nuclear weapons program.[14] For Japanese scholars, this was a startling development. Japan was a strong supporter of the NPT; even public mention of Japan's consideration of nuclear weapons capability had long been considered taboo.

---

14 On October 18, 2006, during a lower house committee session, Foreign Minister Aso said, "It is one idea not to allow discussions or even to talk about [possessing nuclear arms] when a neighbor country is going to have them, but it is important to have various discussions." The next day he was quoted as saying, "Japan is capable of producing nuclear weapons." But he added, "We are not saying we have plans to possess nuclear weapons."

This only reinforced my view that, for any country, the consideration of whether to develop, own, or use nuclear weapons is subject to change at any time, depending on how that country understands its current security situation. It can never be ruled out, as long as the option is open. Changes in the perception of national or regional security can be enough to reverse long-standing policy.

The pendulum swung yet again in the summer of 2008. Pyongyang had a falling-out with Washington because the United States had not removed North Korea from its list of states sponsoring terrorism. Under the Joint Agreement, this was the next action-for-action, once North Korea had taken steps to dismantle its facilities at Yongbyon. The problem, I was told, was that the hard-liners in the U.S. administration were hoping to get "something extra" from North Korea before removing the country from the list: specifically, more progress on the verification of the North Korean declaration.

Naturally, Pyongyang saw this as the United States reneging on yet another commitment. North Korean nuclear experts promptly got the order to begin reinstalling equipment at the dismantled facilities. On October 8, 2008, IAEA inspectors were prohibited from further monitoring the shutdown in Yongbyon.

Three days later, the United States backed down. North Korea was removed from the list of terrorism-sponsoring countries. The next day, North Korea resumed the dismantling process. The IAEA was again granted access to the Yongbyon facilities.

But the spring of 2009 would bring another setback. Despite international pressure not to do so, North Korea went forward on April 5 with a "satellite launch," which was perceived to be a test of its longest-range missile. President Barack Obama called the test a "provocation" and urged the UN Security Council to take action. On April 13, the council condemned North Korea for the launch. Pyongyang responded with predictable anger, declaring that North Korea would never again take part in the six-party talks. Once again, the IAEA's inspectors were asked to leave the country.

North Korea at the time was in an ongoing crisis. Poverty was at extreme levels: the allocation of rice per person had fallen to two hundred grams per day, well below a minimally nutritional diet. Meanwhile, the poor health of Kim Jong Il was causing a struggle between the aging dictator, who wanted to install one of his sons, Kim Jong Un, as successor, and high-ranking army generals, who saw an opportunity to grab power. Any external confrontation was an excuse for the hard-liners to call for dramatic action.

The pendulum had not quite reached the end of its swing. On May 25, 2009, North Korea successfully tested its second nuclear weapon. It was still small by nuclear weapon standards but markedly more powerful than the first. The test was condemned by the UN Security Council and by the five other governments of the now-dormant six-party talks.

The long-alleged enrichment program also resurfaced, this time as a fully outfitted uranium enrichment facility, proudly unveiled by the North Koreans in November 2010 to Siegfried S. Hecker, a Stanford University professor who had once directed the Los Alamos National Laboratory.[15] Hecker and his colleagues were shown a sophisticated control room and an enrichment hall equipped with what the North Koreans said were two thousand centrifuges already producing low-enriched uranium. The facility was housed in a former fuel fabrication center, making clear that the enrichment plant had been constructed after April 2009, when inspectors had last been in the country. The speed of construction led many to conjecture that North Korea must have other uranium enrichment operations elsewhere in the country.[16] The revelation was yet another stunning testament to the futility of attempts to contain proliferation ambitions through confrontation, sanctions, and isolation.

---

15 David E. Sanger, "North Koreans Unveil New Plant for Nuclear Use," *New York Times*, November 20, 2010.
16 David E. Sanger, "U.S. Concludes North Korea Has More Nuclear Sites," *New York Times*, December 14, 2010.

...

To my way of thinking, the second North Korean nuclear test was far more frustrating than the first. Much had been accomplished on the North Korean file during the intervening two years. And the detonation had come at a time when, given the policies of the new American administration, the prospects for progress on global nuclear disarmament were better than they had been at any time in the recent past.

But the biggest source of frustration by far has been watching the cycle of ups and downs in North Korea's relationship with the West. North Korea's actions and reactions have been largely predictable. When Pyongyang has been engaged in a meaningful dialogue, the situation has generally improved. When dialogue has stopped, when perceived insults have occurred, when a policy of isolation has been reintroduced, the situation has deteriorated. It is that maddeningly simple.

Thus the Security Council's condemnation of North Korea's missile launch had of course made the situation worse. Quite possibly, with the new U.S. administration in power, North Korea had been deliberately provocative, in the hope of attracting attention from the Obama administration and extracting better treatment than it had received from the Bush administration. In any case, the North Koreans were certain to overreact, as they had in every earlier situation. Is it possible, I wondered, that diplomats and politicians had become so focused on the specific issue of the day that they had lost sight of the endgame of disarmament?

Invariably, whether dealing with North Korea or another nuclear proliferation case, the Security Council seemed to be either too divided or too restricted in its options to produce anything other than toothless statements or actions that prompted unintended consequences. In case after case, the stances taken by the Security Council in response to threats of nuclear proliferation were hollow and ineffectual. For the council to become effective, several adjustments were clearly necessary: a focus on the root causes of insecurity, and not just the symptoms; greater agility and realism in dealing with noncompliance, intervening early rather than postmortem; effective enforcement measures that would target the regimes in question, not innocent civilians; and consistency of approach when dealing with similar situations.[17]

Nowhere would these needs for adjustment be more striking than in dealing with the nuclear program of the Islamic Republic of Iran.

---

17 Of course, the council also needs to be reconstituted to be representative of the twenty-first century. It is absurd that the P-5, the council's permanent membership, does not include countries such as Brazil, India, and South Africa.

5

IRAN, 2003–2005

The Riddle of Taqqiya

As if two ongoing nuclear verification dramas were not enough, in mid-2002 the IAEA began receiving information about a third. Satellite photos of Natanz, a small town in Isfahan province in central Iran, showed the construction of a large industrial facility with discernable details suggesting that it might be a uranium enrichment plant. In mid-August, the National Council of Resistance of Iran[1] held a press conference in Washington alleging that Iran was building a secret nuclear facility at Natanz.

The Agency began investigating. In September, at the annual IAEA General Conference in Vienna, I looked for Gholamreza Aghazadeh, a small, serious man with two titles: vice president of Iran and the head of AEOI, the Atomic Energy Organization of Iran. I pulled him aside. "Tell me about this Natanz facility," I said. "Is this for enrichment, as the satellite photos suggest? Perhaps we should make a visit."

---

1 The NCRI is an Iranian opposition group based in Paris, self-styled as a coalition of democratic Iranian individuals and groups prepared to form a provisional government if the current regime were to be toppled. Both Iran and the United States have classified the NCRI as a terrorist organization, citing its ties to the Mujahedin-e Khalq, a religious leftist affiliate of NCRI with a history of violence. The NCRI has repeatedly made allegations about Iran's clandestine nuclear program, some of which have been substantiated by subsequent IAEA investigation. Whether the NCRI was used by Western intelligence to disseminate information about Iran's nuclear activities was a question I often pondered.

Aghazadeh smiled. "Of course we will invite you soon," he replied warmly. "And then we will clarify everything."

The ambiguity of Aghazadeh's response was less than reassuring. Still more disturbing was the long list of excuses we began to hear for postponing the promised visit: President Khatami was "traveling"; President Khatami was "sick"; the chosen dates were "inconvenient." This went on for months.

In the interim, during a meeting in Washington with Colin Powell and Richard Armitage, deputy secretary of state, I told them that their policy on Iran—with its heavy reliance on sanctions and a boycott to prevent weapons development—was not working. I believed that punitive actions, actions that failed to address the underlying reasons for a country's pursuit of nuclear development, did not constitute a policy—nor, in any pragmatic sense, a strategy—and would at most delay a nuclear weapons program. If a country like Iran wanted to acquire nuclear weapons, the U.S. approach would not be enough to stop it. Powell did not comment, but Armitage agreed, which I took as a hopeful sign.

At the time, I was drawing on the IAEA's experiences with Argentina, Brazil, and South Africa. Despite years of restrictions on exports to these countries, the first two had acquired the nuclear know-how for the fuel cycle, and the third had actually acquired (and later relinquished) nuclear weapons.[2] From what we had repeatedly observed, a policy of isolation and sanctions only served to stimulate a country's sense of national pride; in the worst case, it could make the targeted country's nuclear project a matter of national priority.

When at last the Iranians settled on a visit during the third week of February 2003, the timing was anything but ideal. North Korea had just withdrawn from the NPT. The UN Security Council was sharply divided over the use of force in Iraq, and a military invasion seemed imminent. Our inspection staff was, to say the least, stretched.

---

2 In each of these three cases, the nuclear program was developed before the country was a party to the NPT.

But we needed answers about Natanz. I accepted the invitation and asked Pierre Goldschmidt, the Belgian nuclear scientist who served as my deputy director general for safeguards, to accompany me, as well as Olli Heinonen.

At the opening meeting in Tehran, Aghazadeh and his AEOI colleagues admitted immediately that the facility under construction at Natanz was a large uranium enrichment plant. They insisted, however, that they had not meant to hide it from the Agency.[3] Based on their safeguards agreement, they noted, they had no legal obligation to inform the IAEA until 180 days before the introduction of nuclear material. And on this point, they assured us, the record was clean: no nuclear material had been used, and no enrichment had taken place at the facility.

The next day we headed to Natanz, a small mountain town noted for its orchards and nestled among scattered religious shrines. Aghazadeh and his deputy, Mohammad Saeedi, were our escorts, along with a cluster of Iranian engineers and technicians. Our first stop was a nondescript sand-colored building that looked like a warehouse from the outside. Inside was a large hall divided into six concrete blocks. This, Aghazadeh announced, was a pilot enrichment facility. Roughly 20 centrifuges had been assembled. Each block would eventually house a cascade of 164 centrifuges, for a total of slightly fewer than 1,000.

Then we headed underground. Even with some foreknowledge of what to expect, we found the cavernous main hall stunning. It was completely empty but built to house more than fifty thousand centrifuges—a far more ambitious project. Aghazadeh and his colleagues were positively chatty, proud to show us around, agreeably answering the technical questions posed by Pierre and Olli.

Two aspects of that visit stood out. The first was the scale of Iran's nuclear ambitions, which required a sharp reassessment on our part.

---

3 Given the size of the Natanz facility, it is likely that the Iranians were not intending to "hide" it per se. Their aim, I believe, was to delay its reporting as far as legally permissible under their safeguards agreement and to delay IAEA inspection until they had completed their construction and received all the needed knowledge and technology, which were being obtained through clandestine channels due to sanctions. I was later told they were worried that declaring the Natanz facilities would expose their supply network.

Up to this point, the hallmark of Iran's nuclear program had been one power reactor under construction at Bushehr, for which Russia had contracted to supply the enriched uranium fuel.[4] But Natanz, when fully operational, would have the capacity to supply the fuel for two or three one-thousand megawatt reactors. What other facilities was the AEOI planning or constructing?

The second aspect was still more disconcerting. Aghazadeh told us that Iran's centrifuge development program was entirely indigenous. The Iranians also insisted they had not used any nuclear material in testing at this site or anywhere else. Our experts were skeptical.

This skepticism was only reinforced by my meeting with the president of Iran, Sayyid Mohammad Khatami. Charming and multilingual, Khatami, a cleric and former head of Iran's National Library, had swept to power in 1997, running on a platform of social reform. Domestically he advocated freedom of expression and supported the empowerment of civil society, and he was known internationally for his advocacy of a "Dialogue Among Civilizations." While he had not achieved all of the promised reforms, Khatami remained popular among moderates and particularly among the Iranian youth, who came to refer to him as "The Man with the Chocolate Robe," for the brown clothes he favored.

At our meeting, Khatami was accompanied only by Ali Akbar Salehi,[5] the Iranian ambassador to the IAEA, who acted as a translator. Khatami greeted me warmly, with the traditional kiss on both cheeks. As a cleric trained in the Quran, Khatami spoke Arabic, which he did for a few minutes before shifting into Farsi, with Salehi translating. "You shouldn't worry at all about our program," Khatami said. "We only used inert gas in running our centrifuge cascade."

The detail in the statement struck me as odd. President Khatami, a cleric by training, had just referred to a means of cold testing a centrifuge

---

4 For a decade, the United States had tried its level best, making demarches around the world, to dissuade the Russians from supplying Iran with the Bushehr reactor. The argument was that if the Iranians were to acquire a power plant, they would have a pretext for also developing fuel cycle capabilities. But the United States was not successful.

5 Salehi would later succeed Aghazadeh as the head of AEOI and vice president of Iran, and was subsequently appointed foreign minister.

without using nuclear material. His point was that Iran had not violated any nuclear material reporting requirements. But why would Khatami know about testing with inert gas? I wondered.

In the months that followed, the IAEA began to uncover some answers.

Intelligence information alerted us to the Kalaye Electric Company, a workshop on the southern outskirts of Tehran where the Iranians had tested a small number of centrifuges of the same model as those at Natanz. Kalaye was not a declared nuclear workshop. Our Iranian counterparts assured us that only "simulation studies" had taken place there and that no nuclear material had been used in these simulations. If this was true, then they were within their rights not to have reported it to the IAEA. But how could we be certain if we were not permitted to verify their assertion? We were caught in the classic catch-22 of the NPT: the Iranians had not declared the Kalaye Electric Company in their safeguards agreements, therefore we were not authorized to inspect it, absent some clear nexus to nuclear material. This was the primary loophole that had led to the invention of the Additional Protocol, but Iran had not signed on to the Protocol.

We decided to call Iran's bluff. Noting Tehran's public and private commitments to full transparency in its dealings with the IAEA, we asked the Iranians to allow us to visit Kalaye. We also asked for permission to take environmental samples.

The response came grudgingly, piecemeal. Iran gave Agency inspectors access to Kalaye but refused to allow samples to be taken. Eventually they relented, and inspectors were permitted to return and take environmental samples using "swipes"—small squares of cloth wiped over selected surfaces. The inspectors noted that the facility had been modified considerably in the months since their first visit and worried that the changes might affect the accuracy of their analysis. But when the swipes were analyzed in Member State laboratories (using double-blind samples to mask the origin), the results were definitive: the spectrum of enriched uranium particles in the samples demonstrated that nuclear material *had* been used in the centrifuge testing. Iran was caught, dead to rights.

Little by little the story began to change. Despite the AEOI's claims that their centrifuge program was indigenous, IAEA centrifuge experts observed a strong resemblance to European designs. When confronted with the results of samples that had also been taken from the pilot centrifuge facility at Natanz—which showed the presence of low-enriched and high-enriched uranium particles—the AEOI said that components had been imported from abroad, and speculated that the particles had come from contaminated parts. In fact, we would find that nearly all of Iran's centrifuge technology had been imported from other countries.

The question of whether Iran's centrifuges had or had not been indigenously produced was important. The answer, one way or the other, would give the Agency information that we sorely needed. If Iran had produced the centrifuges domestically, it would have implied a far more elaborate R&D operation than was acknowledged, almost certainly including testing with nuclear material. If, on the other hand, Iran had imported all the parts, it implied that another country or countries had supplied the technology.

Undeclared nuclear material was also showing up. Stocks of natural uranium imported from China were discovered at the Jabr Ibn Hayan Multipurpose Laboratories (JHL) at the Tehran Nuclear Research Center. Neither the material nor the JHL had previously been reported to the IAEA. Much of this uranium had been converted into uranium metal, a form that has relatively few peaceful nuclear applications. Three cylinders of uranium gas in the form of UF_6—the feedstock for enrichment— were found in storage; one of the smaller cylinders was found to be missing gas. The Iranian counterparts said it must have leaked.

I realized early on that we were dealing with people who were willing to deceive to achieve their goals and that we should not accept any attestation without physical verification. Of course, verification is a central tenet of IAEA inspection under any circumstance, but it was doubly critical in this case because of the deception that, disturbingly, had been endorsed and carried out at the highest levels of the Iranian government. As recently as May 2003, Aghazadeh had given a speech to the diplomatic missions in Vienna in which he had denied, categorically, that Iran had used any nuclear material in its centrifuge testing.

Each of the senior Iranian leaders I had met—President Khatami; Aghazadeh; Mehdi Karroubi, the speaker of the Majlis; and Ali Akbar Rafsanjani, the former president of Iran and the current head of the Guardian Council—had insisted that Iran's nuclear program was exclusively intended for peaceful purposes. They had spoken with eloquence and conviction, their impeccably starched white shirts and well-tailored robes lending their delivery an air of sophistication and piety. Each had come across as well briefed and knowledgeable about the details of the enrichment program.

Rafsanjani, whom I met at his palace[6] and who seemed the savviest politician of the group, had spoken passionately: "I have seen so many of our people killed with chemical weapons during the Iran-Iraq War. I cannot be the one advocating dialogue among civilizations and at the same time developing nuclear weapons."

I was told by a number of people, including President Mubarak of Egypt, that according to Shi'ite theology it is sometimes acceptable to deceive for the right cause. The concept is called *taqqiya*, meaning to protect oneself or those under one's care from harm. I made it clear to our Iranian counterparts that regardless of the origins of this behavior, their denials and ongoing cover-ups had deeply hurt their credibility with the international community. From the outset, they had dug a hole that would undermine their own diplomatic endeavors, what I referred to as starting out with a confidence deficit.

Yet even after being confronted with evidence proving their deception, the Iranians did not seem particularly embarrassed. They pointed to a long history of what they considered double dealings on the part of the West. In the era of the shah, Iran had announced plans to build twenty-three large nuclear power reactors, with the vocal support of the United States, Germany, France, and others. In 1975, a contract was signed with Kraftwerk Union, a German firm, to build the first plant at Bushehr. Iran also acquired a 10 percent share of Eurodif, a multinational company operating a uranium enrichment plant in France. But

---

6 The Palace of Mirrors, one of the shah's old palaces.

after the 1979 revolution, everything changed. Kraftwerk Union refused to continue constructing the Bushehr facility. The United States cut off Iran's supply of research reactor fuel. France also refused to provide Iran with any more enriched uranium, despite multiple attempts and despite Iran's share in Eurodif.

Given their history, the Iranians insisted that their actions had been justified. Peaceful nuclear science and technology remained central to Iran's national goals. They needed a fuel cycle, they argued, because they did not have fuel suppliers from abroad other than the Russians, whom they regarded as not always reliable and who were charging them excessive prices. As for their past secrecy, they were adamant that it had been indispensable: the sanctions imposed on them by the United States and its allies prohibited any import of nuclear-related items, including peaceful nuclear technology. Despite operating under the radar, they had paid double, triple, or more for the technology and materials they had purchased from abroad. Keeping the program secret for as long as possible had been, they insisted, a necessary measure.

In diplomatic circles, back in Vienna, the Americans did not want to consider the Iranian arguments—despite having themselves been in the driver's seat of the effort to isolate Iran for more than two decades. The fact that Iran had lied was, in their view, proof positive that Tehran intended to produce nuclear weapons. This conclusion was, of course, entirely premature in terms of the verification process; what the IAEA needed was hard evidence. But the U.S. statements of certainty regarding Iran's nuclear weapon intentions soon began to be echoed by others in the West. Many representatives of developing countries were, by contrast, more sympathetic to Iran's need to go underground to evade the sanctions.

The precedent set by Iran was troubling, and I was concerned: the IAEA Board of Governors was beginning to split along North-South lines.

Discrepancies and serious questions about Iran's program continued to surface throughout the summer and autumn of 2003. Further sample results and inspector observations made the Iranian account even more implausible. The inspectors were also increasingly convinced that Iran's extensive nuclear program could not have reached its demonstrated level of sophistication without more experimentation and testing than the Iranians were admitting to.

IAEA visits to a laser facility at Lashkar Ab'ad, for example, revealed sophistication in the use of vapor lasers that could have direct applicability for uranium enrichment,[7] yet the Iranians said they had done no laser enrichment. Inspectors also noted that the drawings for IR-40, a heavy water research reactor slated to begin construction in Arak in 2004, did not include plans for "hot cells," special chambers fitted with remote handling equipment so that the processing of radioactive material, including plutonium separation, can occur without radiation risk; yet we had seen evidence of Iranian efforts to procure from abroad the manipulators and leaded windows that would be used in hot cells.[8] And Iran's uranium conversion facilities, at Isfahan and in laboratories elsewhere, were well designed and extensively outfitted, yet the Iranians insisted that no trials of uranium conversion had taken place. Only when faced with contradictory sample results and persistent queries from Agency inspectors did the repeated denials grudgingly turn into admissions that Iran's nuclear scientists had in fact carried out experiments on nearly every phase of uranium conversion.

It was time to confront the Iranians. On October 16, I headed back to Tehran, this time to meet with Hassan Rowhani, the secretary of Iran's National Security Council. The encounter was pivotal. After the requisite exchange of pleasantries, I laid out a series of substantive issues—centrifuge testing, laser isotope separation, uranium conversion, the heavy water reactor project, and the IAEA's sample results—in unambiguous terms. The pattern of deception and backtracking, I told him, could not go on.

Rowhani came to the meeting prepared. Without directly apologizing for past concealment and deception, he said that Iran was ready to turn over a new leaf in its relationship with the Agency. The Iranian leader-

---

7 Uranium enrichment using atomic vapor laser isotope separation, or AVLIS, method.
8 Leaded glass windows or cameras give the operators an inside-the-chamber view of the work they are doing using the remote handling equipment.

ship, he said, had agreed to provide the Agency with a full disclosure of Iran's past and present nuclear activities in the course of the following week. Iran was also ready to conclude an Additional Protocol, and pending its entry into force, to act in accordance with the protocol's provisions allowing the Agency wide-ranging inspection access.

Behind the scenes, Rowhani had been negotiating on Iran's behalf with the foreign ministers of France, Germany, and the United Kingdom (the EU-3). On October 21, the four governments issued a statement they would refer to as the Tehran Declaration, which reaffirmed the basic pledges Rowhani had made to me days earlier regarding Iran's intent to cooperate with the IAEA and to implement an Additional Protocol. The declaration also announced Iran's agreement to suspend its enrichment and reprocessing activities during the course of ongoing negotiations with the EU-3 as a confidence-building measure. In return, the EU-3 agreed to recognize Iran's nuclear rights and to outline specific ways for Iran to provide "objective guarantees" about the peaceful nature of its nuclear program. Once those assurances were provided, the EU-3 would provide Iran access to modern technology, including nuclear technology.

Two days later, the IAEA received a letter from Aghazadeh declaring that Iran was "commencing a new phase of confidence and co-operation." The letter admitted to many activities Iran had previously denied, and it augmented our picture of Iran's nuclear program with significant new information. It turned out that Iran had tested centrifuges with nuclear material at Kalaye using the UF_6 gas that had been "missing" from one of the cylinders at the JHL. It had experimented with laser enrichment throughout the 1990s. It had conducted reprocessing experiments at the Tehran Nuclear Research Center and separated a small amount of plutonium. Additional nuclear material, previously unreported, had been used in extensive uranium conversion experiments. None of these activities pointed explicitly toward a nuclear weapons program, but together they constituted a fairly comprehensive nuclear fuel cycle program, most of it conducted in secret.

On November 10, 2003, I submitted my report to the IAEA Board of Governors. It was detailed and thorough; there was a great deal to convey. I outlined Iran's numerous failures, over an extended period of time, to declare nuclear material and facilities to the IAEA. I characterized Iran's behavior during the recent inspections as following a "policy of conceal-ment" and providing "limited" and "reactive" cooperation. On the other hand, I gave Iran credit for its promise to shift to "full cooperation" with the Agency, its subsequent moves toward transparency, its willingness to suspend enrichment and reprocessing operations, and its decision to sign and implement an Additional Protocol.

None of this would prove controversial. But near the end of the report, I included the IAEA's interim judgment about Iran in terms of nuclear weapons proliferation: "To date," I wrote, "there is no evidence that the previously undeclared nuclear material and activities referred to above were related to a nuclear weapons programme. However, given Iran's past pattern of concealment, it will take some time before the Agency is able to conclude that Iran's nuclear programme is exclusively for peace-ful purposes."

It was a factual statement, dispassionate and straightforward. But it drew a sharp reaction. John Bolton, the U.S. undersecretary of state for arms control and international security, was furious that the IAEA had not taken a more hard-line position against Iran. A pointless dis-pute emerged in diplomatic back corridors over the legal meaning of the term *evidence* as used in the IAEA report. Bolton engineered a harsh rebuttal. The American ambassador to the IAEA, Ken Brill, was ordered to read a statement claiming that "the institution charged by the inter-national community with scrutinizing nuclear proliferation risks is dis-missing important facts that have been disclosed by its own investigation." It would take time, the statement said, "to overcome the damage caused to the Agency's credibility."

Brill was gracious enough to share an advance copy of the statement with me. Even so, I was incensed when it was read aloud to the Board. I asked the chairman for the floor and answered on the spot, without a pre-pared text, defending the integrity of the Agency and its inspectors. I drew attention to the enormous progress we had made in developing a picture of Iran's nuclear program—more progress in ten months than the world's best intelligence agencies had come up with in the previous ten years. And I issued a fierce refutation of the Americans' obsessive—and logically incorrect—focus on what they called the "evidence" of Iran's nuclear weapons intentions. My *Blackstone Legal Dictionary* from my New York University Law School days thirty years earlier was once again pressed into service.

"Frankly," I declared, "I find it disingenuous that this word, *evidence,* has suddenly become a matter of contention. In fact, the credibility of the Agency has increased since Iraq, because of our objectivity." My reference was clear: if anyone had lost credibility over their careless use of the term *evidence,* it was the Americans and their allies in their catastrophic rush to war in Iraq. We were seeing daily evidence in Iraq of the consequences of U.S. and U.K. eagerness to promote unverified intelligence as evidence. To attack the IAEA for its adherence to facts was brazenly hypocritical.

The boardroom was hushed. People were stunned at this public exchange between the Americans and the IAEA Director General in a diplomatic setting. I had remained seated; I had not raised my voice; but the directness of my remarks had been unmistakable. As the Board chairman moved on to recognize the next speaker, I realized I needed to leave the boardroom to regain my composure. A number of delegations told me after the meeting that this had been a "historic day" to see an international civil servant stand up to bullying by the United States.

Soon after the public disclosure of Iran's undeclared activities, I wrote a piece for the *Economist* calling for operation of the nuclear fuel cycle under joint multinational control. This was not a new idea; internationally operated fuel cycles had been the topic of studies and committees as far back as the mid-1970s. Even U.S. president Eisenhower's original "Atoms for Peace" speech in 1953 had hinted at such a goal.

But with nuclear technology and know-how spreading rapidly, through means both legitimate and clandestine, there was a new urgency. If each country were to develop its own fuel cycle, it would open a Pandora's box of proliferation risks. Taking a multinational approach—building centralized fuel cycle facilities under the auspices of multiple countries, for the use of all participants—might put the lid back on the box. Legitimate users of nuclear energy would be assured of a reliable fuel supply for their reactors. The economic advantages were considerable: eliminating the need for hugely expensive, country-specific factories for uranium enrichment and plutonium production. Most important, the risk of nuclear material being diverted to nuclear weapons would plummet.

The article got lots of attention, and the idea took on a life of its own. The United States and its allies began to push for a "Global Nuclear Energy Partnership." Russian president Vladimir Putin suggested creating a web of international fuel cycle centers. Germany proposed establishing a site where the IAEA would operate an international uranium enrichment facility.

A creative approach was taken by Ted Turner and Sam Nunn,[9] head of the Nuclear Threat Initiative,[10] who convinced American investor and philanthropist Warren Buffett to contribute $50 million to finance a fuel reserve under IAEA custody. Buffett's seed fund required governments to match it with $100 million as a symbolic first step on the road to multinationalization of the fuel cycle.

But distrust quickly followed. The United States, Russia, France, Germany, Holland, and the United Kingdom brought a proposal to the IAEA Board that began with largesse—an offer to ensure the supply of reactor fuel—but *only* if recipient countries gave up their rights as granted under the NPT to enrichment and reprocessing.

This pointed to a fundamental difference in approach. In my vision, the creation of multinational fuel cycle facilities was the first phase of a multiphase process that would reduce the divide between the nuclear haves and have-nots—curtailing proliferation and ultimately opening a path toward nuclear disarmament. The six-country proposal addressed only the most immediate objective—preventing "additional" proliferation—and did so in a way that only exacerbated the nuclear divide: essentially, *we keep the technology, and no one else gets*

---

9 Former head of the U.S. Senate Armed Services Committee and one of the foremost American experts on defense policy, as well as a staunch supporter of the IAEA.
10 NTI is a nonprofit organization that funds selected projects to reduce the threat of nuclear weapons proliferation.

it. It was an in-your-face mandate, a blunt demand for participating countries to give up a cherished right.

I could see the train wreck coming: I implored the proposal's sponsors not to make the plan conditional on any country giving up its rights. But the United States insisted: the condition would remain. The proposal was circulated to all Board members.

The result, as I had anticipated, was deep misgivings, not only among developing countries but also from Canada, Italy, and Australia, for example, countries that did not have a full fuel cycle but that wanted to keep their options open for the future. A few additional countries, such as Japan, Germany, the Netherlands, Brazil, and Argentina, straddled the fence: they did not possess nuclear weapons, but they had the know-how to produce nuclear material, which elevated their status. None of the countries with such an advantage was willing to give it up in order to advance a multinational program that would reduce proliferation risk.

This early proposal poisoned the well. The countries without advanced nuclear technology came to view each subsequent proposal with suspicion—as a series of ruses designed to rob them of their rights. The distrust between the nuclear haves and have-nots, already palpable, was exacerbated and continued to dominate the back corridors of international nuclear diplomacy.

From the time that the first A-bomb had fallen on Hiroshima, the possession of nuclear weapons by a limited few had served as an irritant and an incentive for competition to those who had none. The refusal of most of the nuclear weapon possessor states to acknowledge this cause and effect made it no less true. Although the NPT made it clear that the possession of nuclear weapons by five countries was intended as a transitional phase en route to nuclear disarmament, thirty-three years later disarmament was at a virtual standstill. Every statement by one of the nuclear weapon possessor states to "reaffirm" the deterrent value of nuclear weapons, every action to refurbish or modernize a nuclear arsenal, was another signal of a lack of good faith to the nuclear have-nots.

Increasingly, this context shaped the debate among members of the IAEA Board over Iran's past and current nuclear activities. Few if any of them condoned Iran's secret pursuit of a nuclear program, although they understood the reasons for it. Everyone had urged them to come clean. But at the same time, many countries resented the nuclear club's exclusivity and could understand Iran's desire to acquire fuel cycle technology. In the absence of proof that Iran was actually seeking nuclear weapons, these countries were unwilling to condemn Tehran's actions outright. Pressure from Western governments only served to deepen this divide.

The period from late 2003 until the fall of 2005 marked a discrete phase in the face-off between Iran and the international community over Iran's nuclear program. Bracketed by the optimism of the Tehran Declaration and Iran's stated commitment to transparency at one end and at the other, severe international disagreements on how to handle the Iran file, this period was marked by every feature that would come to characterize the extraordinarily complex struggle over Iran's nuclear development: the sacrifice of pragmatism to the vaguest of "principles"; the counterproductive outcome of hard-line tactics; and the constant ratcheting up of stakes that accompanied each new stance of opposition.

From the Agency's perspective, during these years the IAEA—or, more specifically, our Board meetings—became a battleground where clashing positions on Iran were fought out. An early example occurred prior to the Board's March 2004 meeting, which we went into with some concerns about responses we had received from Iran. One issue involved Iran's centrifuge technology. The centrifuges successfully procured by Iran conformed to one design, supplied by Pakistan, designated P-1. However, through inspections and inquiries outside Iran, the IAEA now found reason to suspect that Iran might also have pursued a more advanced P-2 model. Both designs, it appeared, were styled after earlier European models and had been copied by Pakistani nuclear scientist A. Q. Khan during his work at the URENCO, an enrichment facility in the Netherlands.

Up to this point, IAEA inspectors had been given no indication of work on P-2 machines. But we knew that the Iranians had attempted to conduct R&D on as many aspects of the nuclear fuel cycle as possible.

The P-2 model was more advanced than the P-1, with higher enrichment capacity. It seemed unlikely that the Iranians, if given the opportunity, would have declined to work on P-2 production.

Agency inspectors pressed the point. In January 2004, the Iranians acknowledged that back in 1994 they had indeed received drawings for the P-2 centrifuge model. Engineers at a private company in Tehran performed limited testing, under contract with the Atomic Energy Organization of Iran, on a modified P-2 design. Iran neglected to include a mention of this in their October 2003 declaration to the Agency.

Another issue involved the Lavizan-Shian Technical Research Center, located in a suburb of Tehran. This center had been cited as a possible WMD research facility. The Agency received information that radiation detectors had been procured for use at this location. Satellite photos showed that at some point after August 2003, the site had been razed, its buildings torn down, and the grounds cleared, suggesting an effort at concealment.

The Iranians declared that Lavizan-Shian had been a Ministry of Defense facility, conducting research on responding to nuclear attacks and accidents. The site had been razed after the ministry had been instructed to return the land to the municipality of Tehran, following a dispute between the two government organizations.

Naturally, given Iran's past practice of concealment and deception, matters such as the P-2 testing and the demolition of an alleged WMD site immediately raised suspicions. The situation was complex. Overall, Iran had made significant steps forward in its cooperation with the IAEA; since October 2003, because of Iran's provisional implementation of its Additional Protocol, we had been able to visit enrichment and other facilities without disputes over whether nuclear material had been used. We felt that we were at last getting a fuller understanding of Iran's nuclear activities.

But in other ways, Iran was doing itself no favors with actions that made its cooperation appear sporadic. The Agency had scheduled a mid-March inspection of the Pilot Fuel Enrichment Plant at Natanz and visits to locations related to P-2 centrifuge activity. On March 5 the Iranian authorities abruptly postponed the IAEA inspections on the grounds of the approaching Iranian New Year holidays. Of course, this was non-sense: the timing of the new year was not exactly unforeseen, but Tehran seemed unwilling to disclose the real reason for the delay. Once again, the Iranians gave the impression that they had something to hide.

Against this backdrop, Hassan Rowhani came to see me twice to ask that the Agency take Iran's nuclear program off the agenda of the March IAEA Board meeting. This, Iran hoped, would be seen as a signal that our level of concern had lessened. The Europeans came to support Iran's request. The French delegation asked why I would issue a new report on Iran. However, the Americans, who were pressing to refer Iran to the Security Council, were adamant that the agenda item should remain.

I told each delegation the same thing: the Board agenda would not be used as a tool for political negotiation. The contents were a reflection of technical judgment. "I will be happy to remove the agenda item tomorrow," I said to the Iranians and the Europeans, "but only if the outstanding issues in Iran have been resolved. As long as we still have unanswered questions, the Iranian nuclear program will remain on the Board agenda."

In any case, the official instrument for IAEA Member States to register their position on Iran's nuclear program was not the agenda, but the resolutions adopted at Board meetings. Customarily, resolutions are drafted and negotiated by Member State representatives, without any involvement from the Secretariat. In the case of Iran, the drafts usually originated with the EU-3, given their initiative in trying to find a solution, and were then circulated to other countries.

But here, too, the process was a mess. There was an unprecedented split among the Western countries. The Americans, backed by the Canadians and Australians, were calling for the inclusion of strong language condemning Iran. The EU-3 were trying to tone down the resolution. In Iran, the nuclear negotiators had been proclaiming to the Iranian press and political establishment the benefits of expanded cooperation with the IAEA, so they stood to lose domestic support if the IAEA Board issued a negative resolution. The developing countries were also unhappy with the language of the initial draft.

In an unusual step, the Iranians urged me to help. The American ambassador also delivered a message from Colin Powell asking whether I could become involved. In the end, everyone signed off on a consensus resolution that pleased both the Iranians and the Americans. The meeting went off without a hitch, but the wrangling that preceded it demonstrated the degree to which Board actions were becoming a staging ground for showdowns over Iran and presaged deeper divisions yet to come.

A few days after the Board meeting, I headed to Washington to see President Bush. I had been a bit surprised at the invitation. I had recently published an essay on disarmament in the *New York Times* that covered topics on which Bush had also weighed in.[11] Colin Powell called soon after, saying that Bush wanted to meet with me. Naturally I said yes but waited until after the March Board meeting to avoid the appearance of U.S. influence on my report to the Board or on any statements I might make.

Prior to my meeting with Bush, I talked to Richard Armitage, deputy secretary of state. He reminded me of the overture of goodwill that the United States had made to Iran after the devastating December 2003 earthquake in Bam.[12] The plan had been to provide Iran with humanitarian assistance, an offer that was declined, although Iran reversed itself days later. Coincidentally, the earthquake occurred only a week after Iran had signed its Additional Protocol, a significant concession. Some commentators noted that perhaps the convergence of these events presented an opportunity for a thaw in U.S.-Iranian relations, particularly after Colin Powell had spoken favorably about the possibility of future dialogue.[13] But so far there had been no further signs of a thaw.

11 Both my op-ed and Bush's speech, at the National Defense University, reflected an emerging awareness of the clandestine nuclear supply network of A. Q. Khan and his cohorts. A fuller discussion appears in chapter 7.

12 The December 26 earthquake in southeastern Iran, the most devastating quake in Iranian history, killed more than twenty-five thousand people, with tens of thousands more injured and homeless.

13 Paul Reynolds, "The Politics of Earthquakes," BBC News Online, December 30, 2003.

"So, I heard you're a Yankees fan" was one of the first things Bush said to me. We were in the Oval Office. Bush was accompanied by Armitage, Rice, Secretary of Energy Spencer Abraham, and Bob Joseph, who worked with Rice at the National Security Council. I was accompanied by David Waller, the IAEA's American deputy director general for management and a trusted friend.

"Yes," I said, grinning, "and I think we might have paid too much for Alex Rodriguez." The Yankees had just acquired Rodriguez from the Texas Rangers. Bush, I knew, had been co-owner of the Rangers. He explained a few of the terms of the Rodriguez deal, and we soon turned to business. "I hear you have ideas about strengthening the nonproliferation regime," he began.

I rattled off some of the concepts I had talked about in my op-ed. "We first need to get rid of all the high-enriched uranium that exists in the civilian cycle," I said. I mentioned that there were roughly a hundred facilities in forty countries with HEU. Many of these were research reactors, which could be converted to use low-enriched uranium, thus lowering the proliferation risk. Securing all of the HEU, I told Bush, would take about fifty million dollars per year over four or five years.

"Well, that doesn't sound like much," Bush responded. He looked at Spencer Abraham. "Spence, is this doable?"

"Yes, of course we can do it," Abraham replied. As I would later find out, the Department of Energy was already working on a related plan, but following this meeting they got their marching orders from the president.

I talked about the need to control the spread of fuel cycle facilities, noting that there were thirteen countries with either reprocessing or enrichment capabilities. "If we try to prevent others from joining this group," I said, "those who are on the verge of acquiring the capabilities will not be very happy." This comment brought us to the question of Iran. The discussion was going well, so I decided to be bold. "In my view," I said, "theology apart, ideology apart, we need to buy Iran off"—with a package of incentives too attractive to pass up—"and then push for a voluntary moratorium on any additional countries developing a fuel cycle."

"I like this pragmatic guy," Bush declared, surprising me. He said he would like to enact a legal cutoff, allowing those countries with fuel cycle facilities to maintain them but prohibiting new countries from entering the mix. I pointed out that this would deny Member States their rights granted under the NPT. Success would be more likely by combining a voluntary moratorium with assurances of fuel supplies—and, I reminded Bush, a reaffirmation by nuclear-weapon states of their commitment to disarmament.[14] Regarding Iran, I emphasized the need to offer not only threats but also rewards. "A solution based on diplomacy and verification," I concluded, "is the best possible outcome for the Iranian issue."

Bush surprised me again. "It's not only the best solution," he replied, "it's the only solution—other than the Israeli solution. You know there is concern," he added, "that the Israelis might want to use force."

I waited to hear what he might share about the specifics of the Israeli threat, but he was rather vague and did not seem to know whether or when Israel might launch a military strike, or at least he did not tell me. He implied that the U.S. approach of maximizing pressure on Iran was intended to avoid such an action by Israel. I was reminded of a conversation I'd had with Jack Straw and German foreign minister Joschka Fischer in which they said that the EU-3 was trying to act as a kind of "human shield," through their dialogue with Iran, to protect against the risk of military action by the United States or Israel.

At that time there was considerable disagreement within the U.S. government: the hawks seemed to be advocating a military strike and regime change in Tehran, despite the lessons of the Iraq War. They saw Iran as an existential threat to Israel and opposed any dialogue with Iran that might "legitimize" the regime in Tehran. Others—including, from what I could tell, President Bush and Condoleezza Rice, despite their public rhetoric—believed that diplomacy was the preferred pathway but that a set of preconditions must be met in advance of negotiations. Still others, such as Powell and Armitage, favored negotiation and dialogue without preconditions as the route to a diplomatic solution.

---

14 In my October 2003 article in the *Economist*, I had made clear my view that bringing fuel cycle facilities under multinational control was only one step in a process that would ultimately lead toward nuclear disarmament.

I had brought with me a written message from Hassan Rowhani, on behalf of the Iranian regime, saying that Iran was ready to enter into dialogue with the United States on all issues, including both Iran's nuclear program and broader matters of regional security. The message was on a single sheet of paper, without a letterhead or signature, as it had been delivered to me. I handed the note to Bush, explaining its origin, and told him how important I felt it was for the United States to initiate a dialogue with Iran.

"I'd like to talk leader to leader," Bush responded, "but I'm not sure that Iran's leader is ready to engage." He was referring to Ayatollah Khamenei, Iran's Supreme Leader. "I think he is bent on the destruction of Israel."

He raised other issues, including some forty Al-Qaeda operatives of Saudi Arabian or Egyptian origin being held by Iran, individuals in whom the United States had an interest. According to Bush, the Iranians were keeping these detainees as a negotiating card.

I felt that Bush was, in his way, confirming my view that a U.S.-Iran dialogue could bring multiple and mutual benefits, not least of which was the security assistance Iran could provide in Iraq, because of its ties to the Shi'ite population there. Dialogue, I said, was a sign of respect, and respect—particularly in a Middle Eastern cultural milieu—was a first step toward a peaceful resolution of tensions. Many members of Iran's political establishment wanted above all else to reestablish ties to the United States, preferably as part of a "grand bargain" that would address security, trade, Israel's perception of an Iranian military threat, and other issues relevant to full normalization of relations. This was the gist of Rowhani's note. But neither Bush nor Rice seemed, at that time, open to such a prospect.

Toward the end of the meeting, I suggested convening an international summit to discuss how to strengthen the nonproliferation regime. Rice brightened: "I always thought that we needed to have such a summit," she said. The United States was clearly looking for some way to show leadership, particularly in an election year in which weapons of mass destruction and terrorism figured so prominently.[15]

---

15 Unfortunately, the concept of an international summit went no further. I was told that John Bolton had opposed the idea and found a way to keep it from happening.

I was encouraged. My meeting with Bush had turned out to be far more substantive than I had expected. Further encouragement came during my next meeting, in Langley, Virginia, with George Tenet, director of the CIA, a professional who gave us straight talk. I sensed a level of caution, an avoidance of overstatement, which differed markedly from the intelligence claims we had heard in the run-up to the Iraq War.

Tenet himself was convinced that Iran's nuclear program was intended to develop nuclear weapons but acknowledged that he had no concrete proof, no "actionable information," in the intelligence vernacular. He was essentially hoping the Iranians would trip up somewhere during the inspection process.

Tenet's view gave me some insight into the American political rhetoric and media campaign, which kept repeating that the United States "knew" Iran had a nuclear weapons program but presented no concrete evidence. From what I could tell, the CIA, through wiretapping and other surveillance, probably had indications that Iran's Revolutionary Guard had been involved in procurement and other aspects of the nuclear program, yet nothing revealed a link to weapons development. The only U.S. strategy, therefore, was to put pressure on Iran, through the IAEA and the press, in hopes that damning evidence would come to light or that an informant would come forward with a "smoking gun."

Iran was not helping its case. The obfuscation over its work on P-2 centrifuge technology and Tehran's abrupt cancellation of inspections at Natanz and other facilities had heightened the Agency's sense of unease. A stern message was in order, which I decided to deliver in person, with a visit to Tehran.

In each of my meetings during that trip—with leaders ranging from President Khatami to Foreign Minister Kamal Kharazi—I said I was sick and tired of their procrastination and delays. With President Khatami I was deliberately cold, since he had deceived me during our previous discussion. I did not confront him about this directly but made it clear from my behavior that my attitude toward him had changed. I let him and others know that the IAEA Board's patience was wearing thin; Iran was losing support among some Member States and the overall issue was becoming divisive. Anything short of full and consistent transparency on the part of the Iranians would only work against them. I conveyed to Rowhani and Khatami the key elements of my conversation with President Bush: that he was skeptical of the Iranians' readiness for serious dialogue; that the United States urgently wanted the Al-Qaeda detainees repatriated to their respective countries. I mentioned that the Americans had been put off by Iran's initial refusal to accept U.S. aid after the earthquake.

Khatami was indignant about the U.S. skepticism. He pointed to the rapprochement between the countries during the Clinton administration, when Khatami had made the first move by apologizing to the families of the former American hostages in Tehran. Madeleine Albright had responded by acknowledging the CIA's role in the 1953 coup that had overthrown Prime Minister Mohammad Mossadegh and reinstated the shah and by lifting the import prohibitions on certain Iranian luxury items, such as pistachios, caviar, and carpets, a symbolic gesture worth millions of dollars.

It was the Bush administration, Khatami insisted, that had undermined progress in U.S.-Iran relations. Iran had supported the Americans during the war in Afghanistan and in their preparations for the war in Iraq. Khatami mentioned specific meetings in Sulaymaniyah, in Iraqi Kurdistan, and in London in which Iran participated. "In return for our assistance and cooperation," Khatami fumed, "the only thing we got was to be branded as part of an 'axis of evil.'"

Foreign Minister Kharazi was equally indignant about the U.S. offer after the earthquake. "After decades of damaging boycotts and sanctions," he remarked, "the United States wants to insult us by offering ten million dollars as charity?" He shook his head. "These people do not understand the mentality of others." The Iranian government would be happy to discuss the Al-Qaeda detainees, Kharazi said, but he wanted corresponding help from the United States in dealing with the Mujahedin-e Khalq, the militant group of Iranian dissidents that advocated the overthrow of Iran's government.

The Iranians agreed to intensify their cooperation with the IAEA but pointed out that the prevailing perception in Tehran was that working with the Agency had gotten the country nothing. Iran's hard-liners, who had recently gained control of the Majlis, the parliament, were decrying Tehran's voluntary suspension of its enrichment activities as a sellout to the West. The "moderates," who favored a diplomatic solution and normalization with the West, were losing ground. If my upcoming June report to the IAEA Board was negative, Rowhani said, he doubted that he and his colleagues would be permitted to continue their current level of cooperation with the Agency or keep their posts. The moderates hoped, at a minimum, to see positive reactions from the Europeans, so they could say to the Iranian public that their policy was paying off.

The difficulty for the Iranians, as I saw it, was that their government had oversold its nuclear program. They had presented it domestically as the jewel in Tehran's crown, a scientific achievement for the nation. This made it tough to explain why they were suspending it. Of course, they neglected to point out to the Iranian public that the suspension was a consequence of having deceived the IAEA for years. Instead, they argued that U.S. pressure on the Agency was slowing down the verification process.

Here was another hallmark of the Iranian situation, not dissimilar to other nuclear crises, such as Iraq or North Korea: the domestic use, in both Tehran and Washington, of the other nation's supposed ill will. This genie, once decanted, was hard to contain. My treatment at the hands of the Iranian media reflected how public opinion was shaped. For example, an article in the *Tehran Times* reported "observers in Vienna" saying that "ElBaradei . . . has become depressed and passive" due to the extreme pressure I was facing from the Americans.[16] Iranian reporters asked repeatedly, during my visit, how I was dealing with this pressure. "I am under pressure from everyone," I said, smiling. "Americans, Iranians, and everyone else." But I felt less lighthearted than I sounded. It was clear to me, from the questions I was being asked and from the attitudes expressed in the Iranian press, that the nuclear program was becoming a major domestic issue and a matter of national pride. This was not a good sign.

The Iranian authorities also believed they had cards of their own to play. If relations with the Americans did not improve, Rowhani told

---

16 "IAEA Breaches Legal Commitments Towards Iran," *Tehran Times*, February 19, 2004.

me, Iran was confident that it could make the situation in Iraq even more difficult. I discouraged any form of retaliation.

On my return from Tehran, I urged Ken Brill, the U.S. ambassador, and John Wolf, the assistant secretary of state, to search for a way to start a dialogue with Iran or, at a minimum, to make a positive gesture. "If we all share the same objective—that we do not want to see a nuclear weapon in Iran—we need to develop a coherent endgame strategy," I said. I made similar overtures to the EU-3 ambassadors. I explained that Iran's hard-liners were gaining power because of the meager results from cooperation with the IAEA. A policy of pressure alone, I said, would not work, "particularly since no one in the West has clear evidence of an Iranian nuclear weapon program." With no incentives, the Iranians might take any number of actions: they could restart their enrichment program, back away from their Additional Protocol, or even withdraw from the NPT.

Perhaps I ought to have saved my energy. In June, the IAEA Board issued a resolution that "deplored" Iran's lack of "full, timely, and pro-active" cooperation with the Agency. There was, of course, some basis for the criticism. But Iran was infuriated. The Iranian hard-liners in the government could now say, "I told you so." Less than a week later, Iran informed the IAEA that it would resume manufacturing and testing centrifuges, although without using nuclear material. I asked them to reconsider, but it was no use. The Agency's seals were removed, and Iran's centrifuge engineers went back to work, ending their voluntary suspension on enrichment R&D.

I followed the June Board meeting with in-person pleas during meetings with Colin Powell and his colleagues at the State Department to engage directly with Iran. In another six months, absent the leverage of a "smoking gun," Iran's uranium enrichment program would be a fait accompli, and the price for stopping it would be much higher. I also did not think it would do any good to refer Iran to the UN Security Council, as some were again recommending. Iran could withdraw from the NPT, and we would then have another North Korea on our hands.

During my one-on-one with Powell, he said, "If it were up to me, I would meet with Foreign Minister Kharazi tomorrow morning." The problem, in Powell's view, was that feelings against Iran had remained very strong in the United States ever since the hostage crisis. Initiating direct dialogue would be difficult. Condoleezza Rice was also surprisingly receptive, asking me about Rowhani, more or less her counterpart at the time. "What kind of a person is he?" she wanted to know, giving the encouraging impression that she was at least entertaining the idea of engaging the Iranians.

A constructive contribution came from President Vladimir Putin, whom I visited at his summer house in Moscow. Contrary to allegations made at times by the West, Putin strongly opposed Iran's acquisition of nuclear weapons and questioned its need for nuclear enrichment capability; but he concurred that Iran should be offered attractive assistance, including nuclear technology, and he supported an international guarantee of reactor fuel supply. Putin had also put forward an idea for an international repository for spent fuel, which I applauded. A multilaterally controlled repository would help to stem proliferation risks from this sensitive stage of the fuel cycle and would boost the expansion of safe and secure nuclear power. I felt hopeful that Russia might help bring resolution to the Iranian situation.[17]

Meanwhile, IAEA inspectors were redoubling their efforts to determine the origin of the enriched uranium particles found at various locations in Iran. To prove or disprove Iran's contention—that the source was contamination from centrifuge components imported from Pakistan—we needed environmental samples from Pakistani centrifuges to compare with our sample results from Iran's equipment. The IAEA Board had urged all relevant "third countries" to help clarify the matter, but according to Pakistani ambassador Ali Sarwar Naqvi, the Americans had told Pakistan they had given the IAEA enough support. Apparently, some

---

17 I had met Putin once before at the newly renovated Kremlin during the first year of his presidency. While the Iranian nuclear file was not on the table at that time, I found him to be thoroughly engaged on nuclear issues, and he subsequently spoke out in support of the Agency on several occasions to counter U.S. criticism.

individuals in Washington were not anxious to see the contamination question settled.

Tired of this behind-the-scenes shenanigans and the resultant sluggish progress, I pressed the Pakistanis for their assistance. The Pakistanis (who are not party to the NPT) were reluctant to allow inspectors into their enrichment facilities, which were on military sites. But they agreed to take samples for us, using analysis techniques that would minimize any potential for manipulation of the results.

By mid-August 2004 we had our first analyses. The samples from Pakistan correlated strongly with most of the high-enriched uranium contamination we had found at Natanz and the Kalaye Electric Company. The evidence was not yet conclusive, but it tended to support Iran's explanation.

As the September 2004 Board meeting approached, I sensed the beginning of a familiar pattern of political maneuvering. Just before or even during the meeting, an allegation accusing Iran of a new cover-up would be made public. An American-led media blitz would follow, sensationalizing the importance of this unproven "new evidence" and calling for strong action. The Iranians, for their part, might provide the Agency with key information or access to a requested site at the last minute, sometimes shooting themselves in the foot because there was not enough time to include the IAEA's analysis in the Board report.

This time, the push to influence the Board discussions began, as it often did, with John Bolton. Appearing on BBC Two's *Newsnight*, he called attention to Iran's renewed manufacturing of centrifuges. It was no longer enough, he said, for the Iran nuclear file to be handled by the IAEA, "a wonderful but obscure agency in Vienna."[18] Instead, Iran should be referred to the UN Security Council. This was ironic, given that Bolton was hardly an advocate of multilateralism.

Then, on the third day of the Board meeting, just prior to discussions on Iran's nuclear program, the U.S.-based Institute for Science and International Security (ISIS), a think tank that focuses on nuclear pro-

18 Interview with Gavin Esler on "Iran's Nuclear Capacity," BBC Two *Newsnight*, August 26, 2004.

liferation issues, released a series of satellite photos of a military site at Parchin, located roughly forty kilometers southeast of Tehran. The photos were carried on ABC News, with dramatic technical commentary from David Albright, the president of ISIS, about the potential for nuclear-related explosives testing at Parchin.[19] Right on cue, the Associated Press carried an article the next day with an unnamed "senior member of the U.S. delegation" to the IAEA expressing "alarm" and calling it a "serious omission" that I had not mentioned Parchin in my report to the Board.[20]

This was nonsense, and an unsubtle attempt to convince Member States that the IAEA was in some way biased. The Agency had been reviewing data on Parchin for some time and had discussed with Iran our interest in visiting this and other military sites. We knew that Parchin was a military production facility where Iran manufactured and tested chemical explosives. We would continue to probe Iran about the site, but at this stage, we had no evidence whatsoever of nuclear-related activity there. These manipulations did nothing, of course, to help stop Iran's resumption of centrifuge manufacture.

A breakthrough came in mid-October 2004. Representatives of the EU-3, who had not ceased searching for a diplomatic resolution, brought news from Tehran that Iran was open to beginning serious negotiations about the future of its nuclear program. As a precondition for negotiations, the EU-3 leaders asked Iran once again to suspend its enrichment and reprocessing R&D, and the response was positive: the Iranians were open to a voluntary suspension of *all* of its enrichment and reprocessing activities while negotiations were taking place.

The timing was critical. Politics in Iran were becoming increasingly

---

19 "Photos of Suspected Secret Iranian Nuclear Site Released," Agence France-Presse, September 16, 2004. Even in its use of language, this AFP article is a good example of the media tendency to hype such issues. Parchin is described as "a large industrial complex hidden in a warren of valleys and crevices"; the access route is depicted as "snaking between barren hills."

20 George Jahn, "U.S. Alarmed Over Suspected Iran Nuke Site," Associated Press, September 16, 2004.

hawkish. I had just spoken with Sirus Nasseri, a head Iranian nuclear negotiatior and astute political observer. Almost all the candidates for the next year's presidential election, Nasseri believed, would advocate confrontation with the West. An anti-U.S. platform would help them get elected, even though they probably would then try to take credit for achieving a settlement with the United States a year or so later. A confrontation would also likely reinforce the influence of Iran's Revolutionary Guard, setting back reforms that had taken place in the last few years. For domestic reasons, it would be impossible for Iran to terminate its enrichment program permanently, Nasseri believed, regardless of who got elected. No Iranian politician would risk public disfavor by ending a program that Iran had endured so much to achieve. Nor were they worried about the possibility of U.S. or Israeli military strikes against their facilities, a scenario discussed at length, Nasseri said. Having mastered the technological know-how, the Iranians could rebuild underground, in a matter of months, any facility that might be destroyed.

Under these circumstances, a voluntary suspension was a significant opportunity. The problem was that the parties could not agree on how to define the scope of enrichment activities to be suspended.

This was an argument of long standing. The Tehran Declaration of October 2003 had rested in part on Iran's voluntary suspension of "all uranium enrichment and reprocessing activities." But did this include the preparatory stage of uranium conversion? Did it include the manufacture of centrifuges? After hours of wrangling over the definition in Tehran, it became obvious that an outside arbiter was required. The EU-3 ministers and their Iranian counterparts decided to turn to the IAEA.

Once again we found ourselves at an intersection of technology and politics. A purely technical definition would only require suspending the introduction of nuclear material into a centrifuge enrichment cascade. The Iranians would have been happy with this; they wanted the narrowest possible limitation. But since the suspension was intended as a confidence-building measure, the Europeans wanted a broader definition.

Despite the IAEA's efforts to clarify the scope of "enrichment and reprocessing activities," the disagreements had continued throughout 2004. The West had been unhappy that Iran had continued to test its conversion processes, including those that produced UF_6, the feed material for enrichment. Most recently, in August, Iran had begun to process thirty-seven tons of yellowcake, a uranium concentrate, as a large-scale test of its production lines at the uranium conversion facility in Isfahan.

The IAEA ultimately arrived at a reasonable definition that all parties could live with, which cleared the path to an agreement on negotiations. On November 14, in Paris, Iran and the EU-3 signed off on the Paris Agreement, as it would be known. Both sides committed themselves to negotiating in good faith. Iran agreed to suspend all uranium conversion activities, the assembly and testing of centrifuges, and even the import of centrifuge components. Iran's adherence to the suspension was specified in the agreement as a necessary component for negotiations to continue. Optimistically, the projected scope of negotiations went well beyond the nuclear issue, looking toward cooperative arrangements on a range of economic, political, and security matters, including "firm guarantees" for cooperation on peaceful nuclear technology. The EU-3 agreed to support negotiations for Iran to join the World Trade Organization. Both sides agreed to combat terrorism, including the operations of Al-Qaeda and the Mujahedin-e Khalq. Both also confirmed their support for the political process to establish a constitutionally elected government in Iraq.

At the signing, Rowhani emphasized a number of points, as Iran's chief nuclear negotiator, which he asked all the governments involved to acknowledge. First, the suspension was voluntary; it was not in any way legally binding. Second, the negotiations should not try to press Iran to move toward a complete termination of its nuclear fuel cycle activities. This was off the table. The Europeans agreed: they were not seeking such a termination, only "objective guarantees that Iran's nuclear program is exclusively for peaceful purposes."

Iran moved rapidly to implement the agreement. One week later, IAEA inspectors confirmed that the suspension was in place.

The signing of the Paris Agreement set a positive mood for the November Board meeting. At the outset, even the Americans seemed pleased, expressing appreciation for the comprehensive overview I gave of the Iran inspections to date. It was a striking departure from the U.S. attitude of just two months earlier, when they had made such a ruckus over the Parchin photos.

The Americans even refrained from attempting to block the November Board resolution on Iran, although they were not pleased with it. Jackie Sanders, the U.S. representative and a Bolton protegé, implied that nothing of any significance had changed with Iran, telling the Board that its expectations were "sadly familiar." She made clear that the United States would be willing, if need be, to refer Iran to the Security Council on its own, without the Board's consensus. But still they let the resolution pass.

The Iranians, for their part, were hopeful that they had reached a turning point. Sirus Nasseri pretended to fall asleep in the boardroom during Sanders's speech. Hassan Rowhani described the Board's endorsement of the Paris Agreement as a "great victory." Speaking to the BBC, he said that "the whole world had turned down America's calls" to refer Iran to the Security Council. With some hyperbole—in all likelihood playing to his audience in Tehran—he described the U.S. representative to the IAEA as "enraged and in tears." The upcoming negotiations were, he said, a "historical opportunity for Iran and Europe to prove to the world that unilateralism is condemned."[21]

The agreement, it turned out, was the easy part. In my discussions with the Europeans, they seemed to clearly understand how important it was for them to present the Iranians with a concrete, meaningful package, as an outcome of the negotiations. The Germans were the most optimistic. The British were more conservative, trying to keep the Americans happy. The French were somewhere in between. But all three were hopeful, armed as well with an endorsement from the G-8[22] for offering strong concessions to the Iranians.

---

21 BBC News, November 30, 2004.
22 The Group of 8 is a forum of major industrialized countries. Formerly known as the G-7, it included Canada, France, Germany, Italy, Japan, the United Kingdom, and the United States. It became known as the G-8 with the addition of Russia in 1997.

For several months, expectations that the negotiations would lead to an overall diplomatic solution were high. Iran's cooperation with the IAEA stayed strong; there were only a few remaining inspection issues. At the March 2005 Board meeting, Iran's nuclear program was not on the agenda for the first time in almost two years—a fact that Iran's negotiators were quick to point out as progress. The United States was even reported to be considering joining the EU in offering Iran incentives.[23]

But in Iran, concern was mounting. The negotiations were not making visible headway. Rowhani was under pressure from his government to show progress—in the form of concrete "deliverables"—for his cooperative approach. He was pressing his European counterparts to at least agree to let the Iranians resume some aspect of their nuclear operations soon, even at the R&D level. From what I could understand, the Iranian plan had always been to complete a conversion plant and a small pilot enrichment facility, and then to agree, as part of their negotiations with the Europeans, to freeze the industrial-scale enrichment facility at Natanz for a number of years.

In March 2005, Rowhani submitted a paper to the EU-3 with the essence of this proposal. It envisaged that Iran would start enrichment with five hundred centrifuges at its pilot plant, which could build over time to three thousand centrifuges—well short of the planned fifty-four-thousand-centrifuge capacity at the full-scale Natanz facility. This was an initial offer, clearly open to discussion; the key for Rowhani was to be able to send the message to the Iranian public that Iran's enrichment program was still ongoing. The IAEA would be able to closely monitor activity at the pilot facility. Iran would freeze its industrial scale efforts. In return, Iran hoped to receive Western nuclear power and other technologies, trade agreements, and additional incentives.

The Iranian presidential election was coming up in June, and political rhetoric was heated. In May, citing the lack of an offer from the Europeans as a violation of the Paris Agreement, the Iranians threatened to end

---

23 Robin Wright, "Bush Weighs Offers to Iran; U.S. Might Join Effort to Halt Nuclear Program," *Washington Post*, February 28, 2005.

their suspension. The Europeans asked for more time to develop a detailed proposal. Iran agreed to wait until August.

In late June, Iran elected Mahmoud Ahmadinejad, the mayor of Tehran, a deeply religious man and among the fiercest hard-liners of all the presidential candidates. Shortly after the election, and well before receiving the European proposal, Iranian officials began sending messages that they would not continue with the full suspension. The mood in diplomatic circles rapidly turned bleak.

Less than two months later, the bottom fell out of the negotiations. The offer prepared by the Europeans proposed few of the benefits discussed at the time of the Paris Agreement. It did not include nuclear power reactors, only research reactors. The French could have provided nuclear power technology to Iran, except that Areva, the French company, was unwilling to jeopardize its relationship with the United States, its biggest market. The United States had refused to give the green light to Areva, so the Europeans' offer simply made a vague statement about giving Iran access to the foreign nuclear technology markets.

I was told that the Europeans were trying to imitate a bazaar style of negotiation and had refrained from including their full offer up front. The tactic was a disaster. Not only was the proposal meager, but its tone was patronizing, bordering on arrogant. It went so far as to promise that the Europeans would take good care of the Iranian scientists who would become redundant when enrichment was halted in Iran. The Paris Agreement, like the original Tehran Declaration, had talked about Iran's obligation to provide "objective guarantees" about the peaceful nature of its nuclear activities. In direct contravention of every statement made by Rowhani and his colleagues, the European offer translated this obligation into a ban on nuclear fuel cycle activities.

The Iranians tried to get the Europeans to consider the possibility of at least doing uranium conversion. Conversion would allow some face-saving with the Iranian public, a sign that the country had not altogether abandoned its nuclear achievements. The concept was floated that Iran could produce UF_6 and then export it to South Africa for storage. But the Western countries were not willing to allow Iran even this concession. Shortly before the offer was released, I urged the Europeans, taking a suggestion from Nasseri, to mention at least the continuing conversion operations in their cover letter as a possibility for discussion, hoping to forestall a complete collapse of the negotiations. Since the French were putting the package together, I made my request directly to the French political director Stanislas de Laboulaye but was told it was too late. The Europeans had already reached consensus; they could not change it.

Shortly before the EU-3 offer was actually released, the French gave Iran a hint of what was coming. When the Iranians realized how little they would be offered, after months of negotiation, they lost all faith in the process.

On August 3, 2005, Ahmadinejad assumed the Iranian presidency and began working on cabinet appointments. Two days later, Rowhani and his team were replaced; Ali Larijani was announced as the new secretary of Iran's Supreme National Security Council. The Iranians quickly began feeding uranium oxide into an unsealed portion of the conversion facility in Isfahan. On August 10, after formally receiving the European offer, Iran removed the IAEA seals from the rest of the facility.

The IAEA Board met in special session and issued a resolution urging Iran to reestablish its suspension. On September 24, at its next meeting, the Board went further, for the first time characterizing Iran's history of concealment and reporting failures as constituting "noncompliance." The term made eventual referral to the UN Security Council a certainty.

A new phase of the Iranian nuclear crisis had begun.

The standard NPT safeguards agreement makes it discretionary for the IAEA Board to refer "noncompliance" to the UN Security Council. In the case of Iran, I had long been careful to avoid using the word *noncompliance*, opting instead for synonyms such as *breach* or *violation*, so as not to prejudice the Board. The Board had in the past declined to refer Iran to the council, retaining the possibility as a bargaining chip in negotiations. The Americans had wanted to report Iran to the council from day one and specifically criticized the Agency for not using the term *noncompliance*.

What made Iran's eventual referral a cause for cynicism was that there was nothing new in its "noncompliance," which had essentially been known for two years. Recent developments had been positive: the Agency had made substantial progress in verifying Iran's nuclear program. The eventual referral, when it came, was primarily an attempt to induce the Security Council to stop Iran's enrichment program, using Chapter VII of the UN Charter to characterize Iran's enrichment—legal under the NPT—as "a threat to international peace and security."

I have frequently been asked whether I thought the international community missed an opportunity at this point for a peaceful resolution of the Iranian nuclear question. If the Europeans had been more resourceful, or if the Americans had not blocked the export of French technology and understood the value of incentives for Iran, would the crisis have been over by now?

We cannot know what might have happened had this or that variable been different. The situation was extraordinarily complex for each of the players involved—and even more so in combination. The layers of intention on the part of the relevant governments—of Iran, the United States, the EU-3, and others—were nearly impossible to read with certainty.

What is clear, though, is that Iran believed that cooperation with the Agency would prevent its referral to the Security Council and that negotiations with the Europeans were seen as an intermediate step on the path to a grand bargain with the United States. These were their essential policy objectives. When these results did not materialize—a reality that became painfully transparent with the August 2005 offer and the subsequent referral for noncompliance—Iran immediately diminished its cooperation with the Agency, possibly hoping to force a concession from the West.

It also became clear, in the months and years that followed, that the West's insistence on taking a hard line—refusing Iran's request to retain some small element of their nuclear program—achieved nothing. The most amorphous of principles trumped pragmatism. Had the EU-3 offered Iran a reasonable package, with concrete benefits, the Iranians, I believe, would have been willing to suspend their enrichment program, or at least to limit it to a small R&D operation while negotiations toward a grand bargain continued. Iran's requirement was access to Western technology—both nuclear power technology and other technology they had been denied under U.S. sanctions. Because of U.S. opposition, such an offer did not materialize. The result—inevitable and easily foreseen—was a raising of the stakes: Iran resumed uranium conversion operations and, later, enrichment. The more time that passed, the higher Iran's "price" became.

The international community did not immediately give up on finding a negotiation pathway. In November 2005 a new proposal was made to allow Iran to convert uranium at Isfahan and ship the resultant UF_6 to Russia for eventual enrichment for Iran's reactor fuel. But the forces against it were too strong.

6

LIBYA

Discovery and Dismantlement

The first hint of something askew in Libya's nuclear ambitions came to me in a meeting at the British embassy in Vienna. It was May 2003. The principal skeleton being dragged from the closet was Iran, but almost as an afterthought, a senior member of MI6, the British secret intelligence service, mentioned that there might also be some concerns related to Libya. He referred to a research reactor in Tajura, a small city east of Tripoli, without saying why. When I pressed for more details, he promised to invite me to London for an in-depth briefing.

When certain Americans in the State Department got wind that MI6 planned to meet with me, they intervened, urging the United Kingdom not to pass their information to the IAEA. This was characteristic: the United States tended to be reluctant about sharing intelligence, even with the head of the UN organization charged with preventing the spread of nuclear weapons. The British were more relaxed on this front.[1] In any case, eight months later I still had not received the promised briefing.

On December 18, 2003, Graham Andrew, my British assistant and confidant, stopped by my office. Based on a message he had received

---

1 This was not the only difference. The Americans usually had definite views about how to interpret their raw information, whereas the British came across as less opinionated, letting the facts speak for themselves. Interestingly, my contacts at MI6 told me that, although the CIA director briefed the U.S. president each morning, the CIA, unlike MI6, was rarely involved during the actual decision-making process.

from British intelligence, a major announcement about Libya was imminent. It was coming jointly from President Bush and Prime Minister Blair. Graham hinted that it might be prudent for me to postpone my long-planned trip to India the next morning. That night I received a call from Matouq Mohammed Matouq, the Libyan deputy prime minister of science and technology. The foreign minister, he said, was about to go public with a Libyan decision to dismantle its WMD programs. The very existence of Libyan WMD development was news to me. Matouq asked if he could come and brief me in Vienna. My India trip would have to wait.

Matouq showed up the next day with a small Libyan army of nineteen or twenty diplomats, scientists, and other officials. A short man with piercing eyes and hair dyed jet black, Matouq had been part of the senior echelon in Libya for many years. He was respectful and professional, but not in the least apologetic. Following the introductions, we had a one-on-one meeting and got down to business.

The gist of the story was that Libya had been working for years on a uranium enrichment program.[2] They had received equipment, knowhow, and design support through the Pakistani nuclear scientist and businessman A. Q. Khan and from a network of companies and individuals. As Matouq spoke, I became aware that I was in effect receiving my first briefing on the extent and complexity of the nuclear black market. Matouq talked about assistance Libya had received from contacts in South Africa. He related an incident that even in the telling had a multinational flavor: a U.S. and U.K. intelligence tip-off had led to an Italian raid off the coast of Taranto on a German freighter, the BBC *China*, caught in the act of bringing nuclear equipment to Libya that had been manufactured by a company in Malaysia.

Most disturbingly, on A. Q. Khan's most recent visit to Tripoli, he had brought two white shopping bags bearing the name of a Karachi tailor, which contained the designs for a nuclear weapon. "You might

---

2 I was told that the genesis of the Libyan nuclear weapon program—and Gaddafi's other WMD programs—was in retaliation for the April 1986 U.S. bombing raids during which Gaddafi's adopted daughter, Hannah, was killed.

need this in the future," Khan had reportedly told Matouq. Since then, Matouq said, the "Good Looks Tailor" bags had been in his safe.

I was stunned by the extent of Libya's clandestine nuclear activities, as Matouq portrayed them. But my mind was also racing on a parallel track, analyzing the extent to which the Agency was poised to learn about all these activities through inspection, since Libya was party to the NPT.

For nine months, according to Matouq, Libya had been engaged with British and American officials negotiating a deal under which the Libyan government would give up its WMD programs. "We wanted to inform the Agency all along," Matouq said, "but they wouldn't allow it." I bristled but said nothing.

The next day, representatives from the U.S. and U.K. intelligence agencies came to see me at home. I was angry, and I let my indignation show. "What is not clear about your legal obligations under the NPT?" I asked them. "Libya, the United States, and the United Kingdom are all three members of the Treaty. When you discover that a member is in violation of its nuclear safeguards agreement, you are legally obligated to inform the inspecting organization, the IAEA, so that we can take action."

They made no argument in response. Shortly after the meeting, Jack Straw called from London to say that only three or four people in the British government had been privy to the information; he apologized that I had not been informed. Colin Powell called with much the same message: they had kept the information extremely restricted, he said, because of uncertainty about the outcome of the negotiations. They did not want to be embarrassed if their efforts backfired.

Powell's explanation made little sense to me. Later, I heard from an official in MI6 that the real reason for the extreme secrecy governing the Libyan negotiations was to protect the talks from U.S. hard-liners. The fear, I was told, was that they might have tried to torpedo a peaceful resolution of the Libyan case. So they were informed only when the deal was done.

I decided to make the best of the situation and go immediately to Libya. With a small group of IAEA experts, I flew to Tripoli for a few days between Christmas and the New Year. We were taken by our Libyan counterparts to a series of warehouses where nuclear equipment was stored. The scale of the program was small. We were told they had begun installing a few small centrifuge cascades for testing purposes, but only one—a cascade of just nine centrifuges—was actually complete, with electrical and process equipment hooked up. None of the centrifuges had been tried with nuclear material. The Libyans said they had not yet begun constructing an industrial-scale facility nor any of the associated infrastructure. Nor did they have a functioning weaponization program.

All told, it appeared they had about twenty complete centrifuges and components for two hundred more of the P-1 design, the first-generation Pakistani model we had seen in Iran. They had ordered ten thousand of the more advanced P-2 centrifuges; however, many of the P-2 components, including essential rotors, had not yet been delivered.[3] Apparently, A. Q. Khan had tried to have the rotors manufactured by a South African company, and when that effort failed, he had turned to a Malaysian firm. But at the time Libya revealed its program, the rotors had still not been manufactured.

Briefing the press on what we had seen, I characterized the stage of the Libyan program as nascent. Nonetheless, I was worried. The uranium conversion equipment had been assembled methodically and thoughtfully in a modular pattern, evidence of the sophisticated outside assistance the Libyans had received. This modular aspect was especially disquieting; it had the appearance of a sort of "nuclear do-it-yourself kit." The designer, whoever it was, seemed to have ease of replication in mind.

Only a small group had been privy to the transactions with the Khan network—although we heard many opinions, and rumors were abundant. Except for the actual interlocutors, very few senior Libyan officials knew how much Khan had received for his products and services.

3 The rotor is the cylindrical hollow core of a centrifuge through which the uranium feedstock flows. Because these rotors must spin at extremely high speeds for long periods of time, they require high-precision manufacturing and advanced materials to withstand the resultant stresses.

The distressing question plaguing us all was simple: "Who else?" What other customers had gone shopping at this underground nuclear supply chain?

While in Libya, I was invited to meet Colonel Muammar al-Gaddafi, Leader of the Revolution. The meeting took place at the Bab al-Azizia military barracks in the middle of Tripoli. I waited in a chilly room near the entrance, glad I was wearing my coat. Bashir Saleh Bashir, one of Gaddafi's closest assistants, came to greet me and reiterate the government's promise of full cooperation. A short time later, the foreign minister, Abd al-Rahman Shalgem, appeared and invited me inside.

I was ushered into a large heated library. There was little furniture, just a big desk in front of rows of bookshelves holding a meager scattering of books in Arabic. Colonel Gaddafi, seated behind the desk in a traditional robe, invited Shalgem and me to take the chairs facing him. The ambience of the meeting matched the Spartan look of the place.

Gaddafi was more soft-spoken than I expected, his manner an odd mix of friendliness and reserve. His opening line was memorable: "I don't know how to put this," he said, "but why does the Egyptian government hate you?" He added quickly, "The Egyptians are claiming that they can help us get rid of our weapons program better than you and your IAEA colleagues can."

Gaddafi then asked whether I was a Nasserite. "You grew up during Nasser's time in Egypt," he said. "You must be a Nasser fan."

"I am not," I answered, probably to his disappointment, since Nasser was reportedly his idol. "Nasser had a very good vision and set of principles," I added, "but much of it failed in its implementation."

Gaddafi launched into a soliloquy on his decision to terminate his WMD programs. He had reached the conclusion that weapons of mass destruction would not add to Libya's security. They should be gotten rid of, he declared, not only in Libya but also in the Middle East and globally. Of course, I heartily agreed.

Gaddafi digressed. He spoke glowingly about Libya's place in world affairs, anecdotes that were not in all cases admirable. "This little Libya," he said proudly, referring to his country's record of influencing world events.

I realized that Gaddafi was less than fully informed on global security alliances and structures. When I described, for example, the NATO nuclear umbrella that protects its members, Gaddafi pulled out a pencil and a little notebook and began to take notes. But he spoke earnestly of his desire to develop Libya: he wanted better infrastructure; he wanted more roads; he wanted Libyan students to receive scholarships to Western universities; he wanted his country to advance in the fields of science and technology. He asked if I could help to impress these points on George Bush and Tony Blair.

He also urged me to speak publicly about Libya as an example that should lead to a Middle East free from weapons of mass destruction. I assured him again that I was an advocate of a nuclear-weapons-free Middle East. I also agreed to speak to my American and British contacts about supporting Libya economically. And in fact I followed through on this point with Jack Straw and a number of American officials, who said they planned to be responsive to Libya's needs. It would be to everyone's advantage, they felt, if Libya were to improve its financial and economic condition and normalize its relations with the global community.

Not everyone in Washington was pleased that I had gone to Libya immediately after the Bush-Blair announcement. They wanted to be sure that the credit for discovering Libya's clandestine program and for the negotiations with Gaddafi remained exclusively theirs. To me, credit was beside the point. From my perspective, the governments of the United Kingdom and the United States had failed in their obligation to inform the IAEA about Libya's secret nuclear activities. But now that the Agency had the information, it was our legal obligation to follow up.

On January 2, 2004, the *New York Times* ran a story quoting Shukri Ghanim, the Libyan prime minister, urging the United States to hold up its end of the deal—essentially, to lift long-standing sanctions that, among other things, had forbidden U.S. oil companies to work with Libya and frozen $1 billion in Libyan assets.[4] Ghanim also made clear that he considered the IAEA to be in charge of Libya's nuclear disarmament process.

Ghanim's remark, coming right after my visit, clearly struck a nerve. The article also quoted an unnamed "senior Bush administration official" referring to my trip as essentially a "badly advised" publicity stunt. The same official indicated that British and American intelligence officers and nuclear experts would "effectively take charge of the disarmament." The fact that the IAEA has the sole legal jurisdiction to verify nuclear activities in countries party to the NPT seemed not to have entered their calculations.

The Americans were also unhappy that I had characterized the Libyan nuclear program, at first glance, as nascent. The intelligence coup would have seemed more significant had Libya's program been larger or closer to producing a nuclear weapon. In any case, my assessment was confirmed as the IAEA inspection team returned to verify the program exhaustively in the ensuing weeks and months.

A good example was Libya's Uranium Conversion Facility at Salah Eddin. Libyan scientists, as it turned out, had worked on lab-scale and bench-scale uranium conversion activities since the 1980s, with the support of a foreign scientist. In 1984, Libya ordered from abroad a pilot-scale uranium conversion facility, in the form of portable components. The components were received in 1986, then stored in various locations around Tripoli until 1998, when they were partially assembled and moved to a site called Al-Khalla. In February 2002, Libyan scientists had begun cold-testing; but two months later, because of concern over a possible security breach, they dismantled the facility, packed everything up, and moved it all to its current location at Salah Eddin.

So how extensive were the uranium conversion capabilities at Salah Eddin? As our sample analyses would confirm, Libya had never actually used uranium at the facility. The pilot plant had very small capacity and no ability to produce uranium hexafluoride gas, the feedstock for uranium

---

4 "Libya Presses UN to Move Quickly to End Sanctions," *New York Times*, January 2, 2004.

enrichment. Even on a laboratory scale, Libyan scientists had never produced UF_6 domestically.

Similar limitations in scope, capacity, and know-how were characteristic of other parts of the Libyan nuclear fuel cycle. They had essentially no mining or milling operations. Their enrichment capacity, as
I have noted, was limited to a small number of centrifuges with no production or even testing of nuclear material. They had procured precision machine shop equipment for domestic centrifuge manufacture, but
the parts were still in their shipping crates. In their research reactor at
Tajura, they had irradiated a few dozen uranium targets, mostly sized
at about one gram, and from two of the targets separated a miniscule
amount of plutonium. They had done no work on nuclear weaponization.
They had received drawings of nuclear weapons designs, but the drawings had stayed in their shopping bags, locked in Matouq's safe.[5]

While our inspections were still in progress, Reuters and other news
outlets soon began running stories that U.S. and U.K. experts were about
to fly to Tripoli to begin removing the nuclear equipment from Libya. I
immediately rang up Peter Jenkins, British ambassador to the IAEA. If
this were to happen before the Agency completed its work, I told him, I
would convene a special session of the IAEA Board. "Please inform your
government," I said, "that I will report to the Board that I am no longer
in a position to perform my responsibilities under the NPT because of
interference by the British and the Americans." I was tired of playing
games. If necessary, I would go public on the issue. If the United States
and the United Kingdom were determined to circumvent the role and
responsibilities of multilateral institutions, I would not remain silent.

A few days later, Colin Powell called to say he was sending Bolton
and his British counterpart, William Ehrman, to Vienna to discuss with
me modes of cooperation in Libya. "We need to respect your assets,"
Powell said, referring to the Agency's expertise and areas of jurisdiction.
"And of course, we have our assets."

---

5 To our relief, the IAEA's weapon experts determined that these weapon designs were
missing important parts. A. Q. Khan was not a weapon designer, and he most likely
passed to Libya whatever he was able to get hold of in Pakistan.

"I understand," I replied, "but I have a trust that is given to me by IAEA Member States, and I cannot give it away."

Powell did not press the point. "I had meetings with Bolton last night and this morning," he said, "and he is very much looking forward to coming to see you."

I had my doubts about the last part. I had met Bolton once before, shortly after he assumed office, in 2001, as undersecretary of state for arms control and international security. We had agreed to work together on nonproliferation and other arms control issues. "I'm going to have to act in many ways contrary to my own writing," he had said jokingly, alluding, I assumed, to his derisive comments about the United Nations.[6] That was about the extent of his support for the work of the IAEA. But Powell's implicit message was reassuring: Bolton was being sent under explicit instructions not to create problems.

And in fact, in this instance, our interaction was without incident. Our meeting, which took place on January 19, 2004, was staged as a technical briefing at the permanent mission of the U.S., less than a block from IAEA headquarters. Bolton was civil; we shook hands and got right to business. To his credit, Bolton was focused on reaching an agreement, and I made it clear from the outset that I would not waver on the Agency's role. We agreed that the Agency needed to finish its job first— measurements, sampling, and other verification measures—and that only once we were done could the United States and the United Kingdom remove the equipment out of the country, in accordance with their agreement with Libya.

The meeting ended on an ostensibly friendly note, much to the relief of William Ehrman, who apparently had been anticipating a clash. Our agreement also worked well in practice: things went smoothly on the ground between the IAEA inspectors and the American and British experts.

---

6 I believe Bolton was referring to statements such as declaring to a panel of the World Federalist Association, in 1994, "There is no such thing as the United Nations." Bolton had gone on to say, "The Secretariat Building in New York has thirty-eight stories. If you lost ten stories today, it wouldn't make a bit of difference." Quoted in "Bolton: An Unforgivable Choice as UN Ambassador," Council on Hemispheric Affairs, March 10, 2005, retrieved at www.scoop.co.nz/stories/WO0503/S00185.htm.

The path was eased by the Libyans' full and consistent cooperation. Their readiness to provide information and access made the technical verification work refreshingly straightforward for the IAEA inspectors. Matouq came periodically to Vienna to see me, to ensure that inspections were going according to plan and to resolve any outstanding questions. It was a refreshing change from our experiences in Iraq, North Korea, and Iran. By the end of January, Agency inspectors had completed a major portion of the most sensitive nuclear verification work, and soon thereafter, a large assembly of nuclear fuel cycle equipment was dismantled and, in accordance with the Libyan-American agreement, shipped to the United States.

On February 23, I returned to Tripoli for an update. The hotel where I stayed was abuzz with Western corporate types. The word was out: sanctions would soon be lifted and Libya was open for business. In particular, we noticed a glut of oil company representatives standing by, hoping to cut deals for access to Libya's considerable natural resources. Listening to Libyan officials as they tried to cope with rapid changes on many fronts, I could not help feeling that they were in danger of being exploited.

"The problem," Foreign Minister Shalgem told me, "is our lack of managers." This was amply evident. Libya had been isolated for more than twenty years. A large number of their most talented people had left the country. Aside from a handful of Western-educated professionals, including some nuclear scientists, Libya had a very inexperienced bureaucracy.

Moussa Koussa, the head of intelligence, had spent time in the United States, earning a degree in sociology at the University of Michigan, where he had written a biography of Gaddafi as his master's thesis. Shalgem, too, had lived abroad for many years as Libya's ambassador to Italy. Both men had a good grasp of world affairs. We talked about the importance of learning to negotiate and get a fair price for Libya's resources and assets. We also discussed their critical relations with other North African and Middle Eastern countries. Libya was getting a lot of criticism in the Arab world, perceived as "selling out" after thirty years of a so-called "revolutionary" stance on many issues. The Egyptians, in particular, were incensed that the Libyans had not told them about their

WMD programs, nor about their negotiations with the Americans and the British. Just months earlier, President Mubarak had said in a public speech, "I know what Libya has and they have nothing in terms of weapons of mass destruction." In hindsight, of course, his assertion was rather embarrassing.

The Libyans had sent Abdallah el-Senussi, the head of military intelligence and Gaddafi's brother-in-law, to try to smooth things over with Mubarak. However, when criticism of Libya's decision to give up their weapons program began appearing in the Egyptian media, Gaddafi retaliated by putting restrictions on Egyptian citizens crossing into Libya. This was harsh: there were roughly half a million Egyptians working in Libya. But the Egyptians did put a stop to their criticism and sent a group of cabinet ministers to Tripoli to appeal to Gaddafi to reverse his decision. It was easy to get the sense that relations between Egypt and Libya were often driven more by whims and power games than by rational planning.

Libyan officials were in turn very critical of the Egyptian government. Mubarak, they said, had grown too old to provide meaningful leadership, either in domestic policy or in the larger Arab world. "You know," one official told me, "the Arab world cannot go anywhere without Egypt; if the Egyptians take the lead, everybody will follow."

Libya's efforts to maintain its standing in the Arab world were not helped by an exclusive media "show" staged by U.S. secretary of energy Spencer Abraham. I received a call about this on March 16 from Matouq. He was upset. Forty-five journalists had been flown in by chartered jet to the Y-12 National Security Complex in Oak Ridge, Tennessee. The subject of the media opportunity was a dramatic display of Libyan nuclear equipment. Abraham's podium had been strategically placed in front of a collection of large shipping crates, some of them opened to display centrifuge components. He characterized the Libyan developments as a "big, big victory," noting that the equipment on display was only "the tip of the iceberg."

"By any objective measure," Abraham announced, "the United States and the nations of the civilized world are safer as a result of these efforts to secure and remove Libya's nuclear materials."[7]

Leaving aside the implied insult of Abraham's reference to the "civilized world," his assessment of the Libyan program was overblown. His claim that the Libyans had four thousand centrifuges was inaccurate, since the majority of the centrifuges were incomplete. Nonproliferation experts disputed the claims. David Albright at the Institute for Science and International Security issued a rebuttal, noting that the display had shown only centrifuge casings, without the rotors that would make them operational. "Make no mistake," he said. "The Libyan program was very serious and we're glad it's stopped. . . . The problem, from our point of view, is that the White House, which basically organized the briefing, is so focused on claiming credit that it's willing to exaggerate."[8]

Matouq's call reached me in Washington, where I had come for a second meeting with President Bush. Matouq asked me to intercede with the Americans. The Y-12 display, he said, had hurt Libya with Arab public opinion, and domestically, because it had given the impression that the Americans had unilaterally disarmed Libya, one country strongarming another. Either the inherent disrespect in this event was completely missed by the Americans or they didn't care. To the Libyans it was important that the dismantlement had been mutually agreed, after extensive negotiation, and that the steps to disarm the country of its WMD had been conducted under international law and by an international organization. Given the escalating resentment toward the United States in the Middle East at the time, the last thing Libya wanted was to appear to have caved in to American bullying.

I saw Bush the next day. When the topic turned to Libya, he began by

---

7 Jody Warrick, "U.S. Displays Nuclear Parts Given by Libya," *Washington Post*, March 16, 2004. I am often amazed, and saddened, by discriminatory statements like this, made by intelligent, well-educated U.S. politicians, implying that the "civilized world" includes only a certain special group of nations. By inference, I would assume this means that other countries are to be considered "uncivilized."

8 "Was Libyan WMD Disarmament a Significant Success for Nonproliferation?" by Sammy Salama, research associate, Center for Nonproliferation Studies, September 2004, accessed at www.nti.org/e_research/e3_56b.html.

thanking me for the cooperation between the Agency and the United States. I replied that there were a lot of sensitivities involved, and I explained the detrimental effect of flaunting the Libyan nuclear equipment in front of the media. I also said that I believed the United States needed to be careful not to portray Gaddafi to the Arab world as someone who had sold out to the West. Gaddafi already had his critics; if the United States and the British persisted in casting him as defeated, their new partnership with Libya would lose much of its value.

Bush understood immediately. A second display had been scheduled; he had it canceled. He said he would send Bill Burns, the assistant secretary of state for Near Eastern affairs, to Tripoli, as a way to show recognition and respect for the Libyan decision. "I am committed to normalizing our relationship with Libya," Bush said, and asked me, should the opportunity arise, to convey that message of sincerity to Gaddafi.

Still, the push for U.S. preeminence in the disarmament of Libya was not quite dead. In late May 2004, Matouq came to tell me that John Bolton was pressing Libya to sign a bilateral WMD agreement. It would authorize the United States to take special actions, including inspections, if Libya violated its obligations under the agreement or under the NPT. Matouq also said the Americans wanted him to remove the confidentiality clause from the IAEA's records on Libya, so the United States could gain access to them.

I advised Matouq to do neither. The confidentiality clause was standard procedure for all Agency safeguards work; I did not agree that anyone should have access to our files. Also, as I saw it, Libya had no need for additional compliance mechanisms; those in its Safeguards Agreement with the Agency and in the IAEA Statute were sufficient. Unless the Libyans wanted to give the United States the license to intervene at will, under any pretext, it hardly seemed like a sensible move. Convincing Matouq of this was not difficult.

In early June, I saw Shukri Ghanim, the Libyan prime minister and later the minister of oil, at a conference in Talloires, France. We had been friends since his days as director of studies at the OPEC offices in Vienna. He wanted to bring someone to see me in Vienna: Saif al-Islam al-Gaddafi, Colonel Gaddafi's second-oldest son, who had been in charge of arranging the Libyan deal with the Americans and the British.

When they came to my house in Vienna, Ghanim introduced Saif and then left. It was soon clear that Saif was seeking perspective and advice on a broad range of topics. He began by asking how the Libyans were perceived in the United States and in the West in general.

I saw no point in sugarcoating the truth. "They have no trust in you whatsoever," I told him. "You will have to build confidence over time." On the other hand, I said, the Libyans were now demonstrating the seriousness of their intent to take the country in a new direction as a responsible member of the international community. As such, they would be in a position to ask for assistance in terms of education, finance, and other areas of national need.

Saif remarked on Libya's dearth of experienced and well-trained managers in the inner circles of government. It was a recurring theme. I advised him to send some of Libya's midlevel managers abroad for training or to import a managerial training course to Tripoli, with external assistance, to begin addressing this deficiency. The damage to Libya's infrastructure would only be harder to reverse as more time passed.

I realized that Libya's isolation in recent decades had taken a severe toll. In 1964 there had been a direct, nonstop flight between New York and Tripoli, which was then considered a cosmopolitan Mediterranean capital. In 1970, Sheikh Zayed bin Sultan al-Nahyan, at that time president of the Emirates, had come to Libya to get a loan and to have surgery. Since then, the Emirates had evolved into an economic powerhouse, whereas Libya had experienced steady decline.

Gaddafi's style as head of state was, to say the least, singular. At one point he had banned barbershops in Libya, because he had decided it was not a productive profession. For an interim period, Libyans had been compelled to cut their own hair or to meet their barbers in secret locations.

His treatment of world leaders also gained attention. I heard a story that when Kofi Annan paid a visit to Libya, Gaddafi, displeased at recently imposed UN sanctions, announced he would meet Kofi in a tent in the desert in the middle of the night. Gaddafi's entourage drove Kofi to the meeting in a roundabout way, on a pitch-black road, for a couple of hours. The quiet of the night was disrupted periodically with noises from animals Kofi could not see. Another story was of Jacques Chirac's first visit to Libya in November 2004. He, too, was brought to a tent for his meeting with Gaddafi. Cleaners came to vacuum the tent while the discussion was taking place, and later a goat came wandering in. The point of such antics, if true, was not exactly clear. Presumably it was to signify displeasure with certain UN or French policies or to make clear that Gaddafi did not subscribe to external protocols for hosting such dignitaries.

In any case, the consequences of Libya's years of isolation and global inexperience continued to be in evidence—whether in its lack of well-trained managers, its lack of modern infrastructure, or its unique domestic and foreign policies—as Western governments and companies swooped in to scoop up the country's assets.

As I continued to observe Libya's reemergence on the international scene, I was disturbed by a number of insights. First, I was confounded by the ease with which a somewhat isolated country—under international sanctions and with relatively minimal scientific and industrial sophistication—could nonetheless acquire weapons of mass destruction, including the rudiments of a nuclear weapons program.

Second, I found it disconcerting to see the eagerness of some in the international community to apply a "quick fix" to such a situation. In Libya, as elsewhere, the motivations and conditions that gave rise to a clandestine nuclear program developed over decades. These motivations cannot be transformed or eradicated by one agreement—much less through hastily conceived sanctions, a quick bombing campaign, or sporadic bouts of diplomacy. Removing dangerous equipment and material is only the first stage of a complex process. Meaningful change, in such cases, requires a commitment for the long haul—commitment to a relationship based on mutual respect and trust. Libya's relative success at achieving such a relationship with its key international partners will only be understood over time.

Finally, I again was disquieted by the willingness of multiple parties to deceive or withhold information, in blatant contravention of international commitments: Libya, by pretending to be a party to the NPT in good standing while developing secret WMD programs; and the United States and the United Kingdom, by withholding information about clandestine nuclear activity until it suited them to reveal it to the IAEA, and then to inflate its importance to score political points. How much of this behavior would the international community tolerate, I wondered, before the integrity of the entire NPT regime would be called into question?

7

THE NUCLEAR BAZAAR
OF A. Q. KHAN

The revelation of the A. Q. Khan network marked the third in a series of profound changes to the nuclear status quo. The first had appeared in the early 1990s: the emergence of countries such as Iraq and North Korea, both party to the NPT, that deliberately and secretly violated their obligations. Libya was only the latest example.

The second change dates back to the terrorist attacks in the United States on September 11, 2001, which prompted the recognition that not just states but extremist groups were in the market for radioactive material. For nuclear experts, the sophistication of the 9/11 attacks sounded an alarm: what if an extremist group were to gain access to powerful radioactive sources to construct a "dirty bomb"?[1] Or worse: what if they were to obtain enough nuclear material to construct a crude nuclear weapon? This risk escalated when evidence came to light of Al-Qaeda's ambition to acquire WMD.

The international community responded with a dramatic reevalua-

---

1 A dirty bomb is very different from a nuclear weapon. Officially referred to as a "radio-logical dispersal device," a dirty bomb would consist of conventional explosives packaged with nuclear or radioactive material.

Because a dirty bomb is much simpler to construct than a nuclear weapon, and because radioactive material is generally less well protected than weapons-grade nuclear material, the likelihood of a dirty bomb being used by terrorists is generally considered much higher than that of a nuclear weapon. Some experts have expressed surprise that a dirty bomb has not been used to date.

tion of how countries protect their nuclear facilities and radioactive material. Within months, the IAEA's annual nuclear security budget jumped from $1 million to $30 million, funded mostly by voluntary contributions. The IAEA dispatched missions to track down orphaned radioactive materials left behind in the Republic of Georgia and elsewhere in the former Soviet Union. Physical security measures were upgraded at nuclear power plants, research reactors, and other facilities worldwide. Scenarios for the potential sabotage of nuclear facilities were reevaluated.

The response to the threat was not uniform. Western governments and even nongovernmental organizations made significant unsolicited donations to support the Agency's increased nuclear security work. But developing countries, for the most part, opposed any attempt to include this expansion of funding for nuclear security in the IAEA's regular budget. In behind-the-scenes debates, they cited the IAEA tradition of maintaining a balance between funding for nuclear technology promotion—such as the assistance we provide to expand cancer treatment or enhance agricultural productivity—and that for nuclear regulation. They feared that if the massive new investment in nuclear security became a permanent feature of the Agency's budget, they would be required to contribute to it.

This rift was yet another distressing indicator of the North-versus-South divide. Many developing countries believed that the targets of nuclear security threats were primarily the larger industrialized (and mostly Western) countries and felt the West should therefore pay for it. This was shortsighted: the threat was equally significant in smaller, less developed countries, as evidenced by instances we witnessed of attempts to smuggle in nuclear and radioactive material and by the call for our security services worldwide. Indeed, in the years that followed, the IAEA assisted with physical protection upgrades to more than one hundred sites in 30 countries; conducted hundreds of nuclear security workshops and training courses in roughly 120 countries; distributed more than three thousand radiation detection instruments; and secured nearly five thousand radioactive sources in countries across the world.

By early 2004, based on what we were seeing in Iran and Libya, we knew we were facing a third change in the nuclear landscape: the expansion of a black market in nuclear materials and equipment. From a supply and demand perspective, the first two new developments were evidence of demand—whether by states or extremist groups interested in acquiring nuclear material and nuclear weapons technology. The development of an illicit nuclear procurement network headed by A. Q. Khan and his web of colleagues filled in the supply side of the equation. In the coming years, as our monitoring and reporting intensified, our database would come to hold more than 1,300 cases of illicit trafficking in nuclear and radioactive materials. We had begun to uncover a virtual Nuclear Wal-Mart.

What motivates a person like A. Q. Khan? Some answers must be linked to his formative experiences. Khan has said that, as an adolescent in India, he witnessed the massacre of Muslims at the hands of the Hindu majority; he immigrated to Pakistan with his family soon thereafter, during the 1947 partition. Some two decades later, while Khan was in Belgium pursuing his doctorate in metallurgy, Pakistan was devastated by a war with India: its army was decimated and the eastern part of its territory seceded to become Bangladesh. In the early seventies, shortly before India exploded its first nuclear device, Khan went to work for a subcontractor of URENCO,[2] a British–West German–Dutch consortium that developed high-speed centrifuges for uranium enrichment and soon became a major player in the nuclear fuel market.

Was it nationalist zeal that fueled Khan's endeavors? Was it personal ambition and greed? Or was it religious fervor—a personal quest to put nuclear weapons in the hands of Muslims, who he felt were oppressed? It is hard to say definitively; the IAEA has never been permitted to question Khan directly. But it is clear that when Khan returned to Pakistan to head the Engineering Research Laboratories—later renamed the Khan

2 URENCO's name derives from "uranium enrichment corporation."

Research Laboratories—he was equipped with the means to dramatically expand his country's nuclear capacity: stolen copies of URENCO centrifuge designs and a Rolodex of contacts and companies to procure materials and equipment for uranium enrichment and other parts of the nuclear fuel cycle. It is also certain that Khan's exploits on the nuclear black market, which appear to have begun toward the end of the 1980s, netted him a sizable fortune, reportedly over $400 million. By the time it was uncovered, the network of nuclear suppliers, manufacturers, and middlemen Khan had built up was sophisticated, complex, and global in its reach.

After we received our first glimpse of A. Q. Khan's activities in Iran and Libya, Olli Heinonen, the director of the IAEA safeguards group, with responsibility for Iran, dove deep into the investigations of the illicit network. Through the probing done by Olli and a number of his colleagues, we were able to put together many pieces of the puzzle: dozens of transactions, names and locations of key suppliers, and the modus operandi of some of the middlemen. Of course, the major intelligence agencies were all following the same trail, with much larger and more refined operations, in some cases providing us with leads relevant to our primary task, which was to uncover the history of the nuclear programs in Iran, Libya, North Korea, and elsewhere.

Much of the IAEA's investigative work involved tracing the supply chain for the various components. Addresses, company names, and contacts were extracted from purchase orders, shipping papers, operational records, and, where available, financial statements. Equipment labels were used to identify possible suppliers; serial numbers were traced to specific manufacture dates and locations (unless the numbers had been scraped off). And, of course, we conducted interviews: exhaustive efforts to compare the information provided by Iranian and Libyan scientists and officials with the stories recounted by the middlemen who had played a role.

The picture began to emerge.

The first known transaction of the Khan network occurred in 1987, when two of Khan's associates and three Iranians had agreed, in a meeting in Dubai, on the terms of a sale for centrifuge components and designs.

A one-page handwritten sheet was the only record the IAEA was able to recover pointing to the transaction. The page of nuclear-related items Iran sought to purchase resembled a shopping list. As part of the deal, Iran received a list of companies in Europe and elsewhere from which to purchase other technology essential to its program.

Khan's closest lieutenant appears to have been Buhary Sayed Abu Tahir, a Sri Lankan businessman and owner of SMB Computers, a family electronics business based in Dubai, which Tahir and his brother had inherited from their father. Tahir's contact with Khan began when SMB Computers received a contract to sell air-conditioning units to the Khan Research Laboratory. Over time, Tahir grew closer to Khan, eventually acting as his go-between with other middlemen in the nuclear network. When Iran placed a second large order in 1994, it was Tahir who arranged for the shipment of two containers of used centrifuges from Dubai to Iran, using an Iranian-owned merchant ship. Dubai, with its extensive shipping trade and liberal customs regulations, was a convenient center of operations. Khan purchased an apartment on al-Maktoum Road, an elite area of town, from which to direct elements of the network.

Malaysia was another key location: Tahir, whose wife was Malaysian, worked with a precision engineering company, SCOPE,[3] to produce centrifuge components. Urs Tinner, a Swiss and the son of nuclear engineer Friedrich Tinner—a longtime associate of A. Q. Khan—helped Tahir by setting up the SCOPE factory in Shah Alam, Malaysia, and overseeing manufacturing operations. The raw material, high-grade aluminum, was purchased in Singapore. Because the parts were manufactured as individual pieces—some of which might have had application in other household or commercial appliances—the management at SCOPE was unaware of the intended end use and the intended end user.

After pursuing their own investigation and in cooperation with other

---

3 SCOPE, or Scomi Precision Engineering, is a subsidiary of the SCOMI Group, a company in the petroleum services industry. SCOPE's primary business was to manufacture components that required high-precision machining (cutting, turning, milling, etc.) for vehicles or other engineered products.

agencies, the Malaysian police arrested Tahir in Kuala Lumpur in May 2004, on the grounds that he posed a security threat. The IAEA repeatedly pressed to meet with him, and after several months of waiting, our inspectors eventually gained access for an interview.

The Agency learned that the network had no hierarchy; it was a loose-knit arrangement of businessmen, engineers, former acquaintances, and, in some cases, family members. There were many middlemen. Some were eventually made public, as their governments sought to prosecute them under various criminal statutes. Gotthard Lerch was a German citizen living in Switzerland. Peter Griffin, a British citizen living in France, was named in court cases in Germany and South Africa as being part of the Khan network and admitted knowing Khan, but he denied involvement in illicit nuclear programs and was not prosecuted. Johan Meyer was the South African owner of an engineering company. Charges against him were dropped after he reportedly agreed to testify against Gerhard Wisser, a German living in South Africa who was allegedly Meyer's conduit to the network. Daniel Geiges, a Swiss engineer based in South Africa, was also implicated in Meyer's testimony.

We learned as well that, as in other any market, both buyers and sellers took the initiative. Iran, for example, had made independent attempts to procure nuclear and dual-use equipment in multiple other countries in addition to meeting with Kahn's people. A senior official from South Africa's Atomic Energy Commission told me that, in the mid-1990s, the Iranian minister of energy tried to purchase sensitive nuclear technology from South Africa. The offer was rejected; South Africa had recently joined the NPT, and their "technology" was not for sale.

The network's methods were often ingenious. Procurement of tightly controlled components—anything that might raise an eyebrow because of the source government's export controls—customarily was done through an intermediary, using false end-user certificates to camouflage the final destination. As in the case of SCOPE, the supplier was often unaware of the end use—particularly when the component or material also had an application in oil drilling, water treatment, or other industrial operations.

Sometimes the intermediary was a real company; on other occasions, Khan's affiliates would set up a shell company in Dubai, complete the transaction, and then close the company down. Payments were made using accounts in yet another country, so the transaction was difficult to trace. Iran was known to have delivered some of its largest payments in cash; Khan would then use Dubai gold dealers or other businesses accustomed to handling large amounts of currency to launder the money.

One of Khan's simplest and most valuable products was his extensive list of contacts: individuals and companies that could produce or procure the technologies and materials essential to building a nuclear program. During his employment in the Netherlands, for example, he worked on high-strength, or maraging, steel metallurgy for Fysisch-Dynamisch Onderzoek (Physics Dynamics Research) laboratory, a subcontractor of URENCO. He had direct knowledge of the engineering and production firms that could supply maraging steel, an essential material for certain centrifuge rotors. His contacts at those companies gave his clients a foot in the door.

One of the network's more elaborate projects took place in South Africa, at a factory in Vanderbijlpark, a small mining town not far from Johannesburg. It involved the construction of modular process systems for uranium enrichment, minus the centrifuges. The systems were otherwise complete, equipped with the pumps, valves, feed autoclaves, stainless-steel vessels, and auxiliary piping needed to direct the flow of UF_6 into centrifuge cascades. The cascades were configured in stages that would enrich the incoming natural uranium, first to 3.5 percent U-235, and eventually to a high-enriched weapons grade of 90 percent. The factory owner referred to the systems as "a work of art."

In September 2004, South African police, acting on a tip-off in conjunction with South African counterproliferation officials[4] and IAEA inspectors, converged on the factory. The systems had been dismantled piece by piece and placed into containers, ready for shipment.

The revelation of this extensive operation in South Africa was particularly surprising to nuclear experts. South Africa had, after all, long

---

4 The officials were from the Council for the Non-Proliferation of Weapons of Mass Destruction, an agency of the South African Government.

ago relinquished its nuclear weapons program. Its leaders had become outspoken advocates of nuclear nonproliferation and disarmament. This discovery of ongoing private clandestine nuclear activity emphasized the need for more focused national efforts to monitor manufacture and commerce relevant to nuclear and dual-use exports.

South Africa was by no means the only country involved. The details of the network, emerging piecemeal, read like an erratic travelogue. A German supplier had provided the vacuum pumps. A middleman in Spain had supplied two specialized lathes. A Swiss consultant had traveled to Malaysia to produce centrifuge parts based on Pakistani designs that had originated in the Netherlands. A Hungarian-born Israeli ex–military officer working in South Africa was arrested at a ski resort in Aspen, Colorado, for his role in supplying Pakistan with triggered spark gaps, which can be used in nuclear weapon detonators. A British engineer had prepared the plans for the Libyan machine shop set up to produce centrifuge components. Special furnaces were procured from Italy. Frequency converters and other electronics had been manufactured in Turkish workshops using parts imported from elsewhere in Europe. All in all, the IAEA's investigations would ferret out links to more than thirty companies in as many countries.

It was only a year earlier that the IAEA had been searching in Iraq for weapons that were not there. Now, in early 2004, it seemed that wherever we turned we came across tangible new evidence of nuclear proliferation. Libya had confessed to its nuclear weapons ambitions. North Korea was approaching construction of its first nuclear weapon. Iran had recently unveiled, after painstaking investigation, the results of a two-decade-long program to obtain the nuclear fuel cycle. And we had no confidence that we knew how far or where the Khan network had spread.

On February 12, 2004, I published an op-ed in the *New York Times* entitled "Saving Ourselves from Self-Destruction," in which I drew attention to the emergence of the Khan network and noted that both halves of the proliferation marketplace, supply and demand, were flourishing. I proposed a series of measures that would disrupt this trend: toughened export controls; universal sign-on to the Additional Protocol; a prohibition against withdrawal from the NPT; a revival of negotiations over the Fissile Material Cutoff Treaty,[5] which would prohibit the production of nuclear materials for weapons use; increased security for existing nuclear material; and for countries possessing nuclear weapons, a road map for disarmament.

But I realized that these steps addressed only the mechanics of the situation. The true causes of the problem were rooted much deeper, in the extreme economic and social inequalities that prevailed between North and South, the asymmetry of the global security system with its double standards, and the conflicts and tensions that continued to fester in specific regions. "We must also begin to address the root causes of insecurity," I urged in the article.

> In areas of long-standing conflict like the Middle East, South Asia and the Korean Peninsula, the pursuit of weapons of mass destruction—while never justified—can be expected as long as we fail to introduce alternatives that redress the security deficit. We must abandon the unworkable notion that it is morally reprehensible for some countries to pursue weapons of mass destruction, yet morally acceptable for others to rely on them for security—and indeed to continue to refine their capacities and postulate plans for their use.
>
> Similarly, we must abandon the traditional approach of defining security in terms of boundaries—city walls, border patrols, racial and religious groupings. The global community has become irreversibly interdependent, with the constant movement of people, ideas, goods and resources. In such a world, we must combat terrorism with an infectious security culture that crosses borders—an inclusive approach

---

5 In 1993 the UN General Assembly adopted Resolution 48/75L, calling for the negotiation of a multilateral treaty to ban production of fissionable material for weapons. The negotiations remain stalled in the Conference on Disarmament in Geneva.

to security based on solidarity and the value of human life. In such a world, weapons of mass destruction have no place.

Just days before my article was to be published, I received word that President Bush was about to introduce his own set of counterproliferation measures, in a speech on February 11 at the National Defense University in Washington. The *New York Times* agreed to delay the op-ed by a day or two, so it would not appear that I was trying to preempt Bush.

Colin Powell called me a few hours before Bush was to give his speech. The president, he said, planned to announce seven new measures to counter the threat of weapons of mass destruction. Powell went on to imply that he personally did not agree with all of the ideas. "Some proposals are controversial," he said, adding, "they will need to go to the IAEA Board for discussion."

Now he had my attention.

As it turned out, there was a fair amount of overlap in the proposals Bush and I had put forward. Both of us called for tougher export controls, including the need to criminalize actions that deliberately supported proliferation. Bush also proposed more funds to secure existing nuclear material stockpiles. He advocated strong support for the Additional Protocol. He recommended an expansion of the Proliferation Security Initiative.[6] He suggested a cutoff on "newcomer" countries acquiring fuel cycle facilities—a distinctly different approach from mine. Of course there was no mention of nuclear disarmament. But in many of Bush's proposals, there was the clear intent to address gaps in the proliferation regime that had been exposed by what we were witnessing in the Khan network.

Two of Bush's proposals, however, seemed off the mark. The first called

---

6 The Proliferation Security Initiative is a U.S.-led multinational program for the interdiction of ships at sea believed to be transporting nuclear materials. While many countries have signed on to the PSI, it is not conducted under the auspices of the United Nations, as one might expect of an initiative that claims authority over matters governed by international maritime law.

on the IAEA to establish a special Board committee to focus on safe-guards and verification concerns. The second urged the IAEA to pro-hibit any Member State under investigation for possible safeguards violations from serving on its Board.

I was later told by a senior member of the Bush administration that the president's speech had been written by John Bolton and Bob Joseph[7] and had not been vetted by the State Department. The notion of a special safeguards committee, although ostensibly a good way to strengthen the Agency's verification program, was born out of their desire to micromanage the IAEA's verification work and particularly to force a hard-line approach on Iran's nuclear program. The intent behind the proposal to exclude "countries under investigation" from serving on the Board—clearly targeting Iran—was not even well camouflaged and would not have worked. It revealed, more than anything, a lack of understanding: the protocols of multilateral diplomacy and mutual respect that make international organizations effective—much like the laws that govern democratic society—are not well served by prejudice, bullying, or a rush to judgment.

When I met with President Bush in Washington in March 2004, our conversation touched on the threat of the emerging nuclear black mar-ket. I mentioned that, while A. Q. Khan may have been the ringleader, it was clear he was at least in some cases not working on his own. For example, in the case of Iran, elements of the Pakistani army may have been involved, and in the case of North Korea, Khan may have been act-ing as part of state-to-state cooperation.[8]

I based my assessment in part on a letter I had seen, handwritten by Khan himself. He had managed to get the letter out of Pakistan as a sort of insurance policy in the event of his arrest by Pakistani

---

7 From 2001 to 2005, Joseph worked for Condoleezza Rice at the National Security Council, as the senior director for proliferation strategy, counterproliferation, and home-land defense. He was heavily involved with Bolton in the development of the Proliferation Security Initiative and in the negotiations to persuade Libya to give up its WMD.

8 Since Pakistan is not part of the Nuclear Non-Proliferation Treaty and also not a mem-ber of the Nuclear Suppliers Group subscribing to export control guidelines, it is not bound by the obligations of either.

authorities. The letter asserted that he had been instructed by senior officers in the Pakistani Army to cooperate with Iran and North Korea.

Bush agreed that there were definite signs pointing to other Pakistani actors. However, it was clear that the complex relationship between the two countries—including the extensive help Pakistan was providing for U.S. operations in Afghanistan—would make it awkward for Washington to press the Pakistani government too hard.

Striving for a pragmatic approach, I concluded that our first priority was to find out who else had acquired technology through Khan's network.

In the weeks that followed, international support built rapidly for new prohibitions against nonstate actors, designed specifically to criminalize and impede the types of clandestine activities carried out by the Khan network. In May, the UN Security Council passed Resolution 1540, requiring UN Member States to enact and enforce laws targeting individuals who in any way lend a hand to WMD proliferation. The resolution also called for new domestic controls, to tighten up access to nuclear and nuclear-related materials.

Not all the proposals in Bush's speech fared as well, however. The exclusion of Member States under investigation from serving on the Board—a symbolic gesture designed to humiliate—never received serious consideration. And for the next two years, the Americans lobbied the Board to approve a special safeguards committee. I saw a useful role for such a committee if it focused on "ways and means to strengthen safeguards," for example, by beefing up the IAEA's forensic laboratories, which were in a dilapidated state. Once in existence, the committee did not last long. Major North-South differences quickly surfaced relevant to the fairness and effectiveness of the nonproliferation regime. After a series of rather nondescript meetings, the Board allowed it, in the words of one of the ambassadors, to "die a quiet and natural death."

The emergence of the Khan network—the news that a high-level Pakistani government official had been running an international smuggling ring—was an enormous embarrassment for Islamabad. President Musharraf had no choice but to take action. On February 4, 2004, A. Q. Khan was forced to confess on a government-owned television network that he had been the ringleader of the illicit international nuclear network. But the very next day, Musharraf pardoned him, noting his service to Pakistan, although Khan remained under house arrest until 2009. To a non-Pakistani audience, the sequence of events was baffling: why an immediate, official pardon for the man who had single-handedly engineered nuclear proliferation on a massive scale?

Musharraf could not afford to be too critical. Khan's status as national hero—the perception that he had made immense contributions to his country's national security by helping Islamabad build a nuclear capability to counter that of India—gave him a degree of immunity from prosecution. Also, Khan quite likely could have implicated others in Pakistan's government. There has been a great deal of speculation about how much the government knew about Khan's activities and to what extent he had support from other government or military officials. Khan is reported to have used Pakistani government aircraft, on occasion, to transport nuclear-related equipment to non-Pakistani clients.[9] His affluent lifestyle clearly suggested income well above his government salary, a direct indicator of his moonlighting activities. And press reports indicated that Pakistan's National Accountability Bureau accumulated an extensive dossier on Khan but chose not to act on it.[10]

As the Agency's understanding of the Khan network matured, we also learned of the "watch-and-wait" strategy that had been employed by Western intelligence agencies. American officials claimed they had known about Khan's activities all along but had decided not to act. If true, this made nonsense of the American claim that the discovery of Libya's WMD was a triumph of intelligence work. Ruud Lubbers, the former Dutch prime minister, told me that the Dutch had wanted to arrest Khan as early as the 1970s, only to be told not to by the CIA. This

---

9 Douglas Frantz, "From Patriot to Proliferator," *Los Angeles Times*, September 23, 2005.
10 Frantz, "From Patriot to Proliferator."

was corroborated by other sources. Seymour Hersh, writing in the *New Yorker* in March 2004, reported a senior U.S. intelligence officer as saying, "We had every opportunity to put a stop to the A. Q. Khan network fifteen years ago. Some of those involved today in the smuggling are the children of those we knew about in the eighties. It's the second generation now."[11] Robert Einhorn, who held the post of U.S. assistant secretary for nonproliferation from 1991 to 2001, later made a similar statement: "We could have stopped the Khan network, as we knew it, at any time. The debate was, do you stop it now or do you watch it and understand it better so that you are in a stronger position to pull it up by the roots later? The case for waiting prevailed."[12]

"Can you explain what was gained?" I wanted to shout. Where were all the bigger fish who should now be ready for the catch? How could the IAEA expect to make headway against nuclear proliferation if vital information was withheld from us? Was there no recognition in the United States—or in the United Kingdom, or other countries that had known about A. Q. Khan—of their obligation, as a member of the NPT, to inform the IAEA of such underground dealings? Even more to the point, would it not have made more sense to stop the clandestine programs of Iran, Libya, and others in their infancy?

Whatever the circumstances or arguments at the time, in hindsight the decision to watch and wait was a royal blunder. Among the ways in which the strategy backfired was that it alerted members of the network. Interviews with middlemen have suggested that, at least in some cases, they knew for some time that they were under surveillance. This allowed them to destroy extensive records, which in turn made it difficult for the IAEA and other investigators to pin down additional dimensions of the network, including the identities of other customers.

Did Khan have other customers? Robert Gallucci has referred to A. Q. Khan as the Johnny Appleseed of nuclear enrichment for his role

---

11 Seymour M. Hersh, "The Deal," *New Yorker*, March 8, 2004.
12 Robert Einhorn was quoted in Douglas Frantz, "A High-Risk Nuclear Stakeout," *Los Angeles Times*, February 27, 2005.

in spreading centrifuge technology far and wide. Khan's travels took him across the Middle East and Africa. In most cases, there is little record of what happened in those places. But rumors persist and disturbing signs sometimes emerge.

When I visited one of the Gulf States in 2004, for example, a senior member of the royal family told me that Khan had been trying to sell them nuclear hardware for two years. The government had feigned interest, sending an agent to try to elicit information about the network's dealings with Iran. Additional countries came forward with similar stories. In all likelihood, variations on this narrative had taken place in many locations. Is it not probable that, faced with such an opportunity, some customers did more than window-shop?

My ultimate nightmare is that the network's ability to make nuclear material, equipment, and know-how available to anyone with cash in hand might have led to the creation of a small enrichment operation in a remote area such as northern Afghanistan.[13] Given the increasing technological sophistication of extremist groups, this should no longer be regarded as a macabre fairy tale.

The demise of A. Q. Khan may have removed the mastermind from the operation, but there is no assurance that the network is no longer capable of supplying interested clients. As Sam Nunn remarked about the network's trade in nuclear weapon components, "When you see the kind of money involved, and the stakes involved, and the spread of this kind of technology around the world, it's virtually inevitable."[14] Abdul Qadeer Khan made it his life's work to level the nuclear weapons playing field for Muslim countries, to establish security parity with Israel's nuclear weapons program, and to make money in the process. The eradication of his nuclear bazaar may yet take some time.

There are three morals to the story. First, as illustrated by Israel's role in the Middle East and by India's role in South Asia, proliferation begets proliferation. Second, while export controls should be significantly

---

13 Mentioned in Hersh, "The Deal."
14 Steve Coll, "The Atomic Emporium: Abdul Qadeer Khan and Iran's Race to Build the Bomb," *New Yorker*, August 2006.

stronger, they can no longer be considered a remedy: the technology is out of the tube. And third, so long as nuclear weapons exist and bring power and prestige to their owners, we will continue to see proliferation, especially in countries and regions that perceive themselves to be under threat.

8

FROM VIENNA TO OSLO

In the summer of 2004, as my second term leading the IAEA approached its conclusion, my inclination was not to seek a third term, despite the urging of most Member States. The job came with considerable stress, and my family's preference was that I give it up. Then came U.S. interference.

I had been given to understand that should I choose to run again, the United States would respect my decision. In August, while on vacation at my summer home in Egypt, I was told to expect a call from Colin Powell confirming that position. This expression of support was not all that surprising. The past few months had seen a very positive series of meetings with American officials, including Bush himself.

But the call did not come. Shortly after I returned to Vienna, I learned from my deputy David Waller that the tone in the United States had changed. "I've just gotten back from Washington," he said. "We need to talk." Walking with David in Belvedere Park, across from my home, I heard that the U.S. view had shifted. John Bolton had launched a campaign to block my reappointment by invoking the seldom-applied limit of two terms to the tenure of UN Agency heads. Bolton had called David to say that if I agreed to step down, the United States would express effusive appreciation of my work for the past eight years.

I was furious. Bolton was my ideological opposite, a champion of "us-versus-them" foreign policy; he opposed multilateral diplomacy and consistently worked behind the scenes to discredit the IAEA, often blocking efforts to resolve nuclear proliferation issues peacefully. He strove to undermine everything I stood for. That he would presume to dictate whether I ran for a third term was intolerable. The irony was not lost on me: the United States, which had backed my first term as Director General against Egypt's preferred choice was now calling for my ouster.[1]

That evening I talked things over with Aida, my wife. We quickly agreed that I should stand for a third term. If I won, it would be a vindication of multilateral diplomacy and a clear mandate to press for a negotiated resolution in Iran and in other trouble spots. If I lost, I would still have stood up against U.S. bullying. The next morning I wrote to the chairman of the IAEA Board declaring my candidacy for reelection.

The storm began almost immediately after I announced my decision. In September 2004 the Americans tried to amend a draft resolution on Iran to remove the standard statement of appreciation that referred to the Agency as "professional and impartial." To an outside observer this might seem insignificant, but in diplomatic circles it was an overt slap. Peter Jenkins, the British ambassador, told me he found the move "churlish and petty."

The United States began casting around for a candidate to run against me. Approaches were made to Brazil about putting forward UN High Representative for Disarmament Sergio de Queiroz Duarte.[2] They approached Argentina about Roberto Garcia Moritan, an undersecretary in the Foreign Ministry. They asked Japan about Shinzo Abe, their former ambassador to Vienna. They pressured both Australia and Russia to support Alexander Downer, the Australian foreign minister. These requests went nowhere, so the Americans formally asked the Europeans to join them in

---

1 At the time of my first election as Director General, in 1997, Egypt had put its support behind Mohamed Shaker, Egyptian ambassador to the United Kingdom and a close friend of President Hosni Mubarak's family.
2 Duarte at the time was the Brazilian ambassador-at-large for disarmament and nonproliferation. He also served as ambassador to the IAEA.

urging the IAEA Board to postpone the end-of-December deadline for candidates. The Europeans refused.

The campaign to unseat me adopted new tactics. In November 2004, at about the time of George Bush's reelection in the United States, news broke about the missing explosives from Al-Qa'qaa in Iraq.[3] A barrage of misinformation ensued. A concocted story appeared about a clandestine nuclear weapons program in Egypt, tied to Libya's efforts, that I was trying to cover up. Another article claimed that Blix and I had secret bank accounts in Switzerland, payback for our work in Iraq before the war. Still another asserted that Iran had deposited more than $600,000 in Aida's bank account in Switzerland and had given me Persian carpets, each worth $50,000.

As reported by Dafna Linzer in the *Washington Post*, my phones were bugged in an attempt to find information to discredit me.[4] This was not the first time; we had seen earlier evidence of intercepted IAEA text messages and phone conversations. But now the issue had been reported in the news by an authoritative source.[5]

I was told that the tip about wiretapping had been leaked to the *Washington Post* by individuals at the CIA who were unhappy with the actions of certain people in the State Department. This did not surprise me: from mid-2004 to mid-2005, we had received copies of memos, briefings, and other information passed on confidentially from State Department staff who disliked the high-handed, insidious behavior of a few individuals.

In the end, the Americans were alone in their opposition to my candidacy. The four countries that normally follow their lead—Australia, Canada, Japan, and the United Kingdom—stayed for a time on the sidelines, saying privately that they supported me but refraining from any public declaration in order not to embarrass or isolate the United States.

---

3 The full account of the Al-Qa'qaa incident and its aftermath is given in chapter 3.

4 "IAEA Leader's Phone Tapped," December 12, 2004.

5 Reuters reporters later said they were shown by Western diplomats what was purported to be transcripts of intercepted telephone conversations that I had held with the Iranian ambassador to the IAEA. Lou Charbonneau, "Rice on WikiLeaks Spy Charges: We're Just Diplomats," Reuters, November 29, 2010.

One week before the IAEA Board met to make its decision, I was invited to Washington by Condoleezza Rice, now the secretary of state. With some hesitation, I decided to make the trip. At my meetings, Rice and Steve Hadley, her replacement as national security adviser, limited the discussion to the immediate issue at hand: Iran's nuclear program and the U.S. conviction that Iran must be prevented from carrying out any stage of the fuel cycle. When I mentioned the need for some face-saving steps for Iran with respect to its enrichment program, Hadley interjected: "Iran must not have even one centrifuge spinning." From that time forward, the phrase became a U.S. mantra.

Only afterward, at the end of my meeting with Rice, did she address my reelection. The Americans' view on my serving a third term had not been personal, she said, only a consistent application of the U.S. policy of two terms for heads of UN agencies. Looking at each other, we both knew this wasn't true, but I also saw that Rice and Hadley were trying to distance themselves from some of John Bolton's diplomatic blunders. I had heard that Rice, upon taking her new position, had refused to keep Bolton at the State Department. He was instead appointed directly by Bush as U.S. ambassador to the United Nations, which was either the most outrageous mismatch of job qualifications in diplomatic history or the most coherent expression of the U.S. approach to multilateralism at the time.

We left it at that. I understood that the meeting with Rice constituted a shift and the United States would now join the rest of the Member States in their decision.

I smiled. "We should let bygones be bygones," I said to Rice. "No need to talk about past history." Just days later, on June 13, 2005, I was reelected to a third term by unanimous vote.

After a bruising season, the Agency received the most restorative of gifts. It was the morning of October 7, 2005, and I had stayed home from the office. By late morning, I was still in my pajamas. I had recently returned from a grueling trip, but that had never kept me at home before. The reason for my truancy was something quite different.

For the second year running, there were rampant rumors that the IAEA and I were front-runners for the Nobel Peace Prize. In 2004 the rumors had been so persistent that our communications people had drawn up talking points in case we had to deal with the press. On the day of the announcement that year, I had been in Japan for talks with the minister of the economy. When I arrived at our meeting, there were roughly fifty cameramen waiting in anticipation of news from the Nobel committee. During the meeting, my assistant, Ian Biggs, slipped out. He came back a few minutes later and passed me a note with the name of the Peace Prize laureate: Wangari Maathai. When I left the meeting, there was one cameraman outside, who came up to me and said, very kindly, "Sorry."

This year I avoided talking about it with anyone at the Agency. I was told later that no one wanted to jinx our chances. That Friday, I didn't feel like sitting through a morning staff meeting with everyone looking at their watches, especially since the day before, bookmakers had suddenly upgraded our odds of winning.

The announcement was scheduled for 11:00 A.M. The Nobel committee customarily phones the winner half an hour in advance. By 10:45, my stomach had stopped churning and I was at peace with the fact that the committee had chosen someone else. When Aida went into the study to watch the announcement on TV, I tagged along, curious.

Even in Norwegian, I recognized the name: "Det Internasjonale Atomenergibyrået," followed by "Mohamed ElBaradei." I stood there dumbfounded, half-disbelieving; then, as the words were repeated in English, Aida and I embraced, tears streaming down our faces.[6]

In less than a minute, our phones began ringing off the hook. First, my brother Ali, calling from Cairo, glued to the TV. Then my secretary,

---

6 My son, Mostafa, was a studio director at the time, working in the London offices of CNN. The news broke in the middle of his shift. He sent us a three-word text message: "Oh my God!"—then took a ten-minute break outside to regain his composure. He later told us he had fifty British pounds in his pocket, which he gave to the first beggar he saw.

My daughter, Laila, who also lived in London, was in the Underground on the way to her law office. She came out of the station to see thirty messages on her cell phone and was sure that something was terribly wrong—until she was able to reach her brother.

Monika Pichler, ringing from the office to say that the Norwegian ambassador and his deputy had arrived with a huge bouquet of flowers.[7] The ambassador was the only one who had been informed in advance by the Nobel committee. I invited them to come over to the house. Between the multitude of calls coming in and my emotional state, it was all I could do to get dressed.

After a hastily arranged press conference at the IAEA, I gave an impromptu speech to the Agency staff, who had crowded en masse into the boardroom. The room was electric: there were tears, laughter, and recurring waves of applause. To say that we were all thrilled and proud would not begin to describe the enormity of the moment. I do not expect to experience again in my lifetime the joy of sharing such extraordinary affirmation: my colleagues, people from more than ninety countries, had striven together to make the world more secure. The prize was the culmination of our efforts as an institution and of my forty years working for the common good.

The deluge of support rapidly became an avalanche. Emails jammed my in-box. Letters began arriving in stacks: the IAEA mailroom resorted to circulating them in overstuffed grocery bags. The thrill of these messages was that they were coming in from people from all walks of life and of all ages, ethnicities, and religions, from heads of state to schoolchildren. A group of Italian nuns wrote to promise their prayers for our future. Three hundred Spanish children from Fuenlabrada, a suburb of Madrid, sent individual letters of congratulations.[8] Egyptian citizens of

---

7 The Nobel committee later said they were sure that if they called the IAEA the news would leak immediately. The ambassador told me he had bought a large bouquet the year before as well.

8 Two examples:

From Javier, age 7: "I heard we had many people giving you support from Spain so that your inspectors would have more time so that there would be no war in Iraq. That is why we were so happy with your Nobel Peace Prize, and we hope that you will continue fighting for peace in the world. Congratulations!"

From Alicia, age 12: "I am totally against wars, and I thank you very much for your efforts to try to avoid the war in Iraq. Despite the fact that your strategy, based on dialogue, was absolutely not to the liking of the USA, you knew how to stay firm and you showed that there were not nuclear weapons in Iraq, even while gaining the hate of the most powerful country. I hope that in the conflict with Iran you are luckier and that

every description wrote to express their pride. This generous outpouring was at once immensely humbling and immensely uplifting.

I felt a great obligation to convey, through my Nobel lecture, my particular understanding of nuclear proliferation—as part of a much larger context of global inequality and the quest for human security. For some time, I had been trying, in speech after speech, to articulate the connections: the negative societal spiral began with poverty and inequality; which all too frequently coincided with poor governance, corruption, and human rights abuses; which in turn provided fertile breeding ground for extremism, violence, and civil wars, and, in some cases, in areas of unresolved conflict, the temptation to project power or achieve security parity by acquiring weapons of mass destruction.

Laban Coblentz, my communications assistant and speechwriter, and Melissa Fleming, the Agency spokesperson, had told me that the point was being lost on my audiences, even though they themselves understood my reasoning. The connections I saw were there, but I wasn't driving the message home. I needed something more concrete: an image to capture the message.

I found my answer while thinking about how to use the money that accompanied the Nobel recognition. The prize had been awarded jointly to me, as Director General, and to the IAEA, as an organization. The award money totaled just over one million euros. The IAEA Board had determined that half the money would go to support cancer treatment and childhood nutrition in developing countries. My portion, I decided, would be put toward a cause I had known my whole life: the need to care for the orphans of Cairo. My sister-in-law was directly involved in the city's orphanages; she could help me ensure that the funds were well spent.

Here was the image I wanted, the motif for my Nobel lecture: "My sister-in-law," I wrote,

---

things get solved by using dialogue and not through arms. And that the politicians of the USA accept the opinions of the UN, and that they not always do whatever they want for their economic gain. I wish you luck and that you can continue using your main weapon: dialogue. With affection . . ."

works for a group that supports orphanages in Cairo. She and her colleagues take care of children left behind by circumstances beyond their control. They feed these children, clothe them and teach them to read.

At the International Atomic Energy Agency, my colleagues and I work to keep nuclear materials out of the reach of extremist groups. We inspect nuclear facilities all over the world, to be sure that peaceful nuclear activities are not being used as a cloak for weapons programmes.

My sister-in-law and I are working towards the same goal, through different paths: the security of the human family.

The quest for security, I argued, was the motivation driving a multitude of human endeavors. But because our societal priorities were skewed, some nations of the world were spending more than a trillion dollars per year on armaments while two-fifths of the earth's population were living on less than two dollars per day and nearly a billion were going to bed hungry every night. The world's insecurities had gone absurdly awry. Nor was it possible to sustain such a model. "Today," I wrote,

with globalization bringing us ever closer together, if we choose to ignore the insecurities of some, they will soon become the insecurities of all. Equally, with the spread of advanced science and technology, as long as some of us choose to rely on nuclear weapons, we continue to risk that these same weapons will become increasingly attractive to others.

I did not want to end the lecture on a note of gloom. It was Aida who came up with the idea of concluding with an invitation to imagine a better future:

Imagine what would happen if the nations of the world spent as much on development as on building the machines of war. Imagine a world where every human being would live in freedom and dignity. Imagine a world in which we would shed the same tears when a child dies in Darfur or Vancouver. Imagine a world where we would settle our differences through diplomacy and dialogue and not through bombs or bullets. Imagine if the only nuclear weapons remaining were the relics in our museums. Imagine the legacy we could leave to our children. Imagine that such a world is within our grasp.

To say that the ceremonies in Oslo were an unforgettable experience would be a severe understatement. The warmth of the reception offered to us by the Norwegian people and the royal family was stunning. It is an extraordinary thing to witness an entire capital city come to a halt, for three days of the year, in celebration of peace—from poetry and plays written and delivered by schoolchildren to the Nobel Peace Prize Concert, broadcasted to more than one hundred countries from the Oslo Spektrum Arena. I was particularly humbled by the tour of the Nobel museum, where I saw the images of those who had preceded me as peace laureates.

I was still nervous when I was asked to write in the Nobel book, inscribed by all the laureates. "We need to change our mind-set," I wrote. "We need to understand the common values we share. We need to understand that war and force will not resolve our differences or move us forward toward peace. Only through dialogue and mutual respect can we move forward as one human family." (But as luck would have it, I wrote the word "family" with a double "l"—a lapse my wife, Aida, still teases me about even today.)

It was an intensely personal few days. My family was with me—my wife, my mother, my son and daughter, my brothers and sisters—as well as friends and colleagues from the Agency and other close friends. My mother, as always, made me smile. In Cairo, when the announcement had been made in October, an avalanche of Egyptian and international media had poured into her home, where my family had gotten together. She had become an instant celebrity, talking about my childhood with tears in her eyes. In Oslo, despite her eighty years, she was floating happily from event to event. Driving from the ceremony to the hotel, the limousine flanked by a police escort, she announced, "This is like a dream. I feel like a queen."

The Nobel award was a defining moment—not only for me personally but in the broader sense of public recognition for the work of the Agency and, as a corollary, the sense of unity and pride it brought to the IAEA Secretariat. The media had routinely spotlighted only a small fraction of our work—the role of weapons inspectors in a few critical places—when in fact we were verifying, year after year, more than nine hundred facilities in seventy countries. The wording of the Nobel citation made clear that the IAEA's value rested not only in these safeguards verification activities—the work of one IAEA department—but also in our efforts to promote the safe and secure use of nuclear energy in peaceful applications: nuclear medicine to combat heart disease, isotope hydrology to trace and manage underground water aquifers, or plant breeding to grow barley plants that thrive in the altitudes of the high Andes. For such a diverse workforce, coming from a complex spectrum of cultural, educational, and occupational backgrounds, the abrupt elevation in public awareness of our work solidified the internal organizational conviction that all parts of the Agency were working toward a common purpose.

A second benefit was the access that came with visibility and an elevated platform. The IAEA's work in Iraq before the March 2003 invasion had pushed the Agency into the international spotlight, turning it into one of the better-known global institutions. But with the Nobel award came an exponential expansion not only in media attention—an enviable roster of standing invitations from press channels worldwide—but also in our capacity to shape our message and deliver it to target audiences. We gained unprecedented access to political and other leaders on every continent; interactions that customarily had taken place at the ministerial level were now with heads of state. For the Agency, the norm had been redefined.

The Nobel recognition also made clear the importance of the IAEA's independence and in some ways reinforced it. As Director General, I felt far more immune against accusations of being biased or soft and against those who would question my integrity. I also used the spotlight to draw attention to the Agency's limited financial resources, which restricted our technological capability and, in turn, threatened our independence. For example, our reliance on satellite imagery to search for undeclared nuclear facilities could not be based solely on images passed to us selectively by two or three Member States; we needed the financial capacity to select and purchase our own images. Similarly, we needed to beef up the nuclear forensics capability of our own laboratories, rather than being dependent—as we were for the most sensitive types of fission track particle analysis—on a single laboratory operated by the U.S. Air Force. I began speaking out more publicly and with greater vigor about the need to bolster the IAEA's independence with enhanced legal authority, technological capabilities, and financial support.

Of course, the Nobel Peace Prize did not diminish in any sense the formidable challenges we faced. But it certainly strengthened our hand, renewing our resolve for the tasks that lay ahead.

9

IRAN, 2006

"Not One Centrifuge"

By January 2006, the convoluted, stumbling negotiations between the international community and Iran over its nuclear program were at an impasse. The European offer of aid and technological assistance in exchange for Iran ceasing its nuclear development had been deemed insulting in its language and paltry in its benefits and had failed to recognize Iran's security and political needs. When talks over that offer broke down, Iran resumed its conversion of uranium, ending the country's voluntary suspension of nuclear activities. This led the IAEA Board to condemn Iran's "noncompliance" with its obligations under the NPT.

No tangible progress was in sight. Iran was feeling bold: oil prices were high; China was dependent on Iranian oil and gas; and Russia, still constructing the reactor at Bushehr, was concerned with maintaining its good relationship with neighboring Iran.

So Iran took a calculated risk, informing the IAEA on January 3 that it intended to go one step further, by resuming uranium enrichment R&D. A letter followed asking the Agency to remove the seals on Iran's enrichment facility at Natanz.

The size and scope of this calculated risk was to begin operating a small R&D enrichment cascade at the pilot plant. The Iranians did not imagine that the Security Council would impose further sanctions for this small pilot operation. Enrichment for peaceful purposes was, in any case, their right under the NPT; the suspension had always been specified as a voluntary goodwill measure to facilitate negotiations. It hardly seemed likely that the Security Council would take action against Iran given that most of Tehran's "noncompliance" had been corrected over the previous two years, and its small enrichment operation was after all legal. As nearly as I could discern, the Iranians felt confident that there would be no negative repercussions, that negotiations with the Europeans would resume, and they would agree to a moratorium on industrial-scale enrichment.

The Russians, to their credit, tried to work out a compromise, proposing that Iran be allowed to run a small R&D program of thirty to forty centrifuges, the specifics of which would be determined in consultation with the IAEA. The Americans, however, were adamantly against any such compromise and Iran did not openly endorse it, so the Russians withdrew their suggestion.

I thought the Russian proposal made sense and could open up a way out of our stalemate. When Bolton's replacement, Bob Joseph, visited me in Vienna, I told him so. Condoleezza Rice called me shortly thereafter, in my hotel room in Davos. "Our path seems to have diverted since we last met," she said, her tone rather unfriendly. She implied that I supported an Iranian R&D program, thus legitimizing Iranian enrichment. As I told her, I had taken no public position on the issue but believed the benefit of the Russian proposal far outweighed its cost for two reasons. First, the IAEA needed to be able to inspect possible undeclared activities in Iran, thus it was essential that Iran continue to implement its Additional Protocol. Also, we needed to begin negotiations if we hoped to halt Iran's progress toward industrial-scale enrichment. At the end of a tense conversation, I emphasized that IAEA Member States would decide how to proceed, but that I owed them at least my view of things.[1]

In February, the IAEA Board opened a new phase in the Iran saga—by referring the Iran file to the Security Council. The verdict came after more than two years of failed efforts by the EU-3 and Iran to reach an

---

1 After a meeting with Rice, the Russian foreign minister, Sergey Lavrov, publicly denied that there had ever been a Russian proposal. He obviously wanted to maintain the unity of the negotiating parties and did not want to disagree with the United States in public.

agreement on Tehran's nuclear program through diplomacy. The Board vote was split: among its thirty-five members, five developing nations abstained, and three voted against the resolution, on the grounds that Iran's suspension of enrichment activities had been voluntary and not legally binding. This split was a rare event; the Board traditionally has made a point of reaching its decisions by consensus, a practice often referred to as "the Spirit of Vienna." The nonconsensus decision was not a good sign.

Iran struck back by ending the implementation of its Additional Protocol.[2] This was not unexpected; in September 2005, the Iranian Majlis had passed a law directing the government to suspend the Protocol, as a retaliatory action, if Iran should be referred to the Security Council. This step would significantly curtail the tools available to the IAEA to inspect for undeclared nuclear material and activities. In the Iran nuclear saga, positions had now hardened.

Another trip to Washington was in order. In May, I met with Rice and John Negroponte, director of national intelligence. Negroponte agreed entirely with the inspectors' assessment that even if Iran's intention was to develop nuclear weapons, it was at least a few years away, in terms of technological capacity, from doing so. Negroponte kept repeating this view in public, perhaps as a way to fend off the Israelis and hard-liners, who were beating the drum for military action.

With Condoleezza Rice, I wanted to get the relationship back on track. Naturally, we did not always see eye to eye, but after our tense meetings in the leadup to the Iraq War, we had consistently treated each other with respect and even, on occasion, humor. Rice always came across as more sensible and pragmatic than ideological, particularly when we were alone. Clearly, her view did not always prevail and her first obligation was to implement the decisions made by Bush, to whom she was extremely loyal. I seldom felt certain about where she stood; nevertheless, within the Bush administration, I considered her an asset and a proponent of diplomacy.

---

2 The Majlis had never ratified Iran's Additional Protocol, but the Iranians had been implementing it provisionally.

After a bit of small talk that touched on her love of shoes—Rice once told me that she sometimes bought five or six pairs at a time—I moved to the point I had come to make: the United States urgently needed to take part in discussions with Iran. "The dialogue," I told her, "will not move forward without your participation."

Before traveling to the United States, I had met with Ali Larijani, the top Iranian nuclear negotiator. He had asked me to convey a set of messages to Washington: the Iranians were interested in direct talks with the United States. They were ready to discuss not only Iran's nuclear issues, but also Iraq, Afghanistan, Hezbollah, and Hamas. Larijani believed that Iran could be of great influence in matters related to the upcoming midterm U.S. elections: Iran could assist with security in Baghdad and also help establish a national unity government in Lebanon. At that I saw Rice's eyes light up.

I emphasized to her and to Bob Joseph that a small centrifuge R&D program in Iran was a minor issue from a proliferation perspective. If Iran really wanted to perfect its enrichment technology on an R&D scale, it could easily do so underground, and no one would be any the wiser. "In fact," I said, "it is a good sign that they are insisting on having it above board."

I repeated the arguments I had made earlier to Rice on the phone. The important thing was to freeze any move toward industrial-scale enrichment and maintain a robust IAEA verification presence in Iran. "What use is it," I asked, "if we have perfect verification of Iran's declared nuclear activities, but we don't have the Protocol in place to ensure they are not working undetected on an underground program?" Plus, I added, there was a big difference between having the know-how to build a weapon and developing the industrial capacity to actually do it. Once again I made my point that allowing Iran a small R&D operation as a face-saving measure was not a high price to pay.

I was glad to see Rice paying close attention. I realized the only thing she heard, day in and day out, was the compulsive repetition of the "not one centrifuge" position I'd heard advocated by Steve Hadley. This red line had its origin in something the British had said during the previous round of negotiations with Iran, that the United Kingdom had built its nuclear weapons program based on the knowledge gained from running sixteen centrifuges. "Not one centrifuge" had taken on vast importance for those Beltway ideologues who saw the United States as global disciplinarian and who listened only to one another, perpetuating beliefs that were utterly removed from reality. It had always been clear that Iran would never eliminate its entire enrichment program.

Although some Americans wanted no dialogue or rapprochement with Iran whatsoever—in April reports had even circulated of covert U.S. plans to attack Iran's nuclear sites with "bunker-busting" weapons—Rice seemed to hold the view that Iran would ultimately give in. "Iran is not North Korea," she said. "Iran does not want to be isolated. It will buckle under pressure."

"My fear," I replied, "is that increasing the pressure on Iran will backfire." I could see that U.S. policy on Iran was coming down to two simplistic mantras: "not one centrifuge" and "Iran will buckle." There was no flexibility to adjust to the evolving reality.

When alone with me, Rice emphasized that both she and President Bush were working hard to find a peaceful resolution to the Iranian issue, implying that they had no intention of resorting to the use of force. And a few days later, Washington announced that it was ready to take part in direct dialogue with Tehran, provided that Iran suspended all its enrichment-related activities.

The statement was a radical shift in U.S. public rhetoric. It was clearly a compromise that Rice and her contingent had managed to extract from those who adhered to the neoconservative ideology in vogue, maintaining that any dialogue would legitimize the Iranian regime at a time when they were openly calling for regime change. Nonetheless, the United States was still demanding something Iran could not give without imploding internally. Given that the Iranian nuclear program had become a matter of national pride, the Ahmadinejad government was vulnerable on the domestic front. It could not be seen as caving in to the West. Suspending the enrichment program in advance of talks would weaken the Iranians' negotiating leverage. Also, in Tehran's view, the program's resumption in the future would be endangered if it became a concession to be won from the West. This was a risk they would not take.

In June 2006, in the absence of direct talks between Tehran and Washington, the Europeans once again began working on a new package, together with the United States, Russia, and China. They wanted to present Iran with a two-track proposal: a set of incentives in exchange for limits on the Iranian nuclear program and, in parallel, a set of possible sanctions in the case of Iran's refusal of their package. I tried to explain the fallacy of this approach from a cultural perspective: if they simultaneously presented both carrots and sticks, Iran's government would appear to be negotiating under threat. Under such circumstances, they would have no choice but to reject the proposal as a way of retaining self-respect and national support.

My logic had nothing to do with nuclear technology. The Western notion of how to approach Iran was like going into a souk and offering the proprietor a fair sum for the desired merchandise but also threatening to burn down the shop if he didn't accept. While the tactic might play well in a Clint Eastwood movie, it would be doomed from the start in Tehran.

The Europeans tentatively agreed and privately settled on a set of incentives as well as a set of sanctions. However, when they sent Javier Solana[3] to Tehran on June 6 as their representative, he was charged with presenting only the incentives.

This package, unlike the first one in August 2005, was quite generous. It specifically offered to provide Iran with Western conventional and nuclear power technology. It discussed elements of a trade agreement with the West. And it was written without the patronizing tone of the first offer, referring respectfully to Iran's rights. However, it repeated the demand that Iran suspend its enrichment program as a prerequisite of

---

3 Secretary-general of the Council for the European Union and the EU's high representative for common foreign and security policy.

negotiations, and the language seemed to predicate Iran's resumption of enrichment activities on the West's approval.

Iran said they wanted until August 22 to respond. Meanwhile, they continued to expand their enrichment R&D; by this point, they had moved from experimenting with 10- and 20-centrifuge cascades to a 164-centrifuge cascade, still a pilot-scale operation. The activity was not very sustained. They would run a cascade for ten days, stop for a few days, then start again. Our technical experts believed the Iranians could have been proceeding much faster had they wanted to make an all-out effort. At one point, the Iranians mentioned that they might have a second 164-machine cascade in place in another three months. I advised them against it. Building more and larger cascades would only make the negotiations that much harder.

Iran's request for more time was viewed with suspicion by some in the West. The Americans and others asserted that Iran would use the time to build up its enrichment capacity. This was absurd. Iran would hardly be any further along in its R&D program in August than it was in June. I believed the request for time was a function of the slow pace of Iranian decision making. Iran's domestic political processes are full of checks and balances; multiple parties weigh in with their reflections before the formulation of a final strategy. The Iranians never seem to be in a rush, and they are even more resistant to hasty decision making when put under external pressure.

But the United States did not want to wait and insisted that Solana push for a meeting with the P-5 well before Iran's requested response date. Larijani agreed to meet in Brussels, on July 11, because he wanted to clarify details on the terms and scope of the proposed suspension. It was clear from our conversations that he was committed to finding a negotiated solution.

As it turned out, the meeting did more harm than good. In the middle of the conversation, John Sawers, the British director general for political affairs at the Foreign and Commonwealth Office, grew impatient. He forcefully interrupted Solana to demand of Larijani, "We want to know in concrete terms whether you are ready to suspend."

Of course, Larijani was not able to give an affirmative answer. Tehran had not yet agreed on its response. Larijani equivocated, and the conversation ended awkwardly. Solana reported that the meeting had failed and the very next day, the so-called P-5+1[4] announced their intention again to refer the matter to the Security Council.

Soon after, at the G-8 Summit in St. Petersburg, I had a brief talk with President Bush. "ElBaradei!" he called out, coming toward me with a smile. "We really appreciate your work in Iran," he said quietly, after shaking my hand, "because we don't know what's going on there."

Iran was working on an answer to the offer, I told him. I believed they sincerely wanted to find a solution through negotiation and that they simply needed a bit more time.

"We are ready" was Bush's response, signaling that he wanted to hear what Tehran had to say.

In a separate conversation, Tony Blair gave me exactly the same answer—"We are ready"—as if the two men had rehearsed it.

As the Security Council began edging its way toward a resolution, Javad Vaeedi, Larijani's deputy, came to see me. The gist of the conversation was that the Iranians were prepared to agree to suspension, but not as a precondition of the negotiations, only as an outcome. Suspension would also need to be linked to some type of security assurance. "We want to know whether our counterpart is an ally or an adversary," Vaeedi told me. "The issue is not just the nuclear program. It is the entire future relationship between America and Iran."

He explained the situation facing Ahmadinejad domestically. "If he only announces the suspension of nuclear enrichment, without something about security in return, the Ahmadinejad administration will collapse." What Vaeedi said next was both illuminating and disturbing. The previous negotiating team—the group headed by Rowhani, who had served under the Khatami administration—was now opposing any move to suspend enrichment and accept the package. The problem was not the offer itself, which was obviously much better than the previous

---

4 The P-5 (permanent members of the Security Council) plus Germany, who were working more or less as a unit in the negotiations at the time.

year's package. Their concern was that acceptance of the offer and negotiations with the United States toward normalizing relations would
make Ahmadinejad a national hero. That was the last thing they wanted,
so they were busily undermining the very solution they had worked so
hard to achieve.

I sighed. Tehran had been spending way too much time watching D.C.
politics, I thought.

Another opportunity was on the verge of being squandered. I called
Greg Schulte, the U.S. ambassador to the IAEA, and asked him to relay
to Washington that the window of opportunity was still open. The possibility of a broad-based regional security solution was still on the table.
The missing ingredient was only the willingness of the United States
to make a small, and meaningless, concession to get the dialogue
under way.

But it was not to be. At the end of July 2006, three weeks before Iran
had promised to provide its answer, the Security Council adopted Resolution 1696. The resolution made enrichment suspension mandatory
under Chapter VII of the UN Charter, which empowers the Security
Council to act in the face of "threats to the peace, breaches of the peace,
and acts of aggression." By the end of August, I was required to report to
the council confirming that Iran had suspended its uranium enrichment operations.

It was hard for me to imagine a less sensible, more divisive action
than Resolution 1696. First, the investigation of Iran's nuclear program
had, at that point, been ongoing for nearly four years. Waiting three
weeks for Iran's answer, using those weeks to find a solution to the
suspension question—this would have been an eminently reasonable
investment of time and energy. I began to feel that the policy makers
in Washington were perhaps not really interested in resolving the Iranian nuclear issue and talking to Tehran. Could it be that the U.S. leadership was hostage to those who wanted only confrontation, isolation,
and regime change?

Second, the resolution was of dubious legality. There was still no proof
that Iran's nuclear activity involved a weapons program. It was quite a
stretch to say that a small laboratory-scale centrifuge cascade constituted

"a threat to international peace and security" when peaceful uranium enrichment is legal for all states under the NPT.

Third, the resolution lacked logic. If there was genuine concern that Iran was developing a nuclear weapon, stopping its small-scale enrichment operation in exchange for dialogue and normalization made no sense at all. What difference would it make to halt this declared R&D operation if Iran actually had an operative nuclear weapons program? The real focus should have been on continuing IAEA inspections in Iran to investigate any possible *undeclared* enrichment or clandestine weaponization activities. Putting all the focus on the enrichment R&D at Natanz made clear that the concern—the supposed "threat to international peace and security"—was less about an ongoing secret weapons program than about having apparently reached a verdict on Iran's future intentions.

Worst of all, the timing of Resolution 1696 was terrible. Its adoption coincided precisely with a raging war in Lebanon, an intense conflict between Hezbollah and the Israel Defense Forces, in which thousands of Lebanese civilians were caught in the cross fire. Despite repeated appeals from the international community, Rice, Bush, and the British had opposed calling for a cease-fire. In answer to Kofi Annan's request that Bush and Blair support a cease-fire, they had both said, again speaking in unison, "We are not ready."

Later, it was admitted that the United States had joined efforts to halt the violence only when it was clear that Israel's military offensive was not working.[5] Instead of ending the fighting, the United States had rushed the delivery of precision-guided bombs to Israel.[6] The Security Council would not pass a resolution calling for cease-fire in Lebanon until August 11; by that time, more than 1,100 Lebanese and 40 Israeli civilians had been killed and roughly 750,000 Lebanese civilians had been displaced from their homes, all while the world's powers stood idly by.

---

5 "Bolton Admits Lebanese Truce Block," BBC News Online, March 22, 2007.
6 David S. Cloud, "U.S. Speeds Up Bomb Delivery for the Israelis," *New York Times*, July 22, 2006.

I was in Egypt at the time, at my beach house north of Alexandria. The mood on the street was volatile. The anger across the Middle East— at the perceived double standard, at the West's deliberate inaction—was at a fever pitch. Kofi Annan called me while I was there. His tone was despondent. "This war in Lebanon was not considered a threat to international peace and security," he said, his voice subdued but anguished, "but the laboratory-scale activity in Iran was."

Trying to stay focused, shortly after the passage of Security Council Resolution 1696, I had sent a message to Larijani suggesting that the Iranians answer the offer from the West, as planned, on August 22. I proposed that they state their willingness to suspend industrial-scale nuclear enrichment activities for a few years and commit to resolving outstanding verification issues with the IAEA. "If I can report progress on these two fronts," I said, it will change "how the Europeans and others see the situation."

Instead, Larijani sent a message back from Tehran to the West via a press conference. The Islamic Republic of Iran, he announced, would never agree to suspend its uranium enrichment activities.

Certain aspects of the passage of Resolution 1696 were a mystery to me, but part of the problem seemed to be the players behind the scenes in mid-2006.

John Sawers, a sharp diplomat and a former assistant to Blair, who spoke for the United Kingdom, took a hard line similar to the Americans. Over the past couple of years, I had observed differences in style and substance between Sawers and his boss, Foreign Secretary Jack Straw. I had developed a close relationship with Straw; in all our dealings, I found that he had an ability to grasp the big picture, a sense of fairness, a deep respect for cultural nuance, and a pragmatist's willingness to consider commonsense solutions.

But Straw was no longer Sawers's boss. Straw had told me, earlier in the year, that it was clear the Americans no longer trusted him. When reports had circulated alleging U.S. plans to use bunker-busting weapons in Iran, Straw had been quoted saying the idea was "completely nuts," telling BBC News there was "no smoking gun."[7] One month later, Blair had removed Straw as foreign secretary, replacing him with Margaret Beckett, a foreign policy neophyte.[8] I was told that Straw had been removed because of policy differences with Blair. I also understood that it was at the urging of the Americans but when we discussed his detractors, Straw was clear that it was "not Condi." Straw was known to have referred to Blair's policy during the Lebanon war as "disastrous." But Straw's opinion on Iran, Lebanon, and Resolution 1696 no longer mattered to Blair, and Beckett was too new to dissent.

The French foreign minister, Philippe Douste-Blazy, a physician, was also a novice in foreign affairs. I was told he was not taken seriously by the Quai d'Orsay, the French Foreign Ministry, and that the distaste was mutual. In addition, the French were going through a prepresidential election. People had begun to talk about "two Frances"—the first led by Chirac and his national security adviser, Maurice Gourdault-Montagne, and the second by the ministry residing at the Quai d'Orsay—with opposing foreign policy positions. So the French, operating in an unusual mode at the time, were not as coherent in their foreign policy as they might otherwise have been.

The Germans were the ones making an effort to find a solution and a compromise with Iran. In separate meetings with Chancellor Angela Merkel and Foreign Minister Frank-Walter Steinmeier, I found them both to be incisive, humane, and fair in their approaches to foreign policy. But the Germans did not have the clout needed to make headway without the cooperation of their European partners; they seemed happy just to be included in the negotiations.

To me the real surprise was that the Russians and the Chinese in the Security Council had agreed to adopt a resolution based on Chapter VII,

---

7 "UK Dismisses Talk of Iran Attack," BBC News Online, April 9, 2006.
8 Beckett had been working on climate change as the secretary of state for environment, food and rural affairs. She told the *Sunday Times* on June 28 that when Blair told her she was being appointed foreign secretary, her response was "one word, with four letters."

despite their long-standing opposition to such an approach. They knew it could only end in confrontation and complicate any effort to reach a solution to Iran's nuclear program, yet it seemed that their own interests had trumped these considerations.

In my view, Security Council Resolution 1696 was not only counter-productive from a policy perspective, but also a misuse of the council's authority under Chapter VII of the UN Charter. It was staggering to compare the difference in treatment of North Korea and Iran. North Korea had walked out of the NPT and made explicit threats about developing nuclear weapons (and would in fact test its first weapon less than three months later, in October 2006), yet the Americans were ready to join them in a direct dialogue, and Chris Hill seemed to be in Pyongyang every other day. By contrast, Iran, which remained under safeguards and party to the NPT, was penalized for possibly having future intentions to develop nuclear weapons, and the Americans refused to talk to them without preconditions.

I was still in my summer house on August 20, 2006, when Frank-Walter Steinmeier called to say he would like me to meet with Peter Castenfelt, the mysterious Swedish banker who had once talked to me prior to my trip to North Korea. Castenfelt now wore a new hat: adviser to Tehran. He wanted to bring one of Larijani's deputies, Ali Monfared, the foreign policy head of Iran's National Security Council. They were keen to see me before Iran submitted its formal response to the latest EU-3 offer.

Meeting them in Cairo, I stressed the need for the Iranians to respond positively, despite all that had happened. Iran should be clear that it was willing to suspend moving toward industrial-scale enrichment, or at the very least promise not to introduce nuclear material. I believed that their questions about regional security were legitimate, since this was a key issue for them and addressing these concerns could facilitate an agreement on enrichment suspension. We talked for two hours; Castenfelt told me later that he spent five more hours with Monfared trying to put our discussion into appropriate written form.

The Iranians submitted their response, as scheduled, on August 22. They had accepted some but not all of my advice. The twenty-one-page document was long and convoluted, but distilled to its essence, it included a number of positive elements. Despite Larijani's earlier defiant public statement, the Iranians remained open to the notion of suspension, so long as it was not a precondition of negotiations. They were willing to implement the Additional Protocol on a voluntary basis during the negotiations. And they were ready to commit to permanent membership in the NPT, to allay fears of a "breakout" scenario in the style of North Korea.

The reaction was cautious. The EU-3 felt that dialogue was possible; the Russians spoke out against sanctions as a dead-end street; China advised patience. They all called or came by, as did Javier Solana and Kofi Annan, to ask what I thought of Iran's response. But no one seemed ready to take a leadership role.

Eventually, the United States and the Europeans appointed Solana to meet with Larijani to try to determine a way forward. Larijani, however, was not too keen on the idea, since he felt that Solana did not have the authority to make decisions. He was especially set against seeing Solana together with the EU-3 representatives; he still had a sour taste in his mouth from their mid-July meeting in Brussels.

I suggested to Solana that he and Larijani meet alone to agree on a set of four principles as a framework for negotiation. The first principle: Iran would suspend enrichment during the talks. In reciprocation, as the second principle, the Europeans and Americans would suspend Security Council sanctions during this period. The third principle would affirm Iran's right under the NPT to use nuclear energy for peaceful purposes, making clear that the suspension was not permanent. And the fourth: a statement respecting Iran's political independence and sovereignty.

If Solana and Larijani could settle on these principles, then the foreign ministers could meet and declare them the basis for the negotiations. "Both sides would save face," I said to Solana. Tehran could tell its domestic audience that they had accepted the suspension only for the duration of the negotiations. The United States could say they had attended the meeting knowing Iran had agreed. Rice's attendance would be essential as an incentive for Iran.

I repeated these ideas to Larijani. He and Solana fixed a date for early September. I outlined the principles over the phone to Kofi Annan, who planned to visit Iran at about the same time.[9]

Tehran was showing restraint. The IAEA had observed no significant quantitative or qualitative expansion of Iran's enrichment program beyond the 164 centrifuges already in place. Nuclear material was introduced only occasionally and for short periods, which was not the way to build enrichment expertise, had that been the Iranians' objective. We could not tell whether the slow progress was due to a technical problem or a political choice. But in any case, Iran's program was still at a rudimentary level.

On September 5, Condoleezza Rice called me to ask about the set of principles, as conveyed to her by Ambassador Schulte. "Iran cannot accept suspension as a precondition," I explained. "They see this as political suicide. Also, they will need some sort of statement about security."

"This sounds like what we did in North Korea," Rice replied, seeming quite willing to consider the four principles, which was a departure from Washington's unyielding position on Iranian enrichment. "But we will have problems with giving them any security assurances," she said.

"Then make it a statement of good intention," I urged her. "You can fudge it." Rice agreed to at least take some time to mull over the principles and get back to me, but added, "You know we also cannot sit down with Iran until the suspension is in place. But perhaps," she mused, "the Europeans—or maybe the Europeans with the Russians and the Chinese—can have a meeting with the Iranians first." Then, after the declaration of principles and verification of the suspension, the United States could join.

As I headed off to Woodstock in Oxfordshire, England, where my daughter, Laila, was getting married, Peter Castenfelt called, asking to see me urgently. On the night before the wedding, he made his way to

---

9 Annan supported the set of principles, but his visit to Iran never materialized.

the hotel just as our extended family, in from Cairo, New York, and other parts of the world, was about to gather for dinner. The bride was not pleased. "He'd better have something important to tell you," she said.

Castenfelt did more listening than talking. He had just come from Tehran the day before and wanted to know precisely what was required of the Iranians. "Could they do some version of suspension but not full suspension?" he asked.

That would not work, I said. He needed to tell the Iranians that time was running out. Without an agreement, the United States and the EU-3 would go to the Security Council to propose new sanctions on Iran for failure to adhere to the demands of Resolution 1696. "Even if they start with a mild set of sanctions," I said, "Iran will retaliate, and that will start an uncontrolled chain reaction of retaliation, which could lead to a major confrontation, and solve nothing." Castenfelt nodded solemnly, scribbled some notes, and took his leave.

On the following day, September 8, my daughter, Laila, married Neil Pizey, a young British man, at Blenheim Palace. For a few hours, the stresses of Vienna seemed distant. As the solemnity and beauty of the wedding ceremony unfolded, I thought of the part of my Nobel speech that had brought Laila to tears: "I have hope because of what I see in my children and some of their generation . . . my son and daughter are oblivious to colour and race and nationality. They see no difference between their friends Noriko, Mafupo, Justin, Saulo, and Hussam; to them, they are only fellow human beings and good friends."

At the time, Laila had been collecting her courage to introduce me to the man she loved. Laila knew that, at some level, I had hoped she would marry an Egyptian. But as someone who daily observed the ruinous effects of cultural distrust, I blessed my daughter for her choice.

That same day, Solana and Larijani were meeting in Vienna. They spent seven hours together, and Larijani, recounting their conversation afterward, considered the meeting constructive. Suspension remained the central hurdle. Larijani was still trying to deal with the fear emanating from certain quarters in Tehran, that if Iran suspended enrichment they might face insurmountable obstacles to resuming their fuel cycle activities.

As one option, I suggested grouping the discussion of suspension with other topics, such as the other six countries' commitments to providing power reactors and respecting Iran's NPT rights, so that suspension would not stand out as a solo item. "Perhaps you do not even have to declare it," I told him. "It might be enough to stop enrichment activities, de facto, and I could report the suspension."

Larijani mumbled something about suspension as a gentleman's agreement or staggering it over a period of time. Clearly, he was frustrated, trying to find any creative way possible to achieve a solution. Much of this he said he had talked over with Solana.

On one point, Larijani had been quite firm: any future decision to "certify" Iran as qualified to resume fuel cycle activities would be solely a technical judgment, made by the IAEA. The European offer had intimated that the parties to the negotiation would also have a political say in determining whether Iran had achieved the needed level of confidence. Larijani was unequivocal: that was not acceptable. However, Iran was, as Larajani reported, willing to discuss regional issues such as Iraq, Afghanistan, and Lebanon, something the Europeans clearly wanted to do.

Solana was next in line, calling for a reading on what I'd heard from Larijani. Washington, he told me, was not happy with the outcome of their talk. Although an affable person and an experienced diplomat, Solana was in an impossible situation as the point man on Iran for the P-5 + 1: with each country pressing its own opinion and with the Americans in particular breathing down his neck, Solana ended up trying to make something out of the lowest common denominator, which invariably meant an unclear mandate and little with which to negotiate.

I suggested that the proposed four principles be consolidated to two. One principle could cover Iran's nuclear program, including its rights and obligations and the suspension issue. The second could be a commitment to negotiate on economic, political, and security issues, which could include a statement of good intentions vis-à-vis Iran on the part of the Americans, implying that they would not pursue regime change or the use of force. Our conversation concluded with my offer to help in any way and Solana's assurance that he would come to see me in the next few days.

On September 19, Condoleezza Rice and her counterparts from the EU-3, China, and Russia met to discuss next steps. They agreed to give Iran until "early October" to reach agreement on how enrichment would be suspended as part of the negotiations. A staggered schedule of talks—starting without the United States, suspending enrichment in Iran in concert with halting Security Council action, then having the United States join—was put forward as a possibility. With some cynicism, the *Washington Post* reported that the Europeans were giving the Iranians their fourth deadline in four months.[10] This was factually true, but the constant slippage was rooted in the unwillingness or inability of either side to compromise meaningfully.

At the IAEA General Conference in late September, I had a tense meeting with Gholam Aghazadeh, Iran's vice president and head of atomic energy, the only original player still in office. He seemed offended, almost resentful, claiming that the Agency's reports on Iran did not reflect his country's four-year effort to cooperate. My answer, which was somewhat sharp, noted a record of inconsistent, unreliable cooperation on Iran's part. I mentioned as well several long-standing technical questions that Iran had not yet answered.

Aghazadeh followed up by sending me a rather strange personal letter, which he said he was writing as a friend. As he saw it, the IAEA had no intention of ever closing the Iran file. The more Iran cooperated, the more questions they received from Agency inspectors. As a side note, he added that I was not well regarded by the Iranian leadership. He said he would not expect a reply.[11] The frostiness of the letter did not bode well.

Indeed, in a phone conversation with Larijani, I heard discourage-

---

10 Glenn Kessler, "Early October New Deadline for Iran," *Washington Post*, September 21, 2006.

11 It was hard to decipher his intentions. I suspected that Aghazadeh and his colleagues were feeling the heat, because our inspectors were pressing hard for the "full story" that would fill in gaps in the history of Iran's nuclear program. The pressure to suspend enrichment may also have been on his mind; as one of the fathers of Iran's enrichment program, Aghazadeh was not eager to see it disappear.

ment. "These other parties," he said, "do not understand the domestic situation in Iran." He was obviously having just as difficult a time negotiating at home—trying to find a form of suspension acceptable to Tehran—as with Solana and his colleagues. The Iranians were ready to commit not to going beyond the one or two cascades already in operation, but it was highly unlikely they would agree to suspending completely.

Larijani told me extremism was taking hold. From his tone, I understood that he meant in Washington and Tehran.

The early October deadline for Iran to agree to suspend enrichment came and went. The failure of both sides to shift on the key sticking points meant that another Security Council resolution was the inevitable next step. I feared the cycle of retaliation that a new set of sanctions would surely trigger. Late October found me in Washington meeting with Condoleezza Rice and Bob Joseph. The first North Korean nuclear test had just occurred, which perhaps tempered the State Department's inclinations regarding the Iranian impasse. I voiced my concern that a Security Council resolution should avoid provoking or humiliating Iran and should largely be directed toward inducing Tehran to resume the negotiations with the P-5 + 1. Rice seemed to agree.

I put forward a new possibility. "What about having the United States begin talking to Iran directly but confidentially on regional issues, such as security in Iraq?" By introducing dialogue on a less controversial topic, perhaps relations might be smoothed between the key players, making it easier to find a way forward on the nuclear issue. Larijani and his colleagues would be willing to have such discussions, but the United States would need to send someone at a higher level than Zalmay Khalilzad, the American ambassador in Iraq. To the Iranians, Khalilzad had insufficient clout.

Rice seemed somewhat open to starting such a dialogue. "You know," I told her, "that Iran could make more of a mess of the Middle East."

She frowned. "They are already meddling there."

"They could do more," I replied.

In a phone conversation with Solana, he concurred that any sanctions imposed on Iran should be "symbolic." However, the draft resolution, when it came to me from the French mission in Vienna, was far too harsh. Actions such as travel bans on Iranian officials, freezing Iran's foreign assets, and suspending or restricting the IAEA's technical assistance would only be provocative and counterproductive. Similarly, making the IAEA's "transparency visits" mandatory would just backfire.[12] The last thing we needed was to provoke Iran into accelerating its enrichment program or walking out of the NPT.

Sergei Kislyak, the Russian deputy minister of foreign affairs and a good friend for many years who had been deeply involved in the P-5+1 discussions, was of the same view. The draft resolution, he said, was "by no means acceptable" to Russia. "If the Europeans are going to push this resolution, it will change the game completely." I got the impression that Russia might consider exercising its veto.

The resolution that finally passed on December 23, in a unanimous vote, had been considerably toned down. The sanctions, for the most part, only reinforced old measures: a ban on supplying Iran with nuclear-related technology and materials and a freeze of the assets of specific individuals and companies who had supported Iran's enrichment program.

Iran's response, too, was relatively mild. Javad Zarif, Iran's ambassador to the United Nations, declared that "a nation is being punished for exercising its inalienable rights."[13] The Iranian Foreign Ministry issued a statement calling the resolution "an extralegal act outside the frame of [the Security Council's] responsibilities and against the U.N. Charter." More worrisome were signals from Tehran that there was no longer any reason to delay expanding the size of its enrichment program.

---

12 A "transparency visit" was the term used when Iran agreed voluntarily to allow the IAEA to visit a site where the Agency had no clear jurisdiction.

13 Sarah Dilorenzo, "Iran Rejects U.N. Resolution and Accuses Security Council of Hypocrisy," Associated Press, *San Diego Tribune*, December 23, 2006.

If we had not yet reached a point of no return, the stakes had certainly been raised.

The question put to me most frequently in off-the-record conversations—in one-on-one ministerial meetings, or by my seatmates in airplanes, or after reporters have turned off the tape recorder—is usually something like this: "What do you really think—is Iran trying to build a nuclear weapons program?"

My assessment is a gut feeling informed by historical context. First, elements of Iran's nuclear procurement and research programs began in the mid-1980s, in the middle of the Iran-Iraq War. Iran was at the time under dire threat from Iraq; more than one hundred thousand Iranians, including civilians, reportedly fell victim to Iraq's chemical weapons. Faced with this extreme sense of vulnerability, the Iranians might have originally intended to develop nuclear weapons. But at some point—perhaps after the war ended or in the mid-1990s, when records show abrupt adjustments to some of Iran's nuclear programs, or perhaps after the Agency began its investigations—Iran may well have decided to limit its program to the development of the nuclear fuel cycle, legitimately remaining a non-nuclear-weapon state party to the NPT.

In any case, my belief is that Iran has not revealed the whole truth about the beginning of its nuclear program. There might have been some military involvement in nuclear procurement and nuclear experiments. However, these skeletons in the closet are, in all probability, fairly insignificant; the body of evidence would otherwise be greater and harder to conceal.

My impression is that Iran might have intended finally to come clean about any past weapons ambitions during their negotiations with the Europeans, as part of a comprehensive package and a pre-agreed scenario and at a time when the world's focus was on Iran's future and not its past. But when the negotiations fell apart and the environment turned confrontational, the Iranians were left with a dilemma: any revelation of past involvement in a military nuclear program, however minor or distant, coming during a moment of confrontation, would be seen as vindication of the view that Iran was not to be trusted. But if they refrained from giving a full account, they were perpetuating the original sin of concealment.[14]

A second question frequently posed to me is why Iran has remained so intent on pursuing uranium enrichment in the face of sanctions and Western condemnation. My best reading is that the Iranian nuclear program, including enrichment, has been for Iran the means to an end. Tehran is determined to be recognized as a regional power. That recognition, in their view, is intimately linked to the achievement of a grand bargain with the West.

Even if the intent is not to develop nuclear weapons, the successful acquisition of the full nuclear fuel cycle, including enrichment, sends a signal of power to Iran's neighbors and to the world, providing a sort of insurance against attack. Each of the factions in Iran understands that the nuclear program is in itself a deterrent. There is a clear consensus domestically that Iran needs to maintain that deterrence. Overall, though, Iran's goal is not to become another North Korea—a nuclear weapon possessor but a pariah in the international community—but rather Brazil or Japan, a technological powerhouse with the capacity to develop nuclear weapons if the political winds were to shift, while remaining a non-nuclear-weapon state under the NPT.

The furor over Iran's nuclear program cannot be understood without reference to the volatile security situation in the Middle East and the region's fiercely competing ideologies. The elephant in the room is Israel's nuclear arsenal. Israel of course is not in violation of the NPT, having never joined, but that distinction does nothing to temper the anger of its neighbors at the perceived asymmetry in treatment and the imbalance in regional security.

Meanwhile, as all efforts to reach a negotiated agreement over Tehran's nuclear program failed, Iran continued to consolidate its position

---

14 According to rumor, certain Iranian officials had admitted that Iran had appointed a special group in 1987 to look into planning a nuclear weapon option. The group allegedly had been disbanded in the early 1990s. Reportedly, Iran was divided internally about how to confess this matter to the IAEA. The Agency had heard similar intimations through intelligence channels. But we were never able to verify the truth behind these rumors.

as the most powerful Islamic player in the region. The ongoing wars in Iraq and Afghanistan, the continuing plight of the Palestinians, and the West's resistance to a cease-fire during the mid-2006 Lebanon War, among other developments, reinforced the perception of Western prejudice against Muslims. With Iran being one of the few Muslim countries that stood up to the West during this period, it increasingly was viewed by Muslims of many nationalities as the sole defender of their trampled rights.[15]

---

15 Turkey has also taken a number of anti-Western stances under Prime Minister Recep Tayyip Erdoğan's leadership, which has gained him immense popularity in the Muslim world. Turkey is a member of NATO and considered a Western ally, but there has been considerable controversy over its candidacy for membership in the European Union, which has been cited by Muslims as proof of Western bias against them.

10

DOUBLE STANDARDS

In dealing with complex nuclear verification cases, I have consistently made the distinction among three aspects of nuclear programs. The first is knowledge acquisition of the various aspects of nuclear technology, which is easier now than ever before. With the globalization of finance, industry, education, and, most of all, information, it has grown exponentially more difficult to deny states the basic knowledge of nuclear processes and techniques. The second aspect is industrial capacity: that is, the ability to enrich uranium or separate plutonium at an industrial level. Capacity of this sort gives states the ability to produce the nuclear material necessary for use in nuclear weapons. The third aspect relates to a state's future intentions, which are sometimes quite difficult, if not impossible, to judge.

The IAEA Secretariat is able to determine a country's knowledge acquisition and industrial capacity, but we are not in a position to judge future intentions, which are based on the country's risk assessment and are subject to rapid change. Libya's decision to come clean, for example, was the result of a reassessment of its security situation that led, in a very short time span, to a change in its intentions. Japan, which is regarded as having impeccable nonproliferation credentials, had officials calling for a discussion of its nuclear weapons stance after the North Korean nuclear test in October 2006.

It is often difficult for the public—or, for that matter, government officials—to understand or accept the IAEA's unique verification role, with both its limits and its obligations, because it is rare for an international institution to sit in judgment on sovereign governments. Our position is somewhat schizophrenic: on the one hand, Member States pay the Agency's salaries and set its direction and mandate; on the other, we are charged with judging their compliance with international commitments under a treaty they have pledged to uphold. Even though Member States might understand this IAEA role intellectually, in the abstract, and when it applies to others, we inevitably encounter some resistance when we report a government's failure to comply with their obligations.

Despite my attempts to define the scope of the IAEA's jurisdiction consistently and to draw a clear distinction between what the Agency can and cannot judge, the pressure was often extreme for us to behave in a partisan way. When we held fast to our objective evaluation of the facts, when we refused to lend our voice to someone else's interpretation of a country's intentions, we were sometimes accused of playing favorites, of ignoring evidence, or, conversely, of speaking "outside the box," beyond the limits of our jurisdiction.

Invariably, these accusations had political overtones, prompted as they usually were by the supportive or antagonistic relationship between the countries in question. This effort to enlist the Agency for partisan ends is amply illustrated by the evolution of five somewhat unusual encounters—with South Korea, Egypt, Israel, India, and Syria—and by some attempts to deal with the most extreme example of nuclear double standards: the lack of progress on nuclear disarmament.

In early 2004, South Korea began implementing its Additional Protocol. During an inspection that followed soon afterward, the IAEA discovered that experiments had taken place to separate very small amounts of plutonium. Follow-up investigations over the summer found that a few experiments had also involved enrichment of uranium. These activities had not been reported to the IAEA as required.

The South Korean government said it had been unaware of these experiments—they had been carried out by individual scientists at the Korean Atomic Energy Research Institute—and promptly took corrective action, firing staff and establishing a new oversight organization. Nevertheless, it was a huge embarrassment for the government, particularly in light of the ongoing tension regarding North Korea's nuclear program.

The IAEA worked closely with the South Koreans to put the proper perspective on the news and prevent media hype. The Korean government, including Ban Ki-Moon, who was foreign minister at the time, appreciated our handling of the issue. But the slate was not yet clean: I was required to inform the IAEA Board of South Korea's failure to report these nuclear activities to the Agency. The question was whether the Board would then deem that South Korea was in a state of "noncompliance." And if so, would the Board then be obliged to report this noncompliance to the UN Security Council?

The issue of the IAEA Board's obligation to report every noncompliance was the subject of a contentious debate between the Agency Secretariat and the EU-3, on the one hand, and the Americans, on the other. The Secretariat's interpretation was that not every breach or violation of a country's safeguards agreement rose to the level of "noncompliance" within the meaning of the Agency's Statute. The IAEA Board enjoyed discretionary authority to exercise its judgment, to differentiate between cases that involved the diversion of nuclear material or clearly revealed a weapons program, such as Iraq before the first Gulf War—which might require action by the Security Council—and cases that showed no indication of sustained activity, such as South Korea, where a few scientists had conducted unreported laboratory-scale experiments out of scientific curiosity. But the Americans, especially in the case of Iran, insisted that the Board was obliged to report to the Security Council every breach or violation. The United States had pushed for referral to the council since my first report on Iran's undeclared activities. The Europeans' explicit agreement with the Secretariat's interpretation was politically motivated: they wanted to use the prospect of referral to the Security Council as a whip with which to threaten Iran.

Now the defendant on the stand was South Korea, one of the "good guys," a close ally as far as the United States was concerned. The Americans found themselves in a tricky spot. Sticking to their policy guns and referring South Korea to the Security Council for its reporting violations was contrary to the U.S. interest. For one thing, such action could well complicate negotiations with the North Koreans, who might try to use South Korea's noncompliance as justification for their own nuclear activities. South Korea, I was told, was lobbying intensely in Washington against such a referral.

Thus, at the next IAEA Board meeting, the Americans declared that South Korea's violation was not worth reporting to the Security Council. The Board's action was merely "to take note of" my report. The entire incident vindicated and put a seal on the correctness of the Secretariat's interpretation of how and when various degrees of noncompliance ought to be reported to the council—a judgment that contradicted the initial U.S. position of automatic referral, as the Americans were advocating in the case of Iran.

In Egypt, the IAEA encountered a similar case of undeclared nuclear experiments. As part of its ongoing assessment of a country's nuclear file, the IAEA monitors relevant publications and other open sources for professional articles that might have a bearing on that state's activities. In 2004, references in a number of such publications indicated that Egyptian scientists had conducted various types of experiments with nuclear material that had not been reported to the Agency.

The IAEA contacted the Egyptian Atomic Energy Authority, and a series of inspections ensued. The suspected R&D—scattered efforts related to uranium extraction and conversion, the irradiation of uranium and thorium targets in Egypt's two research reactors,[1] and reprocessing—had in fact occurred. In some cases the work had taken place in the 1980s. Egypt had failed to report to the IAEA both the activities and the small amount of nuclear material involved.

---

[1] In these types of experiments, a small "target" of one material is irradiated to produce another material. Thorium, like uranium and plutonium, is a nuclear material that can be used as fuel in a reactor. However, thorium itself cannot be used directly in a nuclear weapon, because it is not "fissile," meaning that the thorium nucleus does not fission, or split, to produce energy. Instead, thorium is "fertile," meaning that it can absorb neutrons to produce uranium-233, which in turn is a fissile material.

The problem appeared to be rooted in a lack of oversight and control, as well as in sloppiness and neglect. The facilities at the Inshas Nuclear Research Center, where some of these experiments took place, were run down; there were rooms that had not been opened in a decade and equipment worth millions of dollars that had never been used. I was told that the Egyptians had tried to delay the IAEA's current inspections just to give themselves time to clean the place up. The head of Egypt's Atomic Energy Agency, Aly Islam Metwally Aly, was not aware of some of the nuclear material and equipment in question, and he was plainly embarrassed. There was no indication that the country had a nuclear weapons program. Nonetheless, the Egyptian nuclear authorities did not come off looking very good.

My February 2005 update to the IAEA Board noted a series of reporting failures on Egypt's part. Despite the small amounts of nuclear material used in the experiments and the openness of the Egyptian scientists in publishing their results in the scientific literature, these failures were a matter of concern and warranted investigation.

More than a year later, another nuclear issue came to the surface when, at a meeting of the ruling party, Mubarak's son, Gamal, suggested that Egypt should develop a nuclear power program. The result was a frenzy of discussion and speculation. The Egyptian media made much of the issue: by advancing in nuclear science and technology, several pundits declared, Egypt would establish parity with Israel's nuclear weapons program. The coverage by government-controlled media was a depressing mix of ignorance, frustration, and manipulation.

My first "official" discussion of the topic came in January 2007, in Algeria, where I happened to see the Egyptian minister of electricity and energy, Hassan Younes. Up to that point, the Egyptian government had not approached the IAEA for advice and expertise, a customary step for any country seeking to develop a nuclear power program. Younes told me that no decision had been made; Egypt was still conducting "studies." He said they were working with a consultant, the American-owned Bechtel Corporation.

"This is not the way to go," I told him. "The least you should be doing is to contact the Agency, so we can help you do an objective national energy assessment, to evaluate the economics, the safety, the environmental aspects. Any other country would be doing this." I was quite blunt, particularly because of the safety considerations. I reminded him of Egypt's history of major train and ferry accidents. Nor was its past record on nuclear safety reassuring. The IAEA had told Egypt more than twenty years earlier that its radiation protection law was not up to standards. In a number of incidents, Egyptians had been injured by undue exposure to radiation sources, and the government still had not updated the law according to the Agency's recommendations.[2] Nuclear power, I told Younes, was not to be taken lightly. Before operating a power reactor, Egypt would need to build the necessary legal, safety, and human resource infrastructure.

Younes said he would write to ask for full IAEA assistance, which he did. I was happy for the Agency to carry out studies to help Egypt approach the topic in a methodical and scientific way. Previous IAEA studies had indicated that Egypt's existing research reactors were severely underutilized. To advance nuclear science and technology in Egypt and consider the merits of nuclear power as part of the country's energy mix, the starting point should be to make greater use of the country's existing facilities. I also advised Younes that Egypt should think about nuclear power development only in terms of the country's energy needs.

I had the opportunity to reinforce this view in a meeting at Davos with Mohamed Rachid, the Egyptian minister of foreign trade and industry, one of Cairo's most competent government officials. The most important thing about the nuclear power option was not to rush, I told him, but to conduct the appropriate feasibility studies, including consideration of existing oil and gas resources, siting, and financing. "Even if you decide you need nuclear energy," I said, "you might need another decade or so just to build the necessary infrastructure." Rachid said he would convey my views to the president—and indeed, not long after our discussion, the tone of the discourse about nuclear technology became more balanced in the Egyptian media.

---

2 In fact, the law was only adopted in 2010.

Egypt's erratic engagement with the IAEA on its nuclear program recurred in 2009, when the Agency attempted to clarify the origin of high-enriched uranium particles found in an environmental sample taken at the Inshas Nuclear Research Center. The Egyptians indicated they thought the source was contamination from an imported container.

A statement about the HEU particles made at an NPT conference by Vilmos Cserveny, the Agency's head of external relations, infuriated Cairo. Vilmos had judged, without consulting me, that transparency required reporting the matter to the conference. The information was about to be published, at any rate, in the Agency's safeguards report a couple of weeks later. Vilmos wanted to avoid fueling accusations that, because I was Egyptian, I was acting in a way that was less than transparent—a theme that was already circulating in some media reports.

Cairo sent a letter via Egypt's ambassador to the IAEA, Ihab Fawzy, accusing the Agency of disclosing classified information and making a statement that was technically and factually incorrect in a political forum. This action could only be interpreted, they wrote, "as either a lack of professional competence or ill intention." Further reactions from Cairo were disjointed: the Foreign Ministry spokesman told the press that the issue of HEU particles was "old and erroneous."[3] But the next day, the Egyptian Atomic Energy Agency said the IAEA and Egypt were working to clarify the source of the particles.

Handling Egyptian nuclear issues was, of course, particularly delicate for me: the Egyptians suspected that I was being extra hard on them, perhaps to reinforce the Agency's credibility. From time to time, the Western media speculated on whether I was extra soft on Egypt. But of course I acted as I would have with any other country, striving to reach decisions with the greatest possible independence and objectivity: I emphasized to my colleagues at the Agency to apply the same standards to Egypt's nuclear file as to any other.

At any rate, the letter from Cairo angered me. The Agency's statement had been factually correct. I reminded Fawzy of the mess we had handled

---

3 "Egypt Rejects Reports of Nuclear Probe," Agence France-Presse, May 7, 2009.

several years earlier. "Egypt did not even have a competent authority with a comprehensive knowledge of nuclear materials and activities in the country," I told him. "The Agency had to go out of its way to help you get your house in order." I asked him to officially withdraw the letter. Otherwise, I said, I would provide the IAEA Board with a response that included a detailed account of the incompetence we had needed to deal with.

Fawzy was taken aback. Within a day we got a different letter, one with no offensive mention of ill intentions or Agency incompetence. We answered professionally and courteously, explaining the technical and factual basis for the Agency's statement.

Egypt's focus on nuclear technology was illustrative of much of the Middle East. While it was true that Egypt needed more energy—specifically, more electricity—and while the Egyptian interest in nuclear power dated back to the eighties, the country's more recent move to incorporate it into its energy mix was, in my view, to a certain extent due to the nuclear tensions unfolding in the neighborhood. Apprehension about Iran's program had started to shape the region's thinking; an increasing number of Middle Eastern countries were approaching the Agency about introducing nuclear power. Paradoxically, the furor over Iran's program had ignited enthusiasm for nuclear technology. No one wanted to lag behind. And without a doubt, the greatest source of frustration and anxiety was the regional asymmetry of military power symbolized by Israel's nuclear arsenal.

The case of Israel and its nuclear program was peculiar. Like India and Pakistan, Israel was a member of the IAEA but not party to the NPT, thus the Agency inspection had no authority in the country. Even so, given the ongoing tensions in the region, the other IAEA Member States had officially requested that I consult with Israel on the application of safeguards to its nuclear facilities and to discuss the potential for establishing a nuclear-weapons-free zone in the Middle East.

I was scheduled to meet with Prime Minister Ariel Sharon in July 2004. Not long before my trip, I received a threat via an email addressed to Aida. If I were to come to Israel, it said, Aida would be made a widow.[4] We investigated the origin; the message had come from some-where in Israel or the Palestinian Territories. We gave it to the Israelis to investigate and went ahead with our plans regardless.

Sharon's office was impressively modest in comparison with those of other heads of state, particularly in the Middle East. Security guards with submachine guns were milling around as we sat in the waiting room, which faced the restrooms. Sharon's office was small, and two sec-retaries shared an even smaller adjacent office. We sat around Sharon's desk, which served as the conference table.[5] Sharon approached in a crumpled suit, taking my hand in a big, firm grip and speaking in a soft voice with a heavy Israeli accent. His demeanor gave no hint of his ruth-less military career—indeed, he talked with pride of his life as a farmer.

I shared my views candidly. "Nuclear deterrence is not going to work for you in the long run," I said, noting the relentless spread of nuclear technology and the efforts by sophisticated terrorist groups to acquire nuclear weapons. No nuclear arsenal would serve as a deterrent against such groups.

Furthermore, Israel's refusal to talk seriously to Arab countries about the possibility of working toward a nuclear-weapons-free Middle East and about its own well-known but unacknowledged nuclear arse-nal, fostered cynicism, anger, and a sense of humiliation across the region. In fact, the situation threatened the legitimacy of the overall nuclear nonproliferation regime in the eyes of the Arab public. Israel's argument—that because of its perceptions of threats to its existence, it could not give up its nuclear weapons before reaching a comprehensive peace with the Arab and Muslim world—did not wash with this audi-ence. Israel's arsenal was seen by Arabs and Muslims as further embold-ening Israel to ride roughshod over the rights of the Palestinians. If Iran

---

4 This was not the first threat I had received. A few years earlier the Egyptian authorities had received information that a militant Egyptian group was planning to target Egyptian public figures abroad. I was on the list. The Egyptian ambassador to Vienna, Mostafa el-Feki, informed me and the authorities in Austria. For a time I was given increased secu-rity, but nothing came of it.

5 Gideon Frank, the director general of the Israel Atomic Energy Commission, attended the meeting, as did Sharon's chief of staff, Dov Weissglass, and his military adviser.

were to leave the NPT, there would likely be overwhelming support from the Muslim world, which would see an Iranian nuclear weapon program as a way of establishing parity with Israel.

Our discussion was substantive, and Sharon listened carefully. He referred from time to time to the briefs prepared by his aides, and his responses were thoughtful and informed. Although the conversation was serious, it was infused with self-deprecating humor and punctuated by irreverent interruptions to Sharon from his advisers.

By the end of the meeting, Sharon had made a commitment, in the context of the Israeli-Arab peace process, to be ready to talk about the establishment of a nuclear-weapon-free zone in the Middle East. This was the first time an Israeli official had ever made such a statement. On previous occasions, the Israelis had repeated their position that any talks about a NWFZ would take place only after a comprehensive peace agreement. Israel had hardened its stance on nuclear discussions during the multilateral talks that began in Madrid in 1991. As a result, Egypt and the other Arab countries had decided to suspend all multilateral discussions, including arms control, resulting in the ultimate collapse of the Madrid process. Sharon's shift in position, I believe, signaled an awareness of the growing anger and radicalization in the Arab world and of the prospects of an extremist group acquiring a nuclear weapon, and perhaps was an effort to show some flexibility on Israel's part. More important, it was also prompted by growing fear of the Iranian nuclear program.

At the end of the meeting, Sharon said, "I heard you like jazz." Smiling, he handed me a small gift, a CD by an Israeli group.

Some of those present at the meeting later tried to tone down what Sharon had told me. I assured them that I had heard clearly and that I would report to the IAEA Board what he had said.

My trip drew heavy criticism in the Egyptian and other Arab media because my agenda had not included inspection of Israel's Dimona nuclear facility. I found myself accused of succumbing to U.S. influence. As the Arab media well knew, the IAEA had no authority to carry out such an inspection. They must have known that I had gone to Israel at the specific request of Agency Member States, including the Arab States.

These facts were ignored in the Arab media, which in turn misled Arab public opinion. In any case, for the common person, legal nuances were trumped by the glaring reality of Israel's nuclear arsenal. Although that arsenal was a source of great apprehension to Israel's neighbors as a glaring regional security imbalance, the international community chose to turn a blind eye; yet it had gone to war in Iraq over fictional WMD claims and was sanctioning Iran for even attempting to acquire advanced nuclear technology. To the Arab Muslim world, the treatment of Israel's nuclear program constituted a staggering double standard, explainable only as an arbitrary distinction between "good guys" and "bad guys."

For some years I had argued that the international community should adopt a new approach in dealing with Israel, India, and Pakistan—the three countries that had never joined the NPT—and engage them as nuclear partners rather than pariahs. They had not violated any agreement by going nuclear. But more important, no arms control negotiations, I felt, could make headway without the participation of all the states possessing nuclear weapons. A nuclear-weapon-free zone in the Middle East, for example, could not be achieved without the engagement of Israel.

In 2006, in keeping with this pragmatic approach, I endorsed the agreement between India and the United States for the two countries to pursue civil nuclear cooperation—meaning nuclear power reactor technology, nuclear safety practices, and other peaceful nuclear applications. For this I drew the ire of U.S. experts and former government officials who had been working in the field of nuclear arms control for many years and who generally were very supportive when I spoke out on disarmament issues. Now they were enraged, charging me with "undermining the NPT" and "taking the side of the Bush administration." They were joined in their criticism by a few officials from other governments.

The history of India's nuclear weapon program was unique. J. N. Dixit, India's late national security adviser, told me that in the early 1960s, before the NPT was finalized, U.S. secretary of state Dean Rusk encouraged Prime Minister Nehru to lead India's development of a nuclear weapon. This reflected the U.S. desire for India to balance the emergence of China as a nuclear-weapon state.

Nehru had refused: India would remain an outspoken advocate of nuclear disarmament. But mindful of its perceived regional security risks, India also declined to join the NPT, thus retaining the nuclear weapons option as a future possibility.

Ten years after Nehru's death, India demonstrated, with its "peaceful nuclear explosion" in 1974—code-named Smiling Buddha—that it had mastered the technology. But India continued to exercise restraint. In 1988, Prime Minister Rajiv Gandhi submitted to the UN General Assembly an "Action Plan Ushering in a Nuclear-Weapon Free and Non-Violent World Order." Only after decades of watching China grow in power and prestige as a nuclear-weapon state, with every technology made available, while India was treated with benign neglect, subject to export restrictions on sensitive technologies, did the Indian government decide to go nuclear. A series of nuclear weapon tests were conducted in 1998, and India declared itself a nuclear-weapon state.

The deal initiated by Indian prime minister Manmohan Singh and U.S. president George Bush in 2005 acknowledged a practical reality: India had long been a possessor of nuclear weapons, and an ongoing refusal by the United States to cooperate on peaceful nuclear technology would have no effect on Delhi's ability to maintain its nuclear arsenal. It would only hamper India's efforts to expand its nuclear power program, part of its strategy to generate the energy needed to lift 650 million people out of poverty. Moreover, the Americans' close cooperation with India in every technology area other than nuclear—a policy pursued by many other countries—was neither coherent nor consistent.

I viewed the agreement as a win-win situation, good for development and good for arms control. It would provide India with access to Western nuclear energy technology and safety insights—an important consideration given India's ambitious indigenous nuclear energy program. Also, although the deal would not bring India into the NPT, it would draw the country closer to the nuclear nonproliferation regime through acceptance of IAEA safeguards on its civilian facilities and a commitment to adhere to the export guidelines of the Nuclear Suppliers Group.[6] This would be an important step toward addressing the lacunae in the export control regime, such as that evidenced by the international community's experience with A. Q. Khan and his collaborators.

During my meeting with President Bush in March 2004, I had mentioned the inadequacies of export controls as a top proliferation concern. I urged him to talk to both India and Pakistan on this topic—to find a way to bring them into the export control regime, at a minimum, but more generally to make them partners in the effort to control proliferation.

In June 2006, I wrote an opinion piece in the *Washington Post*, "Rethinking Nuclear Safeguards," in which I articulated my reasons for supporting the U.S.-India deal. "Either we begin finding creative, outside-the-box solutions," I wrote, "or the international nuclear safeguards regime will become obsolete." The article did not make everyone happy. "An Open Letter to Mohamed ElBaradei," published in *Arms Control Today* on July 24, was signed by many of my friends and supporters, who disagreed strongly with my position. They knew that my endorsement of the agreement with India would boost support for it in the U.S. Congress, where many representatives were undecided.

The Bush administration did in fact make full use of my endorsement. On a number of occasions, Condoleezza Rice took pains to point out that "the agreement has the support of Mohamed ElBaradei, the 'custodian' of the nuclear nonproliferation regime." This was immensely ironic: whenever I talked publicly about the importance of nuclear disarmament or emphasized the need for direct U.S. engagement with Iran, the Americans castigated me, in the press and in diplomatic circles, for exceeding my mandate. Yet, in this case they were quite happy for me to take a clear policy position.

---

6 The NSG, founded in 1974, is a multinational body made up of forty-six Member States that have the capacity to export nuclear technology. The NSG seeks to reduce nuclear proliferation risks by controlling the export of materials that could be relevant to nuclear weapons development.

The Indian government was also deeply appreciative. When I came to Delhi at the invitation of Prime Minister Singh in October 2007, the agreement was facing strong internal opposition from the Communists, who were part of the ruling coalition. There was also ideological opposition by many within the Indian elite, due to their inherent antipathy toward the United States and their fear that the agreement would compromise India's policy of independence.

Prime Minister Singh broke with normal protocol and hosted a lunch for me at his residence, a beautiful old colonial house that was simply furnished. An extraordinarily courteous man, kind and soft-spoken, Singh had lived the first ten years of his life in a village without electricity, clean water, or a sewage system. Yet he had been educated at Oxford and Cambridge and attained a PhD in economics. As India's finance minister in the 1990s, he was the individual most responsible for the policies that transformed his country into an open, free-market economy, with a middle class of three hundred million, a thriving technology export base, and a steady growth rate of roughly 9 percent. And still he remained humble and shy. We shared almost identical worldviews. Of all the world leaders whom I came to know, Manmohan Singh is among those I most admire.

The final steps to make the U.S.-India deal practically effective began at the IAEA, where, after extensive back-and-forth discussions with India, the Board adopted the India safeguards agreement on August 1, 2008, the most extensive such agreement ever with a non-NPT state. The Nuclear Suppliers Group adopted the necessary waiver of restrictions one month later, opening the door for India to import nuclear technology. The final agreement was signed soon thereafter by Condoleezza Rice and Indian external affairs minister Pranab Mukherjee.

The Pakistanis were quite upset by the U.S.-India agreement, because they were not offered the same opportunity. Although I urged them to bide their time and then ask for a similar deal, the problem was that Pakistan's track record was less than stellar; the activities of A. Q. Khan and his network were fresh in everyone's mind. Still, it did not help that Bush, on a trip to Islamabad, made the somewhat pointed statement that

"Pakistan and India are different countries with different needs and different histories."[7]

It was important that Pakistan not be seen to receive different treatment because it was a Muslim country. "It would be helpful," I told Condoleezza Rice, "if you could say that, once conditions are created, the United States could also envisage a similar agreement with Pakistan." I pointed out that it would be a positive gesture, even without an agreement in place, to offer nuclear safety assistance to upgrade Pakistan's aging reactor in Karachi.

Years earlier, the United States had blocked an opportunity to improve the safety of the Karachi reactor. Belgium had been ready to provide relevant equipment to Pakistan in 1999, after the IAEA certified that this equipment was needed for reactor safety, and I had written to the Belgian prime minister in support of this effort. Belgium's offer was derailed by Washington, and I received an angry phone call from my friend Norm Wulf, the U.S. special representative for nuclear nonproliferation. Nuclear safety should not be politicized, I told him; an unsafe reactor could have disastrous consequences for everyone. Wulf answered that Pakistan could shut down the reactor if it was not safe.

This was not a serious response, because Pakistan badly needed the energy. Rather than shutting it down, they did their best to fix it themselves. The result was a less-than-optimal safety situation, which was in no one's interest. The United States had in effect cut off everyone's nose to spite their face. Now there was an opportunity to begin this type of interaction with Pakistan, not by offering them the equivalent of the India deal, which no one was ready to do, but in more limited ways that would have safety benefits and simultaneously begin moving them closer to partnership in the nuclear nonproliferation regime.

One of the strangest and most striking examples of nuclear hypocrisy, multilateral and multifaceted, must surely be Israel's bombing of the Dair

---

7 Peter Wallsten, "Bush: No Nuclear Pact for Pakistan," *Los Angeles Times*, March 5, 2006.

Alzour installation in Syria in September 2007, and the aftermath of that attack. Speculation began almost immediately that the site had housed a nuclear facility. Syria denied the accusations. Israel and the United States remained officially silent, although American officials talked anonymously on the subject to the media. I spoke out strongly, noting that any country with information indicating that the bombed facility was nuclear was under a legal obligation to report it to the IAEA. But no one came forward with such a report. For the six weeks following the bombing—the most crucial period in terms of our seeing inside the facility—we were unable to obtain any high resolution imagery from commercial satellites.

On October 28, in New York, I gave an interview on CNN's *Late Edition* with Wolf Blitzer. In response to Blitzer's question as to whether the Syrian facility was a nuclear reactor, I said we had not seen any evidence to conclude one way or the other. But I was clear on one point: that "to bomb first and then ask questions later," as Israel had done, was deliberately undermining the system.[8] Only the IAEA, I pointed out, had the means to verify allegations of clandestine nuclear activity. In another interview, with Charlie Rose two days later, I pointed out that Israel's 1981 attack on Iraq's Osirak reactor had only served as motivation to accelerate Saddam Hussein's clandestine nuclear program.[9]

Israel obviously did not like the criticism. What followed was a tirade of attacks on me by Israeli officials. Deputy Prime Minister Shaul Mofaz called for me to be sacked: "The policies followed by ElBaradei endanger world peace. His irresponsible attitude of sticking his head in the sand over Iran's nuclear programme should lead to his impeachment."[10] The outspoken and radical Avigdor Lieberman, at the time minister for strategic affairs,[11] said I was part of the problem: "Instead of criticizing Iran, he finds it right to criticize Israel."[12] Deputy Foreign Minister Majalli Whbee

---

8 Transcript retrieved from CNN archives at www.archives.cnn.com/TRANSCRIPTS/0710/28/le.01.html.
9 *Charlie Rose*, October 30, 2007. Transcript retrieved at www.iaea.org/NewsCenter/Transcripts/2007/cr301007.html.
10 "Israel Says UN Nuclear Chief Should Go," Agence France-Presse, November 8, 2007.
11 Lieberman later became foreign minister.
12 "Israel Minister: 'Apocalyptic Scenario' If Egypt, Saudi Arabia Go Nuclear," *Jerusalem Post*, November 8, 2007.

also called on me to step down, accusing me of "criminal negligence."[13] The overt focus of these tirades was my handling of the Iran nuclear file, which did not meet their policy objectives of hyping the Iranian threat, but it was clear that my condemnation of the bombing at Dair Alzour had touched a nerve.

John Bolton was openly supportive of Israel's action. In an interview on CNN's *Late Edition*, Wolf Blitzer asked Bolton what he thought of my public assertion that Israel should have brought its "evidence" to the IAEA. "If you believe that," Bolton retorted, "I have a bridge to sell you. The notion that Israel or the United States would put their national security in the IAEA's hands is just delusional."[14] To hear these sentiments coming from the U.S. ambassador to the United Nations was dreadful.

Attacks notwithstanding, the Agency remained focused on its efforts to get to the bottom of the matter. I met with Ibrahim Othman, the head of the Syrian Atomic Energy Commission. If their denials were factual, I told him, the Syrians should make a categorical public statement to that effect and should invite an Agency team to the site, just to put an end to the nuclear speculation. Othman said he would convey my proposal to the Syrian authorities. I said I also found it strange that no Arab country had made a statement denouncing the Israeli attack on Syria.

Some six months after the bombing, during a visit to Sarajevo, I took a call from John Rood, the acting U.S. undersecretary of state for arms control and international security. A briefing to the U.S. Congress was scheduled for the next day, he told me. The target Israel had destroyed at Dair Alzour was, according to Rood, a nuclear reactor of North Korean vintage. Israel had alerted the United States to the presence of the reactor in 2006; the Americans had come to the same conclusion about the facility on their own in early 2007. Rood added that the United States planned

---

13 *Haaretz*, November 17, 2007.
14 Interview on CNN's *Late Edition* on November 11, 2007. Transcript retrieved from CNN archives at www.archives.cnn.com/TRANSCRIPTS/0711/11/le.01.html. A number of pundits commenting on this interview recalled a comment Bolton had made to *Insight* magazine in August 1999: "It is a big mistake for us to grant any validity to international law even when it may seem in our short-term interest to do so—because, over the long term, the goal of those who think that international law really means anything are those who want to constrict the United States."

to give IAEA safeguards officials an intelligence briefing, and he offered the same to me, either there in Sarajevo or on my return to Vienna.

Rood's information was coming too late in the day. I told him, "The U.S. was obligated to share this information with the Agency, not to wait until Israel went and bombed the facility." At a minimum, I said, the Americans could have let us know immediately after the bombing. By leaving us in the dark for a year before the bombing and six months after, they were undermining the nonproliferation regime. "You are making us look like fools," I concluded. Rood had little to say in defense of withholding information. The United States would have preferred a diplomatic approach, he maintained, and they had not given Israel the green light to bomb the facility.

Back in Vienna, I issued a press statement deploring the fact that the information had not been shared with the IAEA in a timely manner and condemning Israel's unilateral use of force. Neither Israel nor the United States responded to my statement. It seemed they had no wish to engage with me in a public debate; in any case, they would have lost. The Israeli action was a violation of every norm of international law regarding the use of force. It also showed total disregard for the nonproliferation regime. Yet very few countries—and not a single Western country—spoke up to denounce the action.

Israel undoubtedly did not want a reactor developed in any of the Arab countries they considered hostile. Assuming that the Dair Alzour site *was* a reactor, Israel may have concluded that Agency verification would have resulted in Syria putting the site under IAEA safeguards, making it harder for them to bomb it later on. The central issue, of course, was distrust on the part of Israel and the West of these countries' future intentions.

As a next step, I asked Othman to come to Vienna to discuss modalities for verifying the American claims. At the beginning of the meeting, when we were alone, I emphasized the importance of Syria showing maximum transparency and allowing us to come to Dair Alzour and to other sites identified by satellites and thought to be related to the bombed site. He insisted they had no nuclear program at all—the facility, he said, had been a missile-related factory—but they were ready to agree to a visit by Agency inspectors.

We were then joined by Olli Heinonen and a foreign ministry colleague of Othman's. The Syrians called for clarification about why we wanted to go to other sites in addition to the destroyed facility at Dair Alzour. We answered candidly: we had seen satellite photos that showed equipment being moved from the destroyed site to other locations, so it was important to verify the nature of these three other sites.

The next IAEA Board meeting took place in early June. In my opening statement, I said it was "deeply regrettable" that unilateral force had been resorted to before the Agency had been given an opportunity to establish the facts. I emphasized that Syria was obliged to report the planning and construction of any nuclear facility to the Agency. To my dismay, very few countries had anything to add regarding the Israeli attack on Syria. For the most part, Australia, Canada, the European Union, Japan, and of course the United States focused on the need for Syria to cooperate. The only European country to refer to the Israeli bombing was Switzerland. A few nonaligned countries also spoke out. But even some of the Arab countries sitting on the Board, such as Egypt, remained silent.

In a meeting with the twenty-seven European Union ambassadors, I told them they had undermined their credibility a great deal. "When you are not able to speak on a violation of one of the most basic tenets of the UN Charter," I said, "your moral authority to speak up on democracy, human rights, and other issues is also greatly compromised." Many of the ambassadors agreed, behind closed doors. But the European Union's mode of operation on issues of nuclear proliferation was that the French and British monopolized the issuance of "joint opinions," to the irritation of many.

Syria itself made a weak and defensive statement, which was also strange. Even stranger was that, according to the Iranian ambassador, Syria had asked him not to speak on the issue. I had suspected that something was brewing in a back room toward rapprochement between Syria and the United States. Syria's behavior reinforced my view. They did not want to upset the cart.

An intelligence agency brought satellite images for the Agency to see, purportedly of Dair Alzour, which they said had been taken over a span of two years. The images helped clarify the design of the building that was alleged to have housed the reactor. Another intelligence agency provided additional photos, purportedly taken in the vicinity of the building, including inside. A certain individual who appeared in the photos was a North Korean we recognized from our dealings with Pyongyang. This gave the IAEA inspection team additional information on which to press their questioning of Syria. But Syria refused to cooperate in discussing any of the satellite images or other photos, simply maintaining that the building was a missile-related military installation and that the images were all fake.

In June 2008, Olli and his team of inspectors headed to Dair Alzour. The facility had been completely razed, and a new one built. The Syrians stuck to their story that there was nothing nuclear about the facility. The inspectors took environmental samples, and the Agency reached agreement with the Syrian authorities on a process for investigating the allegations about Dair Alzour.

Clearly intent on slowing down the process, Syria asked that additional questions or inspection requests be sent in writing. When the U.S. ambassador to the IAEA, Greg Schulte, came to see me in July, he referred to the destroyed facility as "a one-off thing." It was obvious to me from his remarks that the Americans also were in no hurry to see a report on the Syrian nuclear program—apparently because of ongoing indirect talks between Syria and the United States. "You might have your own political agenda," I told Schulte, "but the Agency's agenda is quite different, and we take our responsibilities seriously."

David Miliband, the British foreign secretary, also seemed to have no interest in seeing the Syria issue pursued further. When I briefed him on the Agency's actions, he responded, "Oh, so you have done a full investigation?" This was not the case; I saw it as his way of indicating that he would prefer to see an end to the inquiries. I was not clear as to the motive, but my gut feeling was that even if Dair Alzour had been a reactor under construction, the threat was now eliminated and the West was eager to bring Syria, an ally of Iran, to their side. This impression of back-room political considerations was reinforced one year later: when Syria failed to accommodate various Western demands, the IAEA Secretariat was urged to pressure Syria by requesting a special inspection, although there was no obvious legal basis for such a request.

The results of the Agency's environmental samples from Dair Alzour came back showing the presence of uranium that, while not enriched, had undergone some chemical processing. In the months that followed, the Syrians gave various explanations for this, beginning with the claim that the material must have come from uranium traces in the munitions used by Israel in the bombing. None of their explanations made complete sense or was verifiable. Israel, for its part, refused to provide the Agency with any information in their possession as to why they had bombed the facility.

Syria also refused to allow the IAEA to visit the three other sites allegedly related to the destroyed facility. They were military facilities, not nuclear related, we were told, and therefore the Agency had no reason to visit them. They also refused to show us where the debris from the destroyed facility had been taken.

During the June 2009 IAEA Board meeting, this stalemate—the result of withholding information from the Agency, and then assigning it the impossible task of verifying what no longer existed—led to a particularly direct confrontation. Once again, I urged Israel to share the information that had led it to use force against the Syrian facility at Dair Alzour. The Israeli ambassador to the IAEA, Israel Michaeli, complained, saying I was making "redundant" demands. Israel, he said, had already provided answers to the IAEA's relevant questions, denying that the uranium traces could have come from Israeli munitions.[15] By pressing Israel to come up with more evidence of Syria's nuclear program, Michaeli declared, I was showing a "political bias." He also implied that

---

15 Israel had provided a one-line answer to the IAEA's questions, merely saying that the source of the uranium found was not Israeli, not even acknowledging that it had been responsible for the actual bombing.

because we had not called for a special inspection on Syria, the Agency was not using all the tools in its toolkit.

Michaeli was out of line, and he knew it, but I also knew he was acting under instructions from his capital. I answered him with a directness that shocked some of the delegates. His stance, I said, was "totally distorted." By refusing to provide us with the necessary evidence, Israel was essentially obstructing the IAEA's investigative process. I made my next remarks looking directly at him:

> The representative of Israel . . . is mentioning that Syria should be deplored and condemned. But Israel, with its action, is to be deplored by not allowing us to do what we are supposed to do under international law. . . . You say we refrain from using tools. Israel is not even a member of the [nuclear nonproliferation] regime to tell us what tools are available to us. [Your country] cannot sit on the fence, making use of the system without being accountable. . . . We would appreciate it if you could stop preaching to us how we can do our jobs.

Regarding his accusation that I was biased, I said I would not even dignify it with a response.

We were stuck. Despite my repeated requests—including those made public in IAEA Board reports—Israel and the United States did not give us further evidence to substantiate their conclusion that the Dair Alzour facility had been nuclear. The Syrians continued to claim that it was not nuclear, but they refused to provide additional information or access to prove their contention.

Sometime later, I sent an appeal through a Syrian businessman with direct access to Syrian president Bashar al-Assad. I pressed for cooperation with the IAEA, making clear that the issue would continue to hang over Syria until it was cleared up. A message came back saying that al-Assad appreciated my efforts; curiously, what was missing was any denial that Dair Alzour had been a nuclear reactor site.

The hypocrisy could not have been clearer: for some Member States, nuclear proliferation concerns were tools to be used, hyped, or ignored according to geopolitical ends, depending on the relationship with the country in the stand.

The most fundamental problem with the nuclear nonproliferation regime is, in itself, a double standard: the inherent asymmetry, or inequality, between the nuclear haves and have-nots, exacerbated by the continuing reliance by the nuclear-weapon states on nuclear weapons and their lack of progress on nuclear disarmament. Worse, rather than moving to fulfill their commitment to disarm, most have modernized their arsenals and continue to develop new types of weapons. For countries that do not have such weapons and do not fall under a nuclear umbrella protection arrangement such as NATO, this reinforces the perception that the acquisition of nuclear weapons is a sure path to power and prestige, an insurance policy against attack.

The UN Security Council also is part of the problem, in part because of the veto power wielded by the P-5, the five nuclear-weapon states. The Security Council's charge is to maintain international peace and security and to be responsive to threats against that peace and security. Certainly, some violations of an IAEA safeguards agreement may not rise to the level of requiring referral to the council. However, on those rare occasions when such referrals are made, the council should be appropriately responsive: it should be agile, resolute, forceful when needed, and above all, consistent in its actions.

By those standards, the record of the Security Council in responding consistently to nuclear threats has been abysmal. In 1981, after Israel destroyed Iraq's Osirak reactor and the Security Council condemned the bombing, it also urged Israel to put its nuclear facilities under IAEA safeguards. Israel ignored the resolution, and the Security Council took no further action. In 1998, after the Indian and Pakistani nuclear weapons tests, the Security Council condemned the testing and asked both countries to cease the development of nuclear weapons and their delivery systems. When those resolutions were ignored, the council again backed off. In the case of North Korea, when the IAEA first reported North Korea's noncompliance in 1993, and in 2003, when the country withdrew from the NPT altogether, the council took no meaningful action, instead letting the United States take the initiative through the Agreed Framework in the 1990s, and in the latter case deferring to China's lead in setting up the six-party talks.

On the other hand, the Security Council imposed sanctions on Iraq in 1990 that led to egregious violations of human rights for millions of Iraqi civilians and culminated in a war in 2003 without the council's consent. To add insult to injury, the council continued to maintain certain sanctions against Iraq for years after the 2003 invasion, long after it was clear to everyone that Iraq had no WMD. The council was unable to agree on how to terminate the UNMOVIC and IAEA mandates in Iraq and close the WMD file. And burdened by the ravages of a war that should never have occurred, Iraq was forced to finance UNMOVIC for more than four years while it sat idle in New York.

While the P-5 exacerbated nuclear insecurity through their actions in the Security Council, their own failure to disarm contributed directly to proliferation itself. Yet the P-5, and the United States in particular, refused to acknowledge the linkage between their lack of progress on disarmament and the growing volume of proliferation-related concerns.

In April 2004 a joint proposal was submitted to the U.S. Congress by the secretaries of state, energy, and defense, to develop "small" nuclear weapons. Their argument was essentially that these weapons would be perceived as more readily usable. If enemy countries believed that the United States might actually use these mini-nukes, the deterrent effect would be stronger. It did not seem to occur to them that the idea of a "more usable" nuclear weapon ran directly contrary to the tenets of the NPT regime and would only tempt more countries to acquire such weapons to defend themselves.

The United States also continued to develop its missile defense shield, which both Russia and China regarded as a threat. The United States claimed that the shield was intended to protect them against missiles by "rogue states," meaning North Korea and Iran. Many experts pointed out that this argument did not make sense. An attack by a small country—or, for that matter, by a group of terrorists—would more likely come in the form of a crude bomb smuggled in through a harbor or across a border, and not through a missile with the country's name on it. The missile shield would be pointless.

I frequently spoke out on these issues, in speeches and press interviews, and the Americans just as frequently complained that I was overstepping the limits of my position, speaking "out of the box." I told them I had "no box," that I felt it part of my responsibility to speak out on matters that had a direct impact on the nuclear nonproliferation regime, a responsibility that, as a Nobel laureate, I felt even more keenly. When it came to reporting on verification issues, my role was to present the facts. But I had witnessed the discrediting and manipulation of the IAEA's work in the lead-up to the Iraq War and would not allow that to happen again on my watch. I felt it was important to leave as little room as possible for media hype or manipulation. And it was my charge to help Member States find peaceful solutions to nuclear tensions, by contributing my perspective and vigorously supporting nuclear diplomacy. I knew, of course, that the states themselves made the decisions in the end.

In early 2007 the British government announced its decision to upgrade its nuclear deterrence force by building new Trident nuclear ballistic missile submarines, a move effectively designed to extend the British nuclear deterrent to mid-century. I was amazed by the hypocrisy. In an interview with the *Financial Times* about Iran's nuclear cycle development,[16] I said that as long as the United Kingdom and other such states continued to modernize their weapons, I would find it very difficult to tell other countries that nuclear deterrence was not good for them.

The *Telegraph* reported my comments under the title "UN Nuclear Watchdog Calls Trident Hypocritical." John Sawers, then the director general for political affairs at the Foreign Office,[17] called to say that my remarks had gone down very badly in London. He expounded on how the British had reduced their nuclear force; it was the smallest arsenal among the P-5, and he felt I was picking on them.

"Don't you understand," I asked him, "that it is difficult to argue that

---

16 "Iran Nears Industrial Nuclear Fuel Production," February 19, 2007.
17 Sawers was later appointed head of MI6, the British secret intelligence service.

some countries should continue to have nuclear weapons and modernize them while others are told they cannot?"

"Yes," Sawers replied, "but we should not be compared with Iran."

The issue was not Iran but the general principle. The United Kingdom seemed to be invoking an odd moral calculus: "We're the good guys; they're the bad guys; trust us."

In the House of Commons, Blair was asked about my *Financial Times* interview. "The United Kingdom," he replied, "has the right under the NPT to have nuclear weapons, and as Mohamed ElBaradei is the custodian of that treaty's implementation, it would be a good idea for him to act accordingly."[18] His rendering of the treaty was a revealing distortion but symptomatic of the behavior of the nuclear-weapon states, who fulfilled their obligations to disarm through lip service only.

It was especially distressing to note that only South Africa publicly protested the United Kingdom's Trident decision. The non-nuclear-weapon states responded with deafening silence, a dismaying response that signaled to me their resignation in the face of a world order that had acquired the appearance of inevitable permanence.

I was reminded of this less than a year later, in a meeting with British foreign secretary David Miliband. We had been talking about Iran; Miliband acknowledged the complexity of the issue, but it was obvious that we did not see eye to eye. At one point he exclaimed, "Why do you think Iran wants to have nuclear weapons?"

"Why does the United Kingdom have nukes?" I was tempted to retort. I found the double standard astounding, but I kept silent.

The IAEA faced many challenges in carrying out its mandate. We were strained for resources. We had insufficient authority. We were spied on by the same intelligence agencies we relied upon to inform us when they detected nuclear anomalies; we were given selective intelligence information, which was often difficult to authenticate. We were dependent on

18 Rebecca Johnson, who had served as an adviser to UNMOVIC, wrote a detailed rebuttal to Blair in the *Bulletin of the Atomic Scientists*, which ended by saying that he owed me an apology. Rebecca Johnson, "Tony Blair's Forgetfulness," *Bulletin of the Atomic Scientists*, February 26, 2007.

Member States, some of whom had their own agendas, to supply us with state-of-the-art technology we could not afford. We were pressured by those who believed that funding the Agency came with the right to influence its work for political ends.[19] And we continued to face complex nuclear verification cases that challenged our resourcefulness and our patience.

But the great, unspoken travesty was that nuclear weapons continued to exist at all, much less that the most powerful countries on the planet held on to their arsenals like a security blanket. We repeatedly heard dire predictions about Iran developing a single nuclear weapon when the world was already blighted by the existence of more than twenty-three thousand such weapons. Many of those weapons were on "hair-trigger" alert—meaning that the leaders of the United States and Russia, faced with the possible launch of a nuclear missile that might well have been caused by computer error or unauthorized use, would have only half an hour to decide whether to retaliate, risking the devastation of entire nations in a matter of minutes. Yet political leaders continued to declare that all this was irrelevant to proliferation.

I had no intention of staying in my box.

---

19 For example, during a meeting at my home with Nicholas Burns, U.S. undersecretary of state for political affairs, and some of his colleagues, he handed me a paper detailing what the U.S. expected from the Agency in handling Iran's nuclear file. Naturally, I was displeased, but I merely put the paper to one side, saying calmly, "We know what to do about Iran." Burns's retort was pointed: "You know," he said, "that we pay 25 percent of your budget."

11

IRAN, 2007–2008

Squandered Opportunities

The U.S. perception of the Iranian regime as a gang of glassy-eyed radicals had deep emotional roots, reaching back to the hostage crisis of 1979–1981. For the Iranians, their sense of the United States as the Great Satan went back still further, to 1953 and the overthrow of the Mossadegh government by the CIA. In both capitals, talk of the relationship was frequently tinged with an element of ideological and even religious fervor.

For the hard-liners in the Bush administration, the very notion of engagement with Iran represented a moral compromise. Their ultimate goal was regime change. But by 2007, the catastrophe of the Iraq War meant that a military strike on Iran no longer appeared to be a viable option, at least for the present. So the administration promoted Plan B: a policy of sanctions and isolation intended to cause Iran to buckle under pressure, particularly on the nuclear issue.

Sanctions served to express the international community's displeasure, but, in my view, they could not resolve the issue. And the notion of Iran buckling was a fiction: although the idea played well inside the Beltway, it had nothing to do with reality. Nonetheless, U.S. hard-liners worked to undermine all European efforts to resume dialogue with Iran, especially when it came to uranium enrichment. At any point that conditions for a breakthrough seemed within reach, the Americans found a way to block progress. To the extent that the United States entered the discussion, on the periphery of P-5 + 1 attempts to restart negotiations, it was only to set the one condition certain to be ultimately rejected: the futile demand that Iran fully give up its enrichment.

The result was self-imposed failure by way of ideology. Provoked by sanctions and harsh rhetoric, Tehran continued to direct the steady buildup of its uranium enrichment expertise. By early 2007, with a few hundred centrifuges operating and more being installed daily, the Iranians were on their way to gaining the technological know-how the Americans deemed unacceptable. The U.S. policy was yielding one achievement only: the price of any eventual agreement was growing ever higher.

To forge a means of bringing the parties back to negotiations, I began to work on a new set of ideas. However, the United States was not the only country that required some coaxing. France, too, had recently veered toward a more uncompromising stance, and I wanted to understand why.

During a mid-January trip to Paris, I heard from Foreign Ministry officials that their recent statements on Iran were designed to keep the Americans engaged in the process. Bush had talked to Chirac some two years earlier about the very real threat of Israeli military action against Iran, and the French remained anxious. I was reminded of Britain's none-too-successful strategy prior to the 2003 invasion of Iraq: the claim that they were staying close to the United States in order to influence U.S. policy.

In addition, the Gulf countries and Egypt had been calling for the West to exert maximum pressure on Iran. Some Arab leaders, for example, had urged Chirac to refrain from sending his foreign minister, Philippe Douste-Blazy, to Iran.

I understood that the French, the tenth-largest oil consumers in the world, wanted to protect both their friends and their interests in the Gulf.[1] But it was disheartening to hear that Arab countries were opposing diplomacy instead of taking a role in mediating the dispute. The EU's

---

1 The French company Total SA is the fourth largest publicly traded oil producer in the world, with operations in Africa, Europe, and the Middle East.

Javier Solana passed on that he, too, was being pressed by Arab leaders not to make concessions or provide incentives to Iran.

The United States had been doing its best to fan the fear of Iran in the Gulf. But to me the actions of the Arab regimes were predominantly a sign of their impotence. For all of Tehran's considerable faults, the Iranians were working on every front, well beyond just nuclear technology, to become more scientifically advanced, to improve their educational standards, and to assert their leadership in the region. The Arab regimes, apparently, were envious and afraid. Rather than working to catch up, to enhance their own knowledge and technology base, and to establish equilibrium across the region—or even to agree on common policies on how to deal with Iran—they were working through their Western allies to bring down the Islamic Republic.[2]

In a meeting with French foreign minister Douste-Blazy, he suggested that I go public and propose the idea of a "double-suspension" as the trigger for all parties to enter into negotiation: Iran would suspend its enrichment activities and the Security Council would suspend its sanctions. The idea was not new, in fact; it was embedded to some extent in the council's most recent resolution. But it had gotten no traction.

I told Douste-Blazy I would be happy to make the call for a "pause" but wanted to avoid using the word *suspension*. The World Economic Forum in Davos, scheduled for the next week, would be a good place to unveil the initiative. "You are the only person who can do this," Douste-Blazy said, "because you are not part of the negotiation, and also because of your status as a Nobel Peace laureate."

This conversation was followed by a call from Sergei Kislyak, the Russian deputy minister of foreign affairs. The Russians were concerned that the Iranians no longer appeared to be talking to anyone. I floated the ideas from my talk with Douste-Blazy, and Kislyak pledged support for such a proposal. Further refinement came from talking to Ursula

2 The release of diplomatic cables from the WikiLeaks Web site in late 2010 pointed toward more efforts by Arab leaders behind the scenes, in which they allegedly urged the United States to conduct military strikes on Iran. See, for example, "Arab Leaders Urged U.S. to Attack Iran, WikiLeaks Says," Mark Hennessy, *Irish Times*, November 29, 2010.

Plassnik, the Austrian foreign minister and a close friend, who suggested using the term *time-out* instead of *pause*. A time-out might sound a bit softer, she said, and therefore appeal more to the Iranians.

That was, in fact, the term I used in Davos, in interviews with both CNN and the BBC. I proposed that Iran take a time-out from its enrichment activities and the international community take a time-out from its implementation of sanctions. Official expressions of support followed from President Putin,[3] the Germans, and the French. The Chinese also lent their support, but they preferred to wait to air their views publicly at the March IAEA Board meeting. The Americans did not reject the proposal but simply said that the latest Security Council resolution[4] was clear on what Iran needed to do. Ali Larijani, chairman of the Iranian Parliament, called to say the Iranians needed some clarification through informal talks before formally pursuing the idea, but they were definitely interested.

While at Davos, I also ran into former president Khatami and took the time to tell him that some of Ahmadinejad's statements—particularly about Israel and the Holocaust—were severely damaging Iran's international image. These statements, together with uncertainty about Iran's nuclear intentions because of inspection issues that remained unresolved, were fomenting distrust throughout the region. Khatami expressed regret about some of what we were hearing from Tehran and said he would carry back the message.

The forum was also an opportunity to meet with Swiss president Micheline Calmy-Rey and State Secretary Michael Ambühl, who were also seeking independently to bring Iran back to negotiations. For two years, I'd been working closely with Calmy-Rey and her team, sharing ideas on possible paths to compromise with Iran on its enrichment program. The Swiss were eager to see a peaceful resolution of the Iran nuclear file and since they represented the U.S. diplomatic interest in Tehran (the U.S. "interest section" in Iran is part of the Swiss embassy), they had a legitimate role to play as an intermediary.

---

3 Putin expressed support for the proposal at the Munich Conference on Security Policy on February 10.
4 SCR 1737, passed on December 23, 2006.

One idea I put forward in Davos was whether Iran could simply stop feeding nuclear material into the centrifuges. This is referred to as "warm standby": the machines continue to spin but without feedstock. I was not sure if the Americans and others would accept the proposal, which would allow me to report that Iran had suspended enrichment as requested by the Security Council and was only conducting R&D. The Swiss agreed to explore the idea with Iran.

A chaotic few weeks ensued, with a frenzied cycle of phone calls, meetings, and brainstorming sessions with various parties. I moved back and forth between Rice and others from the United States, trying to find some way for them to join the dialogue, and Larijani and other Iranians, seeking some form of suspension that would be acceptable on Iran's domestic front.

The Swiss kept up their efforts at shuttle diplomacy. Ambühl met with Larijani in Tehran. Calmy-Rey invited Larijani to Bern. Kislyak called to say the political directors of the P-5 + 1 seemed supportive of "ElBaradei's proposal," as they called it. Mohammad Saeedi, Gholam-reza Aghazadeh's deputy, stopped by for clarification about the possible benefits of agreeing to a time-out to help convince the Iranian leadership. Sweden's foreign minister, Carl Bildt, came to see me, as did Kim Howells, minister of state in the British Foreign Office.

Everyone wanted to get involved. Everyone wanted the same thing. But no one seemed able to find a way to talk sense into the hard-headed conservatives at opposite ends of the equation.

I reshaped the four "principles for negotiation" once again, trying to tailor them precisely to address the core concerns holding both sides back: trust, transparency, and future intentions. Now there were just three principles. First, explicit acknowledgement by all parties of Iran's right to have the nuclear fuel cycle, including enrichment, with recognition that the focus of the time-out was only on the timing and modalities for exercising that right, to create a sufficient opportunity to rebuild trust in the international community regarding Iran's intentions. Second, a commitment by Iran to working with the IAEA, in full transparency, to resolve any outstanding verification issues. And third, a commitment by both sides to work toward full normalization of relations between Iran and the West, including in the political, security, and economic fields.

I began peddling these three principles to the various diplomats working on the issue, including to Larijani. In a February meeting in Vienna, he said the principles seemed fair and should be put in writing. However, suspension, whether in the guise of a time-out or not, was in his view secondary. The primary issue was the distrust between Iran and the other parties, chiefly Europe and the United States. He cited a statement by Tony Blair made during a recent visit to the Gulf, that the West was building a coalition of moderate Arab countries against Iran.[5] These kinds of pronouncements stirred up old suspicions: Larijani recalled Blair saying in 2003 that the only reason Iran was cooperating with the IAEA was a result of the war in Iraq—because the Iranians saw that the West was "serious" and the Iraq War had been a "test case."

These sentiments, Larijani said, undermined every attempt at progress. As long as the West viewed Iran with such distrust, the haggling over suspension was meaningless.

"There are reasons for the distrust," I said, mentioning Ahmadinejad's statements about Israel and the Holocaust.

This was now "under control," according to Larijani. During Iran's celebrations on February 11, Revolution Day, Ahmadinejad had omitted any proclamations about their nuclear program, he pointed out.

Larijani wanted the Americans to understand as well that Iran hoped the al-Maliki government in Baghdad would succeed: the Iranians were not supporting the Shi'ite al-Mahdi militia led by cleric Moktada al-Sadr. Democracy and stability in Iraq was in Iran's interest. Larijani asked me to convey these thoughts to Condoleezza Rice. "She seems to be a person who understands," he said.

The P-5 + 1 and Solana came back with their response to the time-out idea in late February. John Sawers called to say that they would adopt a statement based on the three principles and the idea of a double time-out, but they intended to pursue a dual-track strategy and push for

5 Daniel Dombey, "Blair Seeks Closer Ties with Moderate Arabs," *Financial Times*, December 20, 2006.

another Security Council resolution, with additional "limited" sanctions. The news of another Security Council resolution being in the works dismayed Larijani. "If that goes forward," he said, "it will be the end of the negotiating process."

A conversation with Rice about the Iran situation gave me the chance to urge her to consider the sequencing of the P-5+1's strategy. First, I heard her view on the three principles: she was not keen on the word *normalization*, nor on explicitly spelling out Iran's right to enrichment. Otherwise, she had no problem with the idea of a "simultaneous time-out." This was encouraging. But I told her that going directly to the Security Council to push for sanctions would make it hard for Iran to come to the negotiating table. "You would be better served by airing these ideas with Iran first, before resorting to more sanctions," I said. Otherwise, "you will be empowering the hard-liners and undermining the moderates."

Rice seemed to be listening carefully. Sometimes the way she asked questions, when I suspected she already knew my answer, gave me the impression that our conversations were being recorded and transcribed. The Bush administration was, from what I could tell, fractured internally on foreign policy matters. Rice needed to marshal every argument if she was going to convince Washington's skeptics about reaching out to the Iranians. Maybe she wanted them to hear directly what Larijani had said about Iran's interest in talking to the United States. It was hard for me not to speculate.

Feeling like a broken record, I repeated that she should try to engage Iran directly. "It will help you on Iraq and also on the nuclear issue," I said. The Iranians were talking to the Saudis about Lebanon and Palestine. "People like Larijani," I told her, "are sincerely interested in dialogue." Rice did not disagree but neither did she commit herself.

Two days after we spoke, Washington announced that the United States would participate in a conference on Iraq with "neighboring countries," including Iran and Syria. The Americans insisted they would talk only about Iraq, not about the Iranian nuclear issue. The hair-splitting sounded a little childish to me; but I wasn't about to quibble. It was one step forward.

• • •

Any optimism I felt was fleeting. The opening of one door was immediately followed by other doors slamming shut. The P-5 + 1's march toward another Security Council resolution, however futile, seemed unstoppable, especially since it appeared that neither the Russians nor the Chinese would exercise their veto. Nonetheless, there was a flurry of diplomatic activity aimed at halting the advance.

The Swiss prepared a paper that laid out the lines under discussion. Despite signals from American officials indicating they did not want outside interference, Ambühl presented the paper to Larijani in Tehran.[6] I sent word to Larijani that this was likely the last chance for Iran to avoid another provocative Security Council resolution. The Swiss then tried every argument they could come up with to convince Iran of the benefits of going into full suspension. But to no avail: the Iranians would agree only to a two-stage process, in which they would freeze their enrichment activities—that is, not expand them further—for thirty days of "prenegotiation" during which the parties would jointly determine the "scope" of the double time-out to follow. This time-out would then go into effect for six months while the actual negotiations took place. This was a concession on Iran's part, but it was not enough.

Larijani warned me that if the Security Council passed another resolution, Iran would break off the ongoing IAEA inspections at Natanz. This would be another case of noncompliance, I told him, and could only worsen the standoff. "I know the implications," Larijani said, but the decision was coming from the Iranian government. He had tried to delay this action for six months but would not be able to do so any longer.

In the midst of all the diplomatic commotion, Iran continued to build its uranium enrichment capacity. When our inspectors visited Natanz on March 20, they saw that Iran had installed a total of one thousand centrifuges. It was both ironic and distressing to recall that just one

---

6 The late 2010 WikiLeaks release of cables made clear that Washington was extremely unhappy with the Swiss attempts to work with Iran toward a solution. "U.S. Irked By Over-Eager Swiss Diplomats," Mathieu van Rohr, *Spiegel Online International,* December 14, 2010.

year earlier the buildup of Iran's enrichment program could have been halted at thirty to forty centrifuges. The American argument that Iran should be prevented from having enrichment knowledge was water under the bridge: Iranian nuclear specialists had now been running small cascades of centrifuges for more than a year.

Against this background, I prepared my report on Iran for the IAEA's March Board meeting. Larijani's deputy, Javad Vaeedi, had recently given an interview in which he claimed, falsely, that a comment in my previous report—that the IAEA was not in a position to verify the peaceful nature of Iran's program—had been "embedded" by the U.S. ambassador to the Agency. This made me angry: the Agency had gone out of its way to work with the Iranians objectively and professionally. For Iran to question our integrity was unacceptable.

I decided, in my current report, to be quite blunt: Indeed the IAEA could not reach any verdict on the Iranian program. Iran's position, I wrote, was sui generis; Iran had cheated on their reporting obligations for twenty years. As a result, we had no choice but to reconstruct the full history of their program. Until they responded to our questions and concerns with conclusive and satisfactory explanations, they would remain in the defendant's box.

The Board meeting took place amid much tension. A draft Security Council resolution with sanctions was in the pipeline. Abdul Minty, South Africa's governor on the Board, briefed me on the diplomatic efforts they, too, were making in the Security Council. The United States and the EU-3 would have preferred that South Africa and President Thabo Mbeki, with the weight they carried among developing countries, refrain from trying to find a solution on Iran. But South Africa was keen to play a role. Together with Switzerland, South Africa was ready to engage in an effort to resolve the Iran nuclear issue through negotiation and dialogue in accordance with the tenets of the NPT. In addition, South Africa held a seat on the Security Council and was not afraid to use it. Although the P-5+1 tended to dominate the proceedings, the South African ambassador in New York, Dumisani Kumalo, had declared to the council that his country was not there merely as window dressing.

I told Minty that, unless a breakthrough occurred soon, I believed we were heading toward a train wreck. He said he would speak to his government colleagues, and the very next day South Africa submitted a series of amendments to the draft Security Council resolution. These included the call for a ninety-day time-out. They adjusted the proposed sanctions to focus on the nuclear program. They clarified that any decision to lift a suspension would be based on the IAEA's technical judgment and not the council's political judgment.

The South African amendments could have created problems for the Western powers, who were intent on having the resolution adopted unanimously. The P-5 + 1 ignored South Africa's proposals in public but began acting immediately behind the scenes to exert pressure on the other governments—as well as on Johannesburg—to vote in favor of the unaltered resolution. Their tactics worked; Minty called me the day before the resolution's adoption to say that none of the eight other members of the council had spoken up in support of the proposed amendments. In the end, South Africa's efforts had only delayed the inevitable.

The Security Council adopted Resolution 1747 by unanimous vote on March 24, 2007, calling once again on Iran to comply with suspension of its enrichment program. Sanctions included banning Iran's arms imports and exports, freezing assets, and restricting the travel of individuals engaged in the country's nuclear activities. British ambassador Sir Emyr Jones-Parry read a statement on behalf of the P-5 + 1 expressing readiness to continue talks with Iran. The statement included ideas on restarting negotiations based on the language I had proposed. Of course, my suggestion had been to present these ideas to Iran in confidence, before adopting a resolution, not publicly, in conjunction with punishment.

Interestingly, Jones-Parry's statement claimed that the resolution's purpose was to "eliminate the possibility of Iran acquiring a nuclear-weapon capability." This was a far cry from previous language, used by the United States and others, which had expressed certainty that Iran already had a nuclear weapon program—a certainty that rested, as Jack Straw had once put it, on "not a whiff" of proof.[7] From this point on, the

---

7 As described in chapter 5, I had gotten into a public spat with the Americans in the November 2003 Board meeting, because of their anger when I said that we had not seen evidence linking Iran's nuclear material or activities to a nuclear weapons program.

Americans shifted their vocabulary to speak only of Iran's nuclear weapon "ambitions" or "intentions." It was small comfort.

By mid-May 2007, our inspectors had determined that the Iranians had installed a total of ten 164-centrifuge cascades in the underground industrial enrichment facility at Natanz. Three more cascades were under construction. An additional two cascades were running above ground, in the pilot plant.

According to Olli Heinonen, Iran had achieved its explicit goal of enriching uranium up to 5 percent. Our experts considered that the Iranians had acquired most of the knowledge needed for enrichment. And the pace of expansion was increasing. "They are now installing one cascade per week," Olli said. "By our estimation, if they keep up this pace, they will have three thousand centrifuges in place by the end of June, and eight thousand by Christmas." This would put the Iranians well on the way to industrial enrichment capacity. Obviously, they no longer saw a purpose in holding back.

At this point, I envisioned four possible futures for Iran's nuclear program, which I had the opportunity to lay out explicitly at a meeting in Spain with Prime Minister José Zapatero and his foreign minister Miguel Moratinos.

The first possibility was that Iran would choose voluntarily to return to zero enrichment, or full suspension. That seemed most unlikely.

The second was that the Iranians could be allowed a small R&D enrichment program, as a face-saving gesture. In return, they could be asked to freeze, for a number of years, their efforts to go to an industrial scale. Iran would also have to allow the IAEA to do robust inspections to be able to verify the absence of undeclared nuclear activities—the most important aspect from a nonproliferation perspective. Iran would have to help resolve any outstanding inspection issues. And they would need to commit themselves to remaining indefinitely a party to the NPT.

The third possibility was the status quo: remaining in the pointless stalemate on negotiations, with the West issuing more resolutions and sanctions as Iran moved steadily toward the threshold of industrial-scale enrichment, without adequate inspection or the Additional Protocol and without clarifying concerns about their past and current programs.

There was a fourth possibility. The radicals in the West might bomb Iran. This would produce Armageddon in the Middle East, a region already volatile and chaotic.

In my view, the only option was the second.

Zapatero and Moratinos were among the leaders who took the emerging threat of a major conflagration very seriously and engaged others—including Massimo D'Alema, the Italian foreign minister, and Jean-Claude Juncker, the prime minister of Luxembourg—to be ready to support any diplomatic initiative that might avoid a clash.

Facing the truth of where we were on the issue seemed important, but my efforts to bring clarity caused tempers to flare. On May 15, 2007, I gave an interview to David Sanger of the *New York Times* in which I stated that by now Iran had pretty much gained the knowledge to enrich uranium, even if they still needed to perfect it. "People will not like to hear it," I said, "but that's a fact." I added that the purpose of the demand for suspension—which was to deny Iran this knowledge—had been "overtaken by events."

I repeated the same lines in a long interview with the Spanish news service Grupo Vocento,[8] adding that it was incomprehensible to me that the Americans were ready to talk to the Iranians about security in Iraq but not about "the elephant in the room"—the nuclear issue. I also was critical about the lack of progress on disarmament.

The Americans and the French were furious. Greg Schulte, the U.S. ambassador, dropped by with a message from Rice saying that, to her deep disappointment, my media statements were undercutting the unity of the international community and their diplomatic efforts. I was giving motivation, she said, for those who wanted to use military force.

"Tell Rice," I said to Schulte, "that I am equally disappointed that she did not understand the purpose of my statements, which is to show that the current strategy is not working and that the opportunity still exists

---

8 Interview with Grupo Vocento, by Dario Valcarcel and Borja Bergareche, "Detecto una escalada gradual que aleja una solución pacífica con Irán," ABC, May 17, 2007.

to adjust the strategy." I laid out for him the four scenarios I envisioned as alternative futures for Iran. The worst possible outcome—the use of force—remained a danger. I referred him to an interview that John Bolton had given the same day to Fox News, in which he implied that the United States might yet take this route.[9]

The Americans, Schulte said, did not trust the Iranians. That was pretty obvious, I replied. The United States, he added, needed to maintain its "moral clarity" until Iran abided by the Security Council resolution. It was a poor choice of words; I considered asking when the United States might achieve sufficient "moral clarity" to get rid of its nuclear arsenal, but I said nothing.

As he was about to leave, Schulte hinted that if the Agency was going to be "politicized"—meaning, I assumed, that if I was going to continue to speak in the same vein—Rice had told him the Americans could treat the IAEA budget like that of the Universal Postal Union. The reference was to an argument I frequently made to the Board that Member States should distinguish among UN agencies in terms of their mandates and relative budgetary priorities.

This was a cheap shot, and I told Schulte so. "You are the first ones who have benefited from the Agency," I declared. "And if Member States decide not to pay their dues, I will be happy to shut the Agency's doors."

Two days later, on May 25, Schulte returned with the French and British ambassadors to make a formal demarche. They managed to drag with them a reluctant-looking Japanese deputy ambassador, Shigeki Sumi.[10] He sat quietly during the entire meeting and later told some colleagues that he was embarrassed but under orders to attend. I suspect the Japanese were recruited as stand-ins for the Germans, who had declined to join in.

---

9 Bolton's statement: "If you believe, as I do, that Iran is never going to be chatted out of its nuclear weapons, because it sees the nuclear weapons program as its trump card, then the only recourse is to dramatically ratchet up the economic and political pressure on Iran and keep open the option of regime change or even military force." Interview on *Hannity and Colmes*, Fox News, May 21, 2007. Retrieved at www.realclearpolitics.com/articles/2007/05/interview_with_john_bolton_on_1.html.

10 The ambassador, Yukiya Amano, to his delight, was traveling and unavailable.

The ambassadors repeated the same rhetoric about my public statements: I was dividing the international community and undermining the Security Council and the IAEA Board. The French and the Americans said they also were unhappy about my statements on disarmament, which, according to Schulte, were not part of my mandate. It was my duty, I responded, to advise them from a nonproliferation perspective, and I could see a crisis developing. Additionally, the IAEA Statute charges the Agency with furthering "the establishment of safeguarded worldwide disarmament." When I spoke at outside forums, I noted, it was not as the IAEA Director General, representing the views of the Board, but as an international public servant. "For ten years," I said, "I have been drawing attention to the linkage between nuclear proliferation and the sluggish pace of disarmament, and I will continue to do so."

I reminded Schulte that, when it suited the Americans, as in the case of the U.S.-India nuclear agreement, they referred to me freely as "the custodian of the NPT," but when I spoke against their arms control policies, my role suddenly narrowed. When the French ambassador, François-Xavier Deniau, insisted that Iran had a nuclear weapons program, I reminded him that, at the time of the inspections in Iraq, he had personally informed me that Iraq had retained "little amounts" of chemical and biological weapons, a claim that turned out to be bogus. He did not respond.

Western alarmism notwithstanding, Iran's rapid expansion of its enrichment operations, after an extended period of relative restraint, was indeed cause for concern. It signaled a shift: resignation to the fact that the West would not show flexibility or compromise and determination to pursue the nuclear technology that many Iranians viewed as a national achievement. From the Iranian perspective, the acceleration was also probably intended to put pressure on the West to agree on a compromise that would stop short of Iran fully suspending its enrichment program.

My perception was confirmed by Swiss state secretary Michael Ambühl on his return from yet another visit to Tehran. The Iranian position was hardening. Only two months earlier they had been willing to consider freezing enrichment activities at the R&D level for the duration of negotiations. This time Larijani had not been able to commit to any freeze or time-out during negotiations. He seemed willing only to commit not to enrich uranium beyond 5 percent. For the first time, he had mentioned the possibility that Iran might enrich uranium up to 20 percent to meet the fuel needs of its research reactors.

Given this news, I pressed Iran publicly to consider a self-imposed moratorium on expanding its enrichment. I gave a pointed interview as part of a BBC Radio 4 documentary, underscoring the high stakes at play.[11] "I have no brief other than to make sure we don't go into another war or that we go crazy killing each other," I said. "You do not want to give additional argument to the new crazies who say 'let's go and bomb Iran.'" A military strike against Iran's nuclear facilities, I declared, would be "an act of madness." Everyone wanted to know whom I meant by the "new crazies." I let them draw their own conclusions.

Diplomacy was losing ground. We needed a fresh direction. This time it originated with Larijani. More conservative than moderate, Larijani was nonetheless a persistent pragmatist, with a sharp, clear, logical mind—and a PhD in Western philosophy. As with Rowhani before him, some of Larijani's toughest struggles were at home in Tehran, working within the labyrinthine political establishment. Authority in Iran was diffuse, shared between the army, the Revolutionary Guard, the president, the clergy, the Majis, the Supreme Leader, and other less visible groups. This explained the slowness of Iran's deliberation process and its pendulum swings. Unlike in most of the Arab world, where a single strong-arm leader controlled by diktat, in Iran decisions were made by consensus. I sometimes referred to the regime as "a democracy within a theocracy." Whatever its merits or flaws, the system was proving terribly frustrating for Larijani: he simply did not have the necessary support to move forward on the diplomatic track.

Yet some in Tehran listened to his calls for restraint. I was heartened

---

11 "Inside the IAEA: A Year with the Nuclear Detectives," two-part BBC Radio 4 documentary, broadcast on May 31 and June 7, 2007.

that after the recent Security Council resolution, Iran had not followed through fully with its threat to block IAEA inspections at Natanz. They had applied a few token restrictions and left it at that. Clearly, some inside Iran still saw the value of playing by the rules.

Now, with no progress in sight on the P-5 + 1 negotiation front, Larijani decided to focus his efforts elsewhere. In our discussions, I had been pressing him on the need to clear up the remaining inspection issues and had outlined the multiple benefits to Iran of doing so. These issues included, for example: unresolved concerns related to centrifuge procurement; questions about the source of enriched uranium particles found in certain locations; apparent discrepancies in the AEOI's control of activities at the Gchine uranium mine; questionable procurement activities by a former head of Iran's Physics Research Center; and allegations that Iran had performed weaponization studies. On June 26, Larijani came to see me in Bad Tatzmannsdorf, south of Vienna, where the Agency's senior management were having a leadership retreat. Larijani was accompanied by one of his close deputies, Ali Monfared. With his inability to find a way past the suspension hurdle, Larijani seemed more despondent than at any time in the past. Now there were rumors of a fallout with Ahmadinejad. This meeting felt to me like one final effort on Larijani's part to find a way forward.

Iran, he announced, was ready to hammer out the details of a work plan with the Agency to address some of the IAEA's outstanding concerns. We could start with issues that would be relatively easy to resolve, such as discrepancies on the dates, quantities, and types of material involved in Iran's plutonium experiments. Larijani proposed that the Agency ask for specific inspection measures, without referring to the Additional Protocol, which the Majlis had earlier decided not to implement.

I was pleased to see Iran taking this step to cooperate with the Agency. I promised to send a group to Tehran to begin working out the details. I also urged Larijani to do what he could to halt the expansion of Iran's enrichment capacity. They did not need further development for R&D purposes, and it only served to provoke the West.

Particularly in conjunction with the work plan, a freeze in further expansion of capacity would send a positive signal. In fact, the Iranians made a few immediate goodwill gestures, such as allowing Agency inspectors to visit its heavy water reactor currently under construction at Arak. The inspectors also reported a marked slowdown in the installation of new centrifuge cascades at Natanz. A series of meetings on the work plan ensued in Tehran and Vienna. On certain sticking points, however, we had difficulty in getting a clear commitment from the Iranians. I decided to send a team of "heavyweights" to Tehran for a final push to wrap up the details: Olli Heinonen, who was now the deputy director general for safeguards, accompanied by Vilmos Cserveny, the Agency's head of external relations, and Johan Rautenbach, the legal adviser. To pressure Iran, I arranged for Olli to call me from his Tehran hotel with progress reports; knowing that our conversation would be recorded, I was tough on the telephone vis-à-vis the Iranians.

On August 27, 2007, Olli called to say they had agreed on a three-month timetable for resolving all the outstanding inspection issues. To circumvent resistance by the hard-liners in Tehran, the plan used indirect or vague language on certain topics—a little too vague, for my taste as a lawyer. But we had the upper hand, in that we would be the judges of Iran's implementation of the work plan. We also had an understanding with Larijani that he would do whatever he could to ensure a successful outcome.

Larijani called shortly after the terms of the plan were concluded and adopted by Tehran. His tone was upbeat—more so than I had heard in some time. He thanked me for the hard work of Olli and his team. That Tehran's leadership had signed on to the work plan was obviously a victory for Larijani's advocacy of cooperation with the Agency and rapprochement with the West. He also asked me to continue to speak out about the importance of Iran resuming negotiations with the P-5 + 1.

I told Larijani that the important thing now was to implement the work plan in good faith and according to schedule. Otherwise it would backfire, strengthening the arguments of those who would inevitably insist that Iran was just trying to buy time.

The Americans were quick to do just that. They belittled the importance of the work plan and nitpicked at its more awkwardly worded provisions. They cast doubt on the sincerity of Iran's commitment. The plan made them nervous: an uptick in Iran's cooperation with the IAEA weakened the chance of prodding China and Russia into imposing any further sanctions. Plus, if Tehran succeeding in resolving the outstanding issues about its past and present nuclear program, the Security Council's demand for Iran to suspend uranium enrichment would lose any logical basis.

A full-on blitzkrieg ensued in the media. The *Washington Post* published an editorial entitled "Rogue Regulator."

ElBaradei has made it clear he considers himself above his position as a UN civil servant. Rather than carry out the policy of the Security Council or the IAEA board, for which he nominally works, Mr. ElBaradei behaves as if he were independent of them, free to ignore their decisions and to use his agency to thwart their leading members—above all the United States.[12]

It went on to accuse me of "freelancing," and condemned the IAEA for "striking its own deal with the Iranian regime."

The *Economist* was also critical:

ElBaradei is using the deal with Iran to intervene directly in the policy debate, rather than limiting himself to an impartial look at the safeguards facts. Mr. ElBaradei may think he is making space for diplomacy. But easing the squeeze on Iran may well make it harder to find a diplomatic solution.[13]

Predictably, the *Jerusalem Post* took the attack one step further, with quotes such as "ElBaradei is a man of dubious integrity" and "ElBaradei has been Iran's primary international defender" and even "ElBaradei has used his power to facilitate the proliferation of nuclear energy for military

---

12 "Rogue Regulator: Mohamed ElBaradei Pursues a Separate Peace with Iran," *Washington Post*, September 5, 2007.
13 "In the Crossfire," *Economist*, September 13, 2007.

purposes."[14] A columnist in *Al-Hayat,* one of the leading newspapers in the Arab world, charged that I was acting in defiance of the Security Council resolutions, trying to give Iran a way to avoid additional sanctions and perfect its technology. Even the *New York Times* took a shot, in a lengthy profile that portrayed me as somewhere between "everyone's best hope" and "drunk with the power of [the] Nobel."[15] One journalist thought that the *Times* article had characterized me as a "dictatorial loon."[16]

In Vienna, the Americans reportedly gave their irritation more concrete expression. Abdul Minty, the South African ambassador, said he had heard from a journalist that the Americans were planning to orchestrate a campaign with the Board for a vote of no confidence in me for exceeding my mandate. The journalist had in his notes the names of twenty countries the Americans had targeted to lobby for their support. I was told that the media had received this information from Chris Ford, the U.S. deputy assistant secretary of state for arms control. In any case, after the rumor reached the Associated Press,[17] the U.S. Mission publicly denied that any such campaign was under way.

There was a great deal of irony to these attacks. It was not new for me to be castigated for speaking or acting beyond my brief. On most such previous occasions, the accusation came in response to my calls for more rapid progress on disarmament or my comments on the limited value of Security Council sanctions as a stand-alone diplomatic strategy. This time I was accused of freelancing for attempting to implement the IAEA's core verification mission. As early as August we were able to report progress to the Board due to the work plan: a number of nuclear verification issues had been resolved, because Iran had provided long-sought information. But this success was condemned. The truth was that the

---

14 Caroline Glick, "ElBaradei's Nuclear Policy," *Jerusalem Post,* August 27, 2007.

15 Elaine Sciolino and William J. Broad, "An Indispensable Irritant to Iran and Its Foes," *New York Times,* September 17, 2007.

16 Katrina vanden Heuvel, "Proponent of Diplomatic Solution for Iran Smeared by White House," *Nation.* Reprinted in "Bush, the Bomb, and Iran," *CBS News Opinion,* September 25, 2007.

17 "IAEA Chief ElBaradei Being Pressured on Iran—Diplomats," Associated Press, September 9, 2007.

Americans wanted only to portray Iran as a noncooperative pariah state, in violation of its international obligations and therefore deserving continued punishment. My reports were getting in the way of the Americans' preferred course of action.

For anyone who cared to see, the cards were now on the table. The hard-liners in the West were not concerned with clearing up these outstanding issues. Their focus was denying Iran technology through isolation, confrontational rhetoric, and ideological games. That might have been their business, but it was not mine. And I would not stand idly by while extremists planted the seeds for another devastating war in the Middle East.

The willingness of the press to be manipulated was particularly worrisome. Some of the key phrases used to criticize the Agency were repeated in the mainstream U.S. media, making me wonder whether the American government was behind an orchestrated campaign. I was reminded of the period leading up to the Iraq War. I found it interesting that, in all the analysis, there was not one substantive refutation of the policies or steps I had endorsed. The arguments were focused on casting doubt on my character and motivations.

I hit back. I gave several interviews making it clear that the IAEA had not seen any undeclared facilities in Iran nor any weaponization activities. Therefore, I said, in our assessment Iran did not constitute a clear and present danger requiring any kind of action beyond diplomacy. What was needed across the Middle East was more "soft power": education, intercultural dialogue, good governance, and development. Any use of force, I declared, would turn the Middle East into a ball of fire.

Negotiations with the P-5 + 1, meanwhile, were going nowhere. Despite Larijani's efforts to get back to "prenegotiations," Solana was blocked by the Americans from continuing. He told Larijani they could meet after the work plan was completed. On the other hand, the Russians and the Chinese told the other members of the P-5 + 1 that they would not support another set of sanctions. So the only game in town, for the moment, was the IAEA's work with the Iranians on the outstanding issues.

During the September Board meeting, I had an advance view of the EU-3's planned statement. It was quite negative. It omitted, pointedly, the customary expression of support for the Agency and its Director General as impartial and professional. I knew the French had been trying to delete this phrase for the last couple of Board meetings. This time they had managed to do it. I decided the best response was to walk out during the delivery of their speech, which I did. My seemingly simple act was widely reported in the media. The effect was to send a message to the rest of the Europeans that they should resist being lured into imprudent behavior by one or two countries inside the European Union, in this case, France.[18]

Bernard Kouchner, the new French foreign minister, declared in an interview about Iran on RTL Radio that "We have to prepare for the worst, and the worst is war." His interview occurred just as the IAEA was beginning its annual General Conference. I responded publicly with a reminder that, under international law, there were rules governing the use of military force, including authorization by the Security Council. Many politicians, including the Germans and the Russians, reacted strongly to Kouchner's statement, and he took hasty action to retract what he had said.[19]

After all the commotion over the work plan, in late September the P-5 + 1 endorsed it, urging Iran "to produce tangible results rapidly and effectively by clarifying all outstanding issues and concerns." The Chinese and the Russians had already made clear their support for the plan. I was told that the EU-3 had cautioned the United States that attacking the Agency was counterproductive and could backfire.

For whatever reason, the Americans abruptly reversed their hostile position. Only one week earlier, Condoleezza Rice had taken a swipe at the Agency and, by implication, me.[20] "The IAEA is not in the business of

---

18 In fact, it was not uncommon for me to hear other members of the European Union express private resentment of the "big three"—France, the United Kingdom, and Germany—and particularly the first two. The other European countries seldom felt they were genuinely consulted on what were nonetheless characterized as joint political stances on Iran. In particular, some viewed the United Kingdom as a sort of U.S. Trojan horse inside the European Union.
19 Katrin Bennhold and Elaine Sciolino, "After Talk of War, Cooler Words in France on Iran," *New York Times*, September 17, 2007.
20 Sue Pleming, "Rice Swipes at IAEA, Urges Bold Action on Iran," Reuters, September 17, 2007.

diplomacy," she declared. "The IAEA is a technical agency that has a board of governors of which the United States is a member." Now, in quite a diplomatic about-face, Nicholas Burns, undersecretary of state for political affairs, when asked about U.S. criticism of the plan, implied that the Americans had supported it all along.

The complicated political maneuvering in both Washington and Tehran made progress challenging. When I continued to urge the Iranians not to expand their enrichment capacity beyond three thousand centrifuges and pushed for them to implement the Additional Protocol, Larijani said, "I am doing my best, but you must understand that I am working in a difficult atmosphere." Even with a firsthand view, it was hard to understand the dynamics of the Iranian political situation. The slow-moving, diffuse decision-making structure, added to what seemed like a negotiating culture shaped by the bazaar, made the Iranians inherently difficult to deal with.

The American side was no less opaque. The strategy of dogged repetition, in the absence of any proof, of the argument that Iran intended to produce nuclear weapons seemed to convince the American public, and even the U.S. Congress—and at times the Americans seemed baffled or angry that it failed to convince much of the rest of the international community. Late in 2007, I had an intelligence briefing at the U.S. Mission. Among other topics the Americans went over their suspicions that Iran, at least in the past, had conducted certain experiments and procured certain equipment and components that could only be interpreted as an indication of their intent to develop nuclear weapons.[21] However, they did acknowledge—as in most previous intelligence briefings—that there was no indication that Iran had undeclared nuclear material. After

---

21 In late 2005, the United States had first briefed the IAEA on a package of information they had received claiming nuclear weaponization studies by Iran related to uranium conversion, high explosives testing, and modification of Shihab-3 missiles to carry a nuclear weapon. Iran had called these allegations baseless, and since the United States had restricted giving the IAEA documentation on this topic to share with Tehran, the Agency had been limited in its ability to verify the information.

the Iraq debacle, the U.S. intelligence community had become more circumspect in its assessments. The briefing essentially confirmed what I had been saying, yet this caution somehow did not shape the American public posture.

At the end of this particular meeting, Schulte presented a signed picture of me and Rice, taken at our most recent meeting. She had signed it "With admiration and best regards." It struck me as funny, coming on the heels of a public spat. But the act illustrated the contradictory and fractured nature of the American Iran policy.

Concurrent with my fall United States intelligence briefing, Bush made a series of outlandish comments on the Iran situation. A speech to the American Legion in Reno was punctuated with inflammatory imagery: "Iran's active pursuit of technology that could lead to nuclear weapons threatens to put a region already known for instability and violence under the shadow of a nuclear holocaust."[22] In an October 17 press conference, he remarked, "I've told people that, if you're interested in avoiding World War III, it seems like you ought to be interested in preventing [the Iranians] from having the knowledge necessary to make a nuclear weapon."[23] Speaking on a German news channel on November 14, he casually lobbed another verbal grenade: "If you want to have a Third World War," he quipped, "you need only drop a nuclear bomb on Israel."[24] I didn't know whether the purpose of these statements was to ratchet up the pressure against Iran or to prepare the ground for a military strike, but either way, they were reckless, and disturbingly reminiscent of early 2003.[25]

Yet Rice, at around the same time, made remarks that seemed designed

---

22 Damien McElroy, "Bush Warns of Iran 'Nuclear Holocaust,'" *Telegraph*, August 28, 2007.

23 "Bush Warns of 'World War III' if Iran Gains Nuclear Weapons," Associated Press, October 18, 2007. Retrieved at www.foxnews.com/story/0,2933,303097,00.html.

24 "German TV Interview: U.S. President Repeats 'Third World War' Warning," November 14, 2007. Retrieved at www.world-peace-society.net/eecore/index.php?/site/C78/.

25 Seymour Hersh would report that in late 2007 Bush was lobbying the Congress for up to four hundred million dollars to support covert operations in Iran, in activities "designed to destabilize the country's religious leadership." "Preparing the Battlefield," *New Yorker*, July 7, 2008.

to lower the pitch. "The way forward," she told RTR TV Moscow, "is to give every chance and support to the efforts of Mohamed ElBaradei to resolve outstanding issues on Iran's programs."

Wait. Had I just heard that correctly? Rice continued: "It is not a question of whether Iran has a nuclear weapon today. It is a question of enrichment and reprocessing capability, the so-called fuel cycle."

I tried to find a coherent thread. On the one hand, the Iranian nuclear risk had been characterized as lower than previously thought—no longer a matter of Iran's imminent possession of a nuclear weapon, but in terms of its future intention. On the other, the Security Council had invoked the grimmest chapter in the UN Charter, and Bush was all but ready to pull out his six-guns and begin firing. Meanwhile, a continent away, North Korea, who was raising a generation of children debilitated by malnutrition and diverting every ounce of effort to pull off a successful nuclear test, was being handled with kid gloves.

A handful of concerned American senators and congressmen continued on another track to attempt to maintain some dialogue with Iran. Senator Arlen Specter, still a Republican at that time, contacted me a number of times to facilitate a visit to Tehran.[26]

The last such request came after Ahmadinejad was given a humiliating reception at Columbia University in September 2007.[27] Specter was very upset about what had occurred. "You don't invite a guest to insult him," he said. He wanted to arrange a visit for seven senators and congressmen, including Chris Dodd, Joe Biden, and Tom Lantos. As in any such case, I passed the word to Larijani, urging Tehran to respond positively, as a foot in the door toward dialogue. But the trip did not go forward; the Iranian leadership was in no mood to accept a visit from American public figures.

---

26 Gareth Evans, the head of the International Crisis Group and former Australian foreign minister, requested my assistance for a similar venture.
27 Ahmadinejad was invited to speak at the Columbia University School of International and Public Affairs as part of its annual World Leaders Forum. When he arrived, he was greeted with thousands of demonstrators, and university president Lee Bollinger introduced him with a harsh series of criticisms about Ahmadinejad's political views, which bordered on personal insult.

This period was marked overall by contradictory, haphazard stabs at engagement and, in the now-usual way of the Iranian file, a pattern of doors opening and closing. In mid-October, the French political director Gérard Araud came to see me at the request of Bernard Kouchner. I did not know what to expect, given recent statements by Kouchner and President Sarkozy, who had said that if diplomacy failed, we would be "faced with an alternative that I call catastrophic: an Iranian bomb or the bombing of Iran."[28]

Araud's tone and views, however, were surprisingly positive. The French were eager to work closely with me on any initiative that could return the focus to negotiations between Iran and the P-5+1, he said. Kouchner was keen to invite me to come to Paris. In their view, Iran was feeling self-assured and seemed to be planning to wait out the Bush administration. The French, however, were still worried about possible U.S. military action against Iran in the spring or summer of 2008, before Bush left office.

That same day, Vladimir Putin visited Iran to press for a return to negotiations. According to the briefing I received from the Russians, Khamenei told Putin that Iran "might consider a moratorium on enrichment activities." Putin seemed to have proposed a variation of the double time-out. His visit was seen as a signal that Russia would not stand for U.S. military action. In a speech at the Caspian Sea summit, Putin emphasized the right of all countries to nuclear technology, and the importance of "respecting each other's interests and sovereignty, and refraining not only from any use of force whatsoever, but even from mentioning the use of force."[29]

Despite these positive glimmers, Ali Larijani resigned his post only days after Putin's summit speech. In Tehran, a government spokesman announced that Larijani had previously "resigned a number of times" and that the president had "finally accepted his resignation." Saeed Jalili,

---

28 Elaine Sciolino, "Iran Risks Attack over Atomic Push, French President Says," *New York Times,* August 27, 2007.
29 Muriel Mirak-Weissbach, "Putin Puts Forward a War-Avoidance Plan," *Executive Intelligence Review,* October 26, 2007. Retrieved at www.intellibriefs.blogspot.com/2007/10/caspian-summit-putin-puts-forward-war.html.

deputy foreign minister and a known confidante of Ahmadinejad's, was Larijani's replacement.

Larijani's resignation did not really come as a surprise, despite the success of the work plan. All of his efforts to find a formula for sustained negotiation with the P-5 + 1 had been blocked. But this was not a good development. It meant that Javier Solana, who even under more auspicious circumstances had not succeeded as point man for the P-5 + 1, would now be trying to wring concessions out of a hard-line Iranian conservative. When Solana called to brief me on the results of his first meeting with Jalili, he said nothing much had come out of it. I had expected little else.

Rice and I had not spoken in months when she called me at the end of October. "You seem to be picking on us more than picking on the Iranians," she said. "Well," I replied, "you've been throwing curve balls at me for no good reason." Of course I supported the Security Council's call for Iran to suspend its enrichment activities, I told her, and I continued to press Tehran to do so, or at least not to expand capacity. On that front, we seemed to be having moderate success; our latest reports indicated that Iran had built no new cascades and was not feeding much material into the roughly three thousand centrifuges in operation.

As for sanctions, this was a policy judgment for the Security Council, but I continued to see evidence that sanctions could not be viewed as an overall solution. Pressure only hardened the Iranian position, which was why Larijani had been so frustrated. "The only way in which Iran might suspend enrichment," I said to Rice, "is through negotiation, with active U.S. engagement, plus a face-saving formula and a gesture of good intention."

I mentioned the possibility that I would soon go to Tehran to meet with Ayatollah Khamenei. In that context, I asked her about the American bottom line on the conditions for negotiation. If Iran agreed to a freeze, Rice replied, they could meet with the other members of the P-5+1, but the United States would take part only based on Iran's full suspension.

"Even if the suspension were only for two months," she said, "I would personally be ready to participate in talks with them, and to engage on all issues." But suspension remained a red line she could not cross.

There was some hope that direct interaction with the Supreme Leader of Iran would help explain international perceptions of Iran's actions and reinforce the benefits to Iran of increased levels of cooperation. An opportunity for me to meet with Ayatollah Khamenei had been some time in the making. Two days before I was due to leave for Tehran, however, Olli got a message that, while I had meetings confirmed with President Ahmadinejad, Jalili, and Aghazadeh, it would not be possible at this stage for me to see Khamenei. In that case I wanted to cancel the trip. The reply came the next morning: "The Supreme Leader sends all the best to you," I was told, "but he believes it would be better all around if the visit took place after the next Board meeting."

Two senior members of Iran's negotiating team with whom I had been working for years dropped by to explain that the meeting with the Supreme Leader remained very important as a means of altering the dynamic within Iran—meaning, I assumed, that if I could explain certain perspectives directly to Khamenei, it might be a means of moderating the hard-liners. But Khamenei was concerned that my visit should not be interpreted as an attempt by Tehran to exert pressure on the Agency, which it might if I came to Iran ahead of giving my November report to the Board. I told the Iranians the next chance for a trip to Tehran would not come before the second part of December. The situation was getting precarious, I warned them. "You should not take the prospect of military force too lightly," I said. In the absence of my trip, I took the opportunity to pass along that Condoleezza Rice would be willing to join the negotiations if they were willing to undertake a two-month suspension. The timing was right: the U.S. administration was eager for a foreign policy success.

This was precisely why they were so keen for me to meet with Khamenei, the Iranians said, to explain to him what needed to be done and the potential benefits. The next morning, they called to ask if I would

consider visiting Iran the weekend before the November Board meeting, but the timing was now inappropriate. Without the guarantee of a
substantial breakthrough, the trip would be seen as a publicity stunt
and could backfire for everyone.

With the work plan well under way, but controversies still raging over
Iran's nuclear program and how to deal with it, affirmation of the Agency's
approach came from an unlikely source: a new U.S. National Intelligence Estimate on Iran. On December 3, while I was in Montevideo, I
received the news of the estimate and my office emailed a copy of the
published part, the executive summary. The essence of the NIE findings
was that Iran had pursued a nuclear weapons program in the past, but
that these efforts had ceased in 2003.

From Uruguay, I dictated a press release to one of my assistants, Syed
Akbaruddin, a shrewd, soft-spoken Indian diplomat. "The NIE estimate,"
I wrote,

> tallies with the Agency's consistent statements over the last few years
> that, although Iran still needs to clarify some important aspects of its
> past and present nuclear activities, the Agency has no concrete evi-
> dence of an ongoing nuclear weapons program or undeclared nuclear
> facilities in Iran.

I urged all parties to re-engage in negotiations without delay.

The National Intelligence Estimate was also obviously a surprise to
the Bush administration. Bush made an inexplicable attempt to declare
that the findings changed nothing. Iran, he declared, was still dangerous. And the report and its authors were promptly vilified by U.S. hard-
liners and their supporters in Israel. But the report undeniably took the
wind out of the sails of those who wanted to present Iran as an imminent threat and press for a confrontational approach. On my return to
Vienna, I received a follow-up briefing by U.S. intelligence. They did not
share the supposed evidence that had led them to confirm the existence
of a past Iranian nuclear program, other than to refer to the same unveri-

fied set of allegations about weaponization studies that had already been discussed with the Agency. They did note that Khamenei remained, in their view, as powerful as ever, and they emphasized the importance of my upcoming visit to Iran.

For the IAEA, the National Intelligence Estimate was a breath of fresh air. It validated the Agency's assessment of the Iranian nuclear threat and was a vindication of my past few years of vigorous advocacy for a diplomatic solution. As in the case of Iraq, the Agency's analysis and instincts had proved to be on target. Also as in Iraq, none of the key figures in Western governments bothered to acknowledge the validity of our judgment, let alone apologize for the grief they had caused us.

Coming in the favorable wake of the NIE report, my mid-January 2008 meeting with Supreme Leader Ayatollah Ali Hoseyni Khamenei seemed propitious. I had to wade through a phalanx of officials to get there, but I was willing to be patient.

On the Lufthansa flight to Tehran, a couple of Iranians who lived abroad came to thank me for my refusal to buckle under pressure. They affirmed my sense that even Iranians who were not very fond of the ruling regime supported its quest to acquire technology.

One woman came to my seat to ask about my wife. "She is Iranian, isn't she?"

"No," I said, "she is Egyptian." I pondered how quickly rumors can turn into fact.

On our first evening in Tehran, Aghazadeh hosted the customary opening dinner, in a former palace of the shah, part of a compound of palaces that had been built for him and his family. It was in northern Tehran, not far from where I was staying at the Esteqlal Hotel—itself no palace, if the finest the city had to offer.

The meetings got under way. To each of the Iranian officials with whom I spoke, I made a few core points: I was speaking not only as the Director General of the IAEA, but also as someone who was concerned about the interests of the Iranian people. I had no wish to see Iran subjected to escalating sanctions by the UN Security Council. It was important, I said, for Iran to create the right conditions to enable negotiation with the West—and the United States in particular—and to cultivate better relationships with its neighbors in the Gulf, who were becoming intimidated by the prospect of regional domination by Iran. I stressed the urgency of addressing the escalating concern over the ultimate aim of Iran's enrichment program.

But at every opportunity, I drove home one key point: to seize the moment. The timing was very favorable for Iran, for three reasons: the recent U.S. National Intelligence Estimate; Iran's cooperation with the IAEA under the work plan, which had resulted in a positive report to the Board; and a recent announcement by President Ahmadinejad stating that Iran had mastered nuclear fuel technology based on successfully assembling and operating three thousand centrifuges.

"All this," I said, "puts you in a position of strength. The Americans would be willing to start negotiations if you suspended enrichment for even two months. Why not take the initiative? Rather than waiting for more pressure from the West, declare victory based on having mastered the technology and announce a two-month suspension as a way to show your good intentions."

German foreign minister Steinmeier, I told them, would be meeting with his five counterparts on January 22. Russia and China had requested a strategy discussion before agreeing on any additional Security Council action. "Time is of the essence," I warned them. "The earlier you move forward, the better your chance of preempting a third resolution."

Yet the Iranian officials seemed rather relaxed about the nuclear situation. There was no sense of urgency. Foreign Minister Manouchehr Mottaki pointed out that Iran had tried in the past to compromise—suspending enrichment for a time or voluntarily implementing the Additional Protocol. They had received nothing for their actions. "Now it is up to the other side to also make some compromises," he said.

Clearly, having the upper hand made the Iranians bold. Mottaki told me that Iran had improved security in Iraq. "Who do you think took care of Moktada al-Sadr and his militia?" he asked. Iran's level of trade with countries such as the United Arab Emirates and China was at an all-time high, he said, in the tens of billions of dollars. So in terms of economic hardship, Iran was not intimidated or worried by the threat of additional sanctions. The prospect was more of a thumb in the eye, a matter of disrespect and insult.

What stood out from these conversations was the bewildering display of Iran's political factions and power centers. Each official brought his own view of how to deal with the nuclear situation and with the West in general. Senior figures seemed to analyze the nuclear issue in terms of its impact not just on the country but also on their personal careers and prestige.

From the hard-liners' perspective, a third Security Council resolution would reawaken resentment of the Americans, which would bolster the hard-liners' popularity just as a first round of elections for the Majlis approached in mid-March. Fears of a U.S. military strike had diminished and Iranians were starting to focus on the government's miserable economic performance. For supporters of Khamenei, elections that delivered a more moderate Majlis would put the leader in a much stronger position to deal with the nuclear issue in a more conciliatory manner.

My meeting with Saeed Jalili, Iran's new chief nuclear negotiator, was informative. He viewed the West with undisguised distrust and was especially critical of Javier Solana, his counterpart at the EU-3. At their last meeting, Jalili said, Solana had outlined four points for the dialogue between Iran and the P-5+1: democracy in the region; terrorism and arms control; energy needs; and economic cooperation. I was later told that Jalili had also come to the meeting ready to sign on to a Swiss proposal to limit the build-up of centrifuges, but Solana was not open to such a discussion.[30]

"Before we engage in negotiation with the West," Jalili concluded, "we need to establish a paradigm for what we are doing. Is this supposed

---

30 I had heard none of this from Solana. His report had been only that the meeting had gone badly, achieving nothing after five hours. What I realized was that, despite frequent private assurances that he agreed with my point of view, Solana did not have the flexibility or the mandate to take initiative, particularly in light of U.S. insistence that nothing short of suspension was acceptable as a starting point.

to be a negotiation between two enemies or two friends?" It was a question I heard frequently from senior Iranian officials, reflecting their focus on the larger goal based on trust, mutual accommodation, and respect.

My meeting with Ahmadinejad took place in the president's palace, another of the former shah's residences, but the furnishings did not match in any way the grandiosity of the building.

Olli Heinonen and Vilmos Cserveny accompanied me. Ahmadinejad was soft-spoken and friendly in his reception. His personal style was in distinct contrast to his demonization in the West. He was courteous and reasonable throughout the exchange, although he plainly had strong views on what was right and wrong. I made my points firmly but did not try to confront or challenge him, intent as I was on moving things forward.

I avoided raising Ahmadinejad's inflammatory statements about Israel and the Holocaust. I had been told by Farsi speakers that his notorious comment about Israel being "wiped off the map" had been a Western media misinterpretation. Ahmadinejad, they said, had been speaking not about the State of Israel but about the "Zionist regime." I was reminded of an encounter in Jerusalem in 1977 when Menachem Begin, Israeli prime minister at the time, had given a speech to the Egyptian delegation in which he had invoked the assertion that there was "no such thing as a Palestinian people," only Palestinian Arabs and Palestinian Jews. His statement, too, was emotionally charged; the question, then as now, was how to get past it and embark on meaningful dialogue. In any case, Ahmadinejad had been repeating a quote originally made by Iran's first Islamist leader, Ayatollah Khomeini. However ill-advised, he would be unwilling to retract what he said and there was nothing to be gained by addressing it at this meeting.

Ahmadinejad responded positively when I stressed the need for Iran to improve relations with its neighbors. He mentioned that he had attended the Summit of the Gulf Cooperation Council. The Saudis, he said, had invited him to the Hadj. Clearly, public expression of cordial relations with Iran by many leaders in the Gulf contrasted pointedly with their private statements of fear and distrust.

With Ahmadinejad and Jalili, I again raised the notion of inviting the U.S. senators and congressmen. "It clearly would be in your interest," I said, "to engage in rational discussions with influential Americans who can come to Tehran and hear your views firsthand." Ahmadinejad said he would consider this proposal. I was told that they would likely come back to me with a positive answer within a couple of weeks. In fact, this never went any further.

My most significant meeting was with the Supreme Leader of the Islamic Republic of Iran. He rarely meets with non-Muslim foreign leaders. For his lofty title, Ayatollah Khamenei operates out of a very modest place, far simpler than Ahmadinejad's offices. His working and living quarters reminded me of a very modest country house. We met in what appeared to be a living room, plain to the point of austerity. We sat on simple chairs; the other attendees were seated on a bench. As always, tea was served, with dried fruit and nuts.

I had come alone. Khamenei was accompanied by his foreign policy adviser, Ali Akbar Velayati, a former foreign minister. Aghazadeh and Saeedi were also present. I found it curious that neither Ahmadinejad nor Jalili had been invited.

In keeping with custom, we embraced in Iranian and Muslim tradition. Khamenei, tall and thin, had the look and manner of a father figure, reserved but affable and sensitive. At times I thought he almost seemed a bit frail. But he was in full command of the details and undeniably in charge.

Our meeting began with a brief public segment, which was televised. Speaking to the cameras, Khamenei declared that the Islamic Republic of Iran would never be brought to its knees—meaning, from what I could gather, that no amount of sanctions would get Iran to suspend enrichment or end what they recognized as their legitimate right.

When the camera crews had shuffled their way out, I opened the exchange. I told Khamenei I was speaking primarily as a friend of the Iranian people. I repeated the set of messages I had articulated to the other Iranian officials: the progress on Iran's file at the IAEA, the readiness of the P-5+1 to return to negotiations, and the benefits of moving rapidly to take advantage of the current dynamic. Missteps, I said, had been taken by both sides; but we now had an opportunity to learn from the past and move forward.

Khamenei listened attentively. He thanked me for the independence I had maintained in the face of external pressure. This, in his view, had added to the Agency's credibility. Iran was committed to work with the IAEA to resolve all remaining nuclear issues, he said. In fact, the IAEA should be Iran's only interlocutor; it had been a mistake to discuss Iran's nuclear program with others. Once the Security Council returned the Iranian file to the Agency, he added, Iran would be ready to implement the Additional Protocol.

But with a small motion of his hand, Khamenei dismissed suspending or freezing Iran's enrichment operations. This, he said, was merely a distraction invented by the Americans. The real issue was U.S. anger over Iran's emerging role in the region. Khamenei was ready to engage with the West on all issues of regional security and trade, but he saw no reason for Iran to show flexibility about enrichment. Iran, he insisted, had never had a nuclear weapons program; to do so, he told me, would be against Islam. I knew he had repeatedly made this statement publicly.

I mentioned how important I believed it was to restore relations with Egypt and Iran's other neighbors. Khamenei nodded, replying that Iran had been ready to take this action for some time; however, he did not believe that Mubarak was "able to take such a decision." I couldn't tell whether he was referring to Mubarak's lack of leadership or to the pressure Mubarak was under from the Americans and his own Egyptian intelligence chiefs. I did not pursue the topic.

As part of our visit, the Iranians offered to take us to visit their R&D laboratory, where they were working on their "next-generation" centrifuges: a modified version of the P-2 machine, which would be much more efficient than the P-1 model in use at Natanz. A number of prototypes were in development, which they planned to test in the pilot enrichment facility at Natanz. The laboratory itself presented a striking image. It resembled any Western lab: clean, organized, and filled with young scientists and engineers working on various instruments and computers. The conspicuous difference was the young women in traditional chadors, skilled in advanced software and ultramodern design techniques, hard at work enhancing Iran's uranium enrichment capability.

Aghazadeh, who accompanied our group, mentioned proudly that most of the material and equipment in use was now being indigenously produced in Iran. For both Olli and me, the implications of this were immediately apparent: tracking Iran's enrichment activities would be more difficult, since there would be less import-export activity and procurement reporting. In Olli's view, the shift to indigenous production also implied that Iran had no plans to go to industrial-scale operation at Natanz for a couple of years. It would make little sense to use up their limited supply of certain materials—for example, maraging steel—just as they were about to embark on developing a more efficient model.

I gave no media interviews during my time in Tehran. I knew the Iranian press would spin whatever I said. I issued a short press statement upon my return to Vienna, saying we had agreed to accelerate the process of cooperation.

Back in Vienna, I was flooded with phone calls. David Miliband rang on my first day back. Steinmeier and Kislyak came to see me. I gave each of them—and all the other members of the P-5+1—a detailed briefing emphasizing the likely negative impacts of pushing for a third Security Council resolution with additional sanctions. The provocation of another resolution could well induce Iran to cut its cooperation with the Agency, just as we were poised, under the work plan, to discuss the details of the alleged past weaponization studies and the potential involvement of the Iranian military in the nuclear program. I also mentioned what I'd heard about the likely impact of such a resolution on the outcome of the Majlis elections in mid-March.

Steinmeier was not optimistic that the six countries would agree on any other way forward. "The U.S. has not understood this region for the past thirty years," he said. "If the council decides to go for a third resolution," I urged him, "at least try to make it somewhat encouraging to Iran." Instead of more sanctions, why not give Iran credit for its recent cooperation with the IAEA? "And please," I pressed, "try to allow us time to complete the work plan." We were somewhat behind the original schedule but still making steady progress, and now was not the moment to take action that might induce Iran to withdraw cooperation.

The P-5+1 met in Berlin on January 22. To my considerable disappointment, Steinmeier made a public statement that the six countries had agreed on the content of a new Security Council resolution to be considered in New York "in the coming days and weeks." To me, he had promised that no resolution would be adopted before the end of February.

In the midst of the chatter about a new resolution, support for dialogue with Iran came from a surprising quarter: in an interview on CNN, Colin Powell said, "We're talking to them in Baghdad every few months about security matters. And if we can do that in Baghdad with our ambassador and their representatives, I don't see why we can't speak to them in other fora." It was the first time I had heard Powell—now out of office—taking a swipe at the Bush administration's policy on Iran:

> America is a strong, powerful nation. We are politically powerful, economically powerful, militarily powerful. And it seems to me that with all of this power and all of this influence in the world, we should be willing to talk to nations that are basically weaker than we are. And we should not be afraid to be seen talking to them.[31]

But Powell might as well have held his breath. Nicholas Burns called on February 13 to ask me to make a public statement in support of a third resolution by the Security Council. "That would make a tremendous difference," he said. Although I told him I would see what I could do, of course I could not make such an endorsement. It was bizarre that this request was coming from the same U.S. administration that continued to complain about my getting involved "in politics." And when I saw the draft Security Council resolution, I noted a striking paragraph "commending the IAEA for its efforts to resolve outstanding issues relating to Iran's nuclear programme in the work plan"—this from the people who had so vociferously condemned the plan. If it was now considered a sensible approach, why issue sanctions that would have every chance of derailing it?

---

31 Transcript retrieved at www.archives.cnn.com/TRANSCRIPTS/0802/10/le.01 .html.

• • •

I was to see yet one more erratic shift in the Iranian story, this time on a trip to France to meet with President Sarkozy, Foreign Minister Kouchner, and other French officials. A Western foreign minister had said that, in his view, French foreign policy had become "crazy." I had heard similar thoughts through other diplomatic back channels: the French were getting on the Europeans' nerves.

Sarkozy showed up to the meeting without a jacket and immediately ordered coffee for himself. After a while he looked at me and asked if I wanted coffee. No one else present was offered anything—a peculiar contrast to my meeting a few years earlier with Chirac, and to the formality generally associated with the Elysée.

Sarkozy jumped right in, scoldingly aggressive. "Mr. ElBaradei," he intoned, "I'm a friend of the U.S. and Israel."

I was tempted to say, "So what?" but I held my tongue.

"I want to tell you how I feel," he went on. He underscored the "mortal danger" of Iran's program. The Iranians, he said, were using me and the Agency. His fear was that the Americans or the Israelis would bomb Iran. As he was making his case, his cell phone began vibrating. He stepped out to take the call. I saw the subtle looks of disapproval around the table. Sarkozy returned and picked up where he had left off.

At last he paused. I saw no point in holding back. "Mr. Sarkozy," I told him, "you need to understand how poorly the West has mismanaged the Iranian file. When Iran was already suspending its enrichment program, all it got in return was an offer made of hot air. That was largely because of the French. Your countrymen were too afraid of opposition by the Americans to promise Iran Western nuclear power technology. That was the critical element that made the Iranians feel they were being taken for a ride. And that is how this series of diplomatic failures began."

After that disillusioning experience, I told him, the Iranians had decided to make uranium conversion, and subsequently uranium enrichment, a fait accompli. I explained that enrichment, for Iran, was an insurance policy. It did not mean, necessarily, that they were going for a weapon. But by adding more sanctions, the West was provoking certain retaliation by Iran, which would lead to continuous escalation.

I, too, feared the worst. "What do you think the effect would be across the entire Muslim world," I asked, "if military force were used to counter Iran's nuclear program? It could lead, among other things, to an extremist regime in Pakistan, where they already have more than fifty nuclear weapons."

The only solution, I told Sarkozy, was to engage the Iranians. I suggested proposing a freeze—that is, no further expansion—on Iran's enrichment activities, in exchange for an end to sanctions, a commitment from the West to provide the Iranians with French reactors, and a commitment by Iran to allow the Agency to conduct a robust inspection program. Complete suspension of enrichment, I explained, was no longer a meaningful request. It would not reduce "risk" in any sense; Iran already had the knowledge. They could always continue to work underground. Insisting on suspension would only make Iran lose face. From a proliferation perspective, robust inspection was much more important.

To my complete surprise, Sarkozy abruptly shifted gears. Without consulting any of the top brass sitting around the table or even looking at them, he said he would agree to support my proposal, including supplying Iran with French reactors. I could see the anxiety break out on the faces of his associates. Clearly, he had made the decision on the spot.

I told him I would contact the Iranians to see if I could get a positive response, and the meeting wrapped up soon afterward. As Sarkozy was escorting me out, I congratulated him on his marriage. He beamed.

I met separately with Kouchner, a very likable, affable person. The French had tried a number of times to engage Tehran, he said, including inviting officials to Paris the previous November. They had gotten no response. Kouchner thought the Iranians might have concluded it would be better to wait for a new U.S. administration. He gave me his mobile telephone number, saying I should call him directly if I heard back from the Iranians.

Over the weekend, in Vienna, I rang Aghazadeh and asked him to come see me early the following week. But on the very day I was supposed to see him, I received a call from François-Xavier Deniau, the

French ambassador, saying I should not convey any message to the Iranians before the French sent me some "clarifications." This was embarrassing, I said. Aghazadeh was on his way to see me. If they had "clarifications," why could they not have provided them in Paris?

Deniau's answer, three days later, was to show up with a *note verbale* saying that, in effect, the French would engage with Iran directly, not through me. With surprise and dismay, I told him this was neither diplomatic nor appropriate. "Usually," I said, "I take the words of a president at face value." Obviously, the people around Sarkozy had convinced him that the Americans would react negatively to his agreeing to my proposal. France would be seen as taking a lone initiative, outside the framework of the P-5+1.

Deniau tried to convince Philippe Jamet, one of my French colleagues at the IAEA, that I had in fact "misunderstood" what Sarkozy had said. Jamet, who had been at the meeting himself, replied sarcastically, "This is a clever way of rewriting history."

The much-maligned, then much-commended work plan furnished the meat of my positive February 2008 report to the Board on Iran. We had made significant strides: the last of our questions about the low- and high-enriched uranium particles we had detected at various locations in Iran had finally been answered. The Iranians had explained their polonium experiments, their activities at the Gchine mine, and the procurement activities of the former head of the Physics Research Center. The last of the discrepancies about Iran's past procurement of P-1 and P-2 centrifuges had been addressed in my November 2007 report. While there had been a few minor delays, the Iranians had held steadily to their commitment to the work plan. It was the most consistent and committed cooperation we had experienced in years.

Only one issue remained: the alleged weaponization studies that had come to us from U.S. intelligence. These included the so-called Green Salt Project,[32] high explosives testing, and designs for a missile reentry

---

32 "Green salt" is another name for uranium tetrafluoride (UF_4).

vehicle to accommodate a nuclear warhead. Taken together, these elements pointed to a possible nuclear weapons program, particularly given the indication of administrative interconnections between the various aspects of these studies.

The problem was, no one knew if any of this was real. The allegations had supposedly originated from a laptop computer that held extensive supporting documentation. U.S. intelligence said they had been handed the laptop in mid-2004. They told us it had come from Iran but refused to reveal their source. They said only that their source had gotten it from a third party and that there was reason to believe this person was now dead.

"I can fabricate that data. It looks beautiful, but is open to doubt." This statement, from an anonymous "senior European diplomat" quoted in the New York Times, was a typical reaction that was echoed by multiple nuclear experts.[33] The documentation on the laptop seemed damning but only if it could be proven authentic. Not being able to trace the source made the information extremely tough to verify. Worse still, the United States refused to release copies of most of the documentation so that we could share it with Iran to begin the investigative process. What little we could pass on, Iran dismissed as fabricated and baseless.

After many months of a mutual stand-off on these alleged studies, the IAEA was given additional pieces of the documentation—although still a relatively small portion—that we could discuss with Iran. Working to cover every angle, Agency inspectors also identified a range of procurement activity by various entities in Iran that we thought might relate to the alleged studies. Iran agreed to address the weaponization issue under the work plan, and our discussions began. But as the February report showed, we still had some way to go.

Then, two days before the Board was scheduled to review the report, the Security Council adopted a third resolution, with more sanctions on

---

33 William J. Broad and David E. Sanger, "Relying on Computer, U.S. Seeks to Prove Iran's Nuclear Aims," New York Times, November 13, 2005.

Iran. To put it another way, the council issued the verdict before the deliberation. I had in fact seen a draft resolution that did not even refer to my report.[34] Not only was this a procedural fault, it gave the impression—perhaps accurately—that the council was taking action based on predetermined policy objectives rather than on the facts.

Reactions to the report itself were all over the map. The United States was complimentary, saying the report was damning for Iran, presumably because some of the allegations about weaponization studies had been openly stated for the first time. The Iranians declared it "a total victory, vindicating our program," presumably because of all the issues that had been resolved. Of course, everyone read from the report selectively.

Reactions in the media were equally split. Danielle Pletka and Michael Rubin, writing in the *Wall Street Journal*, blasted me as anti-West and having a hidden agenda:

> Mr. ElBaradei's report culminates a career of freelancing and feckless-ness which has crippled the reputation of the organization he directs. He has used his Nobel Prize to cultivate an image of a technocratic lawyer interested in peace and justice and above politics. In reality, he is a deeply political figure, animated by antipathy for the West and for Israel on what has increasingly become a single-minded crusade to rescue favored regimes from charges of proliferation.[35]

Not to be outdone, another Israeli official, Housing Minister Zeev Boim, called for my resignation, saying that my behavior was that of a "planted agent."[36]

Thankfully, these criticisms were balanced by other analyses, among them an article in the *Financial Times* by Joe Cirincione and Ray Takeyh from the Council on Foreign Relations. Despite the attacks against me, they said, I was quietly succeeding in disarming Iran:

---

34 I had alerted South Africa to this omission, and mention was made in the resolution but not to any substantive effect.
35 "ElBaradei's Real Agenda," *Wall Street Journal*, February 25, 2008.
36 "Israeli Minister Says Sack ElBaradei over Iran," Reuters, March 9, 2008.

The point that Mr ElBaradei's critics miss is that he is judiciously achieving the goals that they seemingly desire—the disarmament of the Islamic Republic. . . . Instead of sanctions, the west should appreciate that a nuanced diplomacy of reconciliation could both regulate Iran's nuclear programme and help stabilise the Middle East. It is the much maligned Mr ElBaradei that has paved the way for success.[37]

On April 8, the first signs appeared of Iran's reaction to the Security Council resolution, when Ahmadinejad announced plans to expand enrichment operations at Natanz to six thousand centrifuges. This was obviously a show of defiance for his domestic audience. It may also have been meant to put pressure on the United States and Europe to take a different tack.

In any case, his pronouncement was not put into place. The Iranians continued to install centrifuges but at a rate slower than predicted. Their primary focus was on gaining experience operating the existing three thousand P-1 machines and testing their higher-capacity next-generation machines—which they referred to as IR-2 and IR-3 models.

The most regrettable outcome of the resolution was that Iran's cooperation with the IAEA essentially stalled on addressing the facts of the alleged weaponization studies. In the weeks that followed, we made little progress.

Just before I issued my May 2008 report on Iran, the Iranians offered to give us access to key individuals and crucial information—precisely what we had been pressing for. This would prove, they said, that to the extent the alleged activities had taken place, they were not nuclear-related. But there was a condition: the IAEA had to guarantee in advance that we would conclude the issue prior to the June Board meeting.

This was ludicrous. We could not provide a guarantee before the fact, and they knew it. In my report, I criticized Iran for its recent lack of transparency. To keep things in perspective, I emphasized that we had seen no indication of the use of nuclear material in relation to the alleged

---

37 "ElBaradei Is Quietly Managing to Disarm Iran," *Financial Times*, February 27, 2008.

activities, but from what I could tell, Iran was playing wait-and-see with the coming shift in the U.S. administration. If the weaponization work had in fact occurred, the Iranians would likely try to reveal it only during negotiations with the United States as part of a comprehensive settlement of Iran's nuclear issues. And if the documentation on the laptop was fabricated, as Tehran claimed, the Iranians would likely try to get a high price for the damaging effect of the accusations.

Two days after the June report was released, Olli Heinonen gave a technical briefing that raised the hackles of many observers. Speaking to Board representatives, he mentioned that the IAEA now had intelligence from about ten countries that tended to support claims that Iran had engaged in weaponization studies in the past. When he mentioned a uranium metal document Iran received in 1987 through the A. Q. Khan network, he used the term *alarming*. Some of the developing country representatives got the impression that Olli had bought into the U.S. accusations.

Adding fuel to the fire, former UNSCOM chief inspector Scott Ritter wrote an article accusing Olli of working for the CIA and characterized him as "the pro-war yin to the anti-confrontation yang of his boss, IAEA Director General Mohamed ElBaradei."[38] Ritter had gained a reputation as a truth teller for speaking out against the Bush administration's policies on Iraq and Iran. In this case, however, he was dead wrong. Olli was among the most experienced members of my team. We did not always see eye to eye, but I valued his keen insight, and we spent long hours together dissecting the finer points of Iran's nuclear program. Unfortunately, this would be the first of many stories, from various quarters, alleging that Olli and I were in disagreement behind the scenes as to how to deal with Iran's nuclear program.[39]

---

38 Scott Ritter, "Acts of War," Truthdig, July 29, 2008. As usual, Ritter was quite emphatic: "Olli Heinonen might as well become a salaried member of the Bush administration, since he is operating in lock step with the U.S. government's objective of painting Iran as a threat worthy of military action."

39 As in any institution, there were differences of view among the many people providing input on complex issues, including between the lawyers and the technical people. My reports to the Board on Iran customarily went through ten to fifteen drafts, with painstaking efforts to get the facts straight and ensure objectivity in our assessments. But in each case, Olli and I agreed on the final report before its issuance.

Meanwhile, calls for direct U.S. negotiation with Iran were coming from many quarters. The Iraq Study Group, led by former U.S. secretary of state James Baker and U.S. congressman Lee Hamilton, had recommended talks with Iran as far back as December 2006. In a March 2008 interview with Bloomberg News, former secretary of state Henry Kissinger had weighed in, saying, "I think we should be prepared to negotiate about Iran."[40] In May, former president Jimmy Carter had strongly criticized the Bush administration for refusing to engage in dialogue with countries with whom the United States had serious differences, calling it a "terrible departure" from past U.S. presidential practice.[41]

The debate heated up further when the Democratic presidential candidate Senator Barack Obama was first reviled and then praised for saying he would, if elected president, engage in direct negotiations with Iran "without conditions." In a remarkable forum at George Washington University on September 15, five former U.S. secretaries of state—Colin Powell, Madeleine Albright, Warren Christopher, James Baker, and Henry Kissinger—all came out in favor of direct U.S. talks with Iran on its nuclear program.[42]

These sentiments, however, did not translate into progress. On the contrary, the notion of negotiations went into more or less a holding pattern. No one expected the Bush administration, in its final months in office, to make an about-face on dialogue with Iran. From the EU-3 to Iran, everyone seemed resigned to waiting on the outcome of the U.S. elections. Germany's foreign minister, Frank-Walter Steinmeier, told me that, based on his conversations with Condoleezza Rice, she was quietly getting ready to hand over the Iranian file to the next team.

The P-5+1 had gone through the drill of preparing a package to entice Iran into negotiation, and Javier Solana had traveled to Tehran in mid-June to present it as a "new and improved" offer. But the package

---

40 Camilla Hall and Mike Schneider, "Kissinger Backs Direct U.S. Talks with Iran," Bloomberg News, March 15, 2008.
41 Joy Lo Dico, "Jimmy Carter Calls for US to Make Friends with Iran after 27 Years," Independent, May 26, 2008.
42 "Five Former U.S. State Secretaries Urge Iran Talks," Reuters, September 16, 2008.

clung stubbornly to the hard line of demanding suspension of enrichment as a precondition. When Saeed Jalili met with Solana and the P-5+1 in Geneva in July, British political director Mark Grant demanded an answer on the package within two weeks. Iran, as always, took this domineering style as disrespect and a threat.

This by-now pro forma discussion of course went nowhere. Tehran, operating from a position of strength, was in no rush. And Solana and his colleagues were only going through the motions. With their pile-on of Security Council resolutions, they had firmly driven the nail into the coffin.

12

IRAN, 2009

In Pursuit of a Breakthrough

The Bush administration had maneuvered itself into a corner. By insisting that dialogue could be only a reward for good behavior rather than a tool to accomplish that behavior, Washington had created a hamstrung approach to diplomacy: all principle, no pragmatism. In Iran, the nuclear saga had stumbled from quagmire to quagmire, with negotiations repeatedly short-circuited by the absence of the United States. With the election of Barack Obama as president on November 4, 2008, I hoped to see a return of pragmatism. Two days later, Ahmadinejad sent a congratulatory message to Obama, hoping for "major, fair and real changes, in policies and actions."[1] It was widely reported as the first such message from Tehran to a newly elected American president since the 1979 Iranian Revolution.

In his inaugural speech, President Obama was particularly gracious in signaling a change in foreign policy: "To the Muslim world, we seek a new way forward, based on mutual interest and mutual respect. To those leaders around the globe who seek to sow conflict, or blame their society's ills on the West—know that your people will judge you on what you can build, not what you destroy."

---

1 Thomas Erdbrink, "Ahmadinejad Congratulates Obama, Urges 'Real' Change," *Washington Post*, November 7, 2008.

It was a message perfectly attuned to the moment. The stage was set for something new.

A year earlier, Richard Holbrooke[2] had suggested that I be ready to come to Washington during the presidential transition phase in late 2008 to advise on engagement with Iran, and possibly to mediate. At the time, Holbrooke was advising Senator Hillary Clinton, then a front-running presidential candidate, on foreign policy. He had asked whether I thought Iran was ready for dialogue with the United States and whether Tehran would make it a precondition that Israel give up its nuclear weapons program. Iran had been ready to engage in dialogue for the past four years, I told him, and I had never heard mention of such a precondition.

I was eager to engage anew with Washington on Iran, yet I was soon surprised at how little contact I had with the new U.S. administration. Hillary Clinton, now secretary of state, sent a letter jointly with Secretary of Energy Steven Chu applauding Agency efforts to develop an "assurance of supply" mechanism for nuclear fuel. Clinton also spoke publicly about the Iranian nuclear program in a way that was less strident than that of her predecessors, and she emphasized the importance of working through the IAEA.[3]

But that was all. There were no calls for a Washington briefing, no attempts to build on what the IAEA had learned. Gregory Schulte, a steadfast advocate of Bush administration policies, remained in place as U.S. ambassador to the IAEA until June. I knew that Obama and his team had inherited a daunting list of domestic challenges, exacerbated by the global financial crisis in late 2008. I knew that Iran's nuclear program was not the only foreign policy issue on their plate. But I was mindful of my own constraints: my third term as Director General would be complete at the end of November 2009. I had a limited window for collaboration.

---

2 Former assistant secretary of state and former U.S. ambassador to the United Nations.
3 On April 9, 2009, Clinton made the following comments during a joint press conference with Australian foreign minister Stephen Smith and U.S. defense secretary Robert Gates: "We don't know what to believe about the Iranian program. . . . One of the reasons why we are participating in the P-5+1 is to enforce the international obligations that Iran should be meeting, to ensure that the IAEA is the source of credible information."

The events associated with the Iranian presidential election in June 2009 provoked expressions of concern in many Western countries. There were allegations of rigged votes and outrage at the reports of violence against anti-Ahmadinejad demonstrators. I, too, was distressed by the violence, even as I could not fail to register the double standard in the West's dealing with Iran. As the leader of the opposition, Mir-Hossein Mousavi had received 33 percent of the vote. His supporters were able to mobilize hundreds of thousands of people to demonstrate in the streets of Iranian cities. By contrast, most of the countries in the Arab world have either sham elections or none at all, yet they are virtually protected from criticism from Western leaders because they are largely supportive of Western policies. Of course, this double standard is not lost on Arab public opinion.

On ABC News, on July 5, 2009, Vice President Biden said that the United States was watching the election results with interest, waiting "to see how this sort of settles out." Then he seemed to put his foot in his mouth. On the one hand, he said that the U.S. offer to meet with Iran on its nuclear program remained "on the table." On the other, he implied that Israel, "as a sovereign nation," had the right to attack Iran's nuclear facilities.[4] Obama tried to contain the damage with a statement on CNN affirming that the United States was committed to a diplomatic solution to the Iranian question.[5]

While I waited for a word from Washington, two accusations began circulating: that I was hiding information incriminating to Iran in its pursuit of nuclear weapons; and that I had suppressed a secret analysis of Iran's nuclear state of play by Agency inspectors. These accusations were tied to a strident behind-the-scenes push by the United States and the EU-3, starting as far back as late 2007, for me to publish a summary of Iran's alleged weaponization studies in order to put pressure on Tehran.

The IAEA had shared with the Board whatever it could in relation to

---

4 Ryan J. Donmoyer, "Biden Says Israel Has 'Sovereign Right' to Hit Iran," Bloomberg News, July 6, 2009.
5 "Obama: No Green Light for Israel to Attack Iran," CNN, July 7, 2009.

these alleged studies. In my May 2008 report, for example, I listed in detail the documents we had been permitted to show to Iran, including those related to the allegations of "green salt" production, high explosives testing, and the missile reentry vehicle. But I could not reach a verdict on these allegations, which, if proven, had the potential to spell the difference between war and peace—without first being able to verify the authenticity of the documents passed on by U.S. intelligence. Nor would I have done so with any other country.

In response to my reticence, I was now targeted by attacks claiming that I was more concerned with my legacy than with telling the truth. An Associated Press article wrote:

> Mohamed ElBaradei is faced with the tough choice of sharing all his agency findings about Iran's alleged arms programs, or leaving the decision to his successor later this year. The existence of a secret IAEA summary of Iran's alleged weapons experiments based on agency investigations and U.S. and other intelligence was confirmed to The Associated Press over the past few days by three senior western diplomats from nations accredited to the IAEA, as well as a senior international official who follows the Iran nuclear issue.[6]

An article in *Haaretz*, the Israeli daily, made much the same claims.[7] An editorial the same day said that I had, for years, intentionally downplayed evidence of Iran's nuclear program "by using vague language and barely comprehensible jargon intending more to conceal than to reveal." It also implied that Olli and I were in sharp disagreement over whether such information should be published:

> It is no secret that Heinonen does not see eye to eye with his boss. There have been many cases in which he would have preferred the reports to use clear, unequivocal language, and he has said so periodically. But like

---

6 "Outgoing IAEA Chief Has Tough Choice on Iran," Associated Press, August 20, 2009.
7 Barak Ravid, "Sources: UN Watchdog Hiding Evidence on Iran Nuclear Program," *Haaretz*, August 19, 2009.

any good diplomat, he accepts ElBaradei's decisions, even if with gritted teeth.[8]

At the crux of these accusations was the willingness, on the part of Israel and the West, to treat allegations as fact. The alleged studies were, in truth, an unprecedented challenge for the Agency. We were equipped to verify operations involving the use of nuclear material, where we could establish the facts through measurements and environmental sampling. We did not have the tools or expertise, however, to verify the authenticity of documents.

The second part of the media accusations, what the Associated Press called the "secret IAEA summary," referred to an internal analysis, a rolling text compiled by the Agency's Department of Safeguards that included all the various pieces of information that had come in from different intelligence organizations, most of which IAEA inspectors had been unable to verify or authenticate. As such, by definition it was a series of best guesses, as if to say, "If all these claims were true, what would they mean?" It was not something that Olli Heinonen, head of the safeguards department, had assessed, signed off on, or even suggested for inclusion in my Board reports. Nor had it been vetted by relevant IAEA offices responsible for other dimensions of safeguards verification—legal and policy aspects, for example.

Providing this kind of preliminary analysis to the Board would have gone against every principle of due process and would have lent an aura of credibility to unverified accusations. The key missing ingredient—for which we had been pressing for months—was the ability to corroborate the allegations. The critical information on which the analysis was based

---

8 Yossi Melman, "Israel, U.S. Lost Faith in IAEA Long Ago," *Haaretz*, August 19, 2009. In October 2010, two months after Olli Heinonen retired from the IAEA, he gave an interview to *Haaretz* in which he addressed the rumors that our relationship had been tense: "It is true that we had some arguments. And it is true that there were some at the organization who tried to drive a wedge between us by spreading rumors. I am a technical person, and [Mohamed] deals on the diplomatic-political level. Sometimes there was disagreement between us regarding the timing and the course to take; but, in fact, none of these arguments and differences of opinion did any harm to the agency's mission of reporting what we saw." Yossi Melman, "Behind the Scenes of UN Nuclear Inspection of Iran," *Haaretz*, October 22, 2010.

was all paperwork. We had no "green salt" to examine, no components to inventory or trace, no high explosives tunnels or missile reentry vehicles to measure or inspect.

Absurdly, we were limited with regard to what documentation we were permitted to show Iran. I constantly pressed the source of the information to allow us to share copies with Iran. How can I accuse a person, I asked, without revealing the accusations against him? The intelligence crowd refused, continuing to say they needed to protect their sources and methods.

Iran, for its part, continued to dismiss most of the allegations as fabrications. Since the Iranians' cooperation on the work plan had been rewarded with yet more Security Council sanctions, their cooperation on the alleged weaponization studies had been minimal. Their predicament, they said, was that proving the studies were unrelated to nuclear activities would expose a great deal about their conventional weaponry, particularly their missile program. They suspected this was what some of the inspectors were after. The inspectors, of course, rebuffed this line of reasoning.

Was this really the reason for the Iranians' reticence? Or were they intent on hiding something because the timing was not right for a confession? Or was it a combination of both? I could not tell. It was undeniably frustrating to be caught in the middle, unable to get to the bottom of the issue. I continued to press both sides, but no one was budging.

In the late summer of 2009, the Israelis provided the IAEA with documents of their own, purportedly showing that Iran had continued with nuclear weapon studies until at least 2007. Unlike with the U.S. intelligence, the Israelis said we could share these documents with Iran, with no restrictions about protecting their sources. The Agency's technical experts, however, raised numerous questions about the documents' authenticity, and we sent Israel a list of questions.[9]

From what I could tell, Israel's purpose in bringing these allegations to the IAEA was threefold. First, they wanted to contradict the conclusion

---

9 The accuracy of these accusations has never been verified; however, it is significant that the conclusions of the U.S. National Intelligence Estimate were not changed, indicating that they, at least, did not buy the "evidence" put forward by Israel.

of the December 2007 U.S. National Intelligence Estimate, which said that Iran had halted its nuclear weapons program in 2003, but they could not publicly undermine the United States, so the IAEA was the most credible secondary vehicle. Second, they wanted to exert pressure on China and Russia to agree to tighten the sanctions on Iran. Third, and most worrisome, they wanted to create the impression that Iran presented an imminent threat, perhaps preparing the grounds for the use of force.[10]

This was the background for the September Board meeting. A few days ahead of the meeting, Bernard Kouchner took a shot at me, telling journalists that I had documents in my possession, "annexes" to the Iran report showing Tehran was working to develop nuclear weapons.[11] He was referring, of course, to the IAEA internal analysis.

My opening speech to the Board addressed the issue head on. These dismaying accusations made by Member States and fed to the media were baseless and politically motivated. I was clear that "All information made available to the Agency relevant to Iran's nuclear programme which has been critically assessed by the Agency in accordance with its standard practices has been brought to the attention of the Board." In effect, I said, the allegations were attempts to influence the Secretariat and undermine its objectivity and independence.

The French tried to have the last word, asserting that some information had been presented by the Agency in a technical briefing that was not reflected in the report.

I threw down a direct challenge: "Here are the people who supplied the information available to us," I declared. "If any of you have any information that we have not shared with the Board, please step up right now, or forever hold your peace." No one responded.

I could not understand for the life of me, I said, how any information that might have been presented at a technical briefing with 150 Member States present could be regarded as "withheld." I then focused on our

---

10 In January 2011, the outgoing Mossad chief Meir Dagan said he did not believe that Iran would have a nuclear weapon for at least another four years. Yossi Melman, "Outgoing Mossad Chief: Iran Won't Have Nuclear Capability Before 2015," *Haaretz*, January 7, 2011.
11 "France Accuses UN Watchdog of Hiding Iran Nuclear Evidence," Agence France-Presse, September 3, 2009.

limitations in authenticating the alleged weaponization studies. *If* all the documents provided to us were authentic, I said, choosing my words carefully, then there was a high probability that Iran had engaged in nuclear weaponization studies. "But I have to underline this *if* three times," I stressed, "and that is why we are stuck."

It was something of a relief that, the day after this unpleasant confrontation, the Board conferred on me the title of Director General Emeritus. The tone shifted entirely, and for me this was a deeply moving experience. There were tributes from forty-one speakers in all. Together they represented the entire membership of the Agency. I will always remember two tributes in particular: "We are here to honor honor," the Cuban ambassador said, quoting the poet Alphonse de Lamartine; while the Brazilian ambassador said I had "used the power of argument, and not the argument of power."

Stories about the IAEA's "secret annex" of information did not entirely disappear. A September Associated Press article referred to copies of this supposedly secret analysis.[12] And in October, the U.S.-based Institute for Science and International Security (ISIS) published a paper on its Web site that included short excerpts from the document.[13] Clearly either the document had leaked—and there were only six people within the Department of Safeguards who had access to it—or it had been obtained via someone hacking the Agency's computers.

More important, however, was that a chance for a dramatic breakthrough with Iran had been unfolding behind the scenes.

It had started a few months back, with a request from Tehran for IAEA support in getting a new fuel core for its research reactor, which was used to produce radioisotopes for medical purposes. The enrichment level needed for the reactor was 20 percent, significantly higher than the

---

12 George Jahn, "Nuke Agency Says Iran Can Make a Bomb," Associated Press, September 17, 2009.
13 "Excerpts from Internal IAEA Document on Alleged Iranian Nuclear Weaponization," ISIS, October 2, 2009. Retrieved at www.isis-online.org/uploads/isis-reports/documents/IAEA_info_3October2009.pdf.

4–5 percent enrichment needed for power reactors and higher than the level Iran had set for itself at Natanz. The old fuel core had been imported, but Iran was now under sanctions, so the request was a hot potato: while it was perfectly legal for the Agency to support a Member State in getting fuel for a facility under safeguards, Iran was currently in violation of Security Council resolutions.

To test the water, I decided to have Vilmos Cserveny share Iran's request with only two countries at first: Russia and the United States, using their representatives in Vienna. I asked Vilmos to explain the delicacy of the situation. If Iran were denied a fuel core from abroad, it would have every justification to proceed with higher-level enrichment at home to satisfy its own fuel needs. Finding a way to help Iran secure nuclear fuel for this legitimate use could send a positive signal.

A proposal put together by the United States and Russia was brought to the IAEA in early September. The proposal supported Iran's request, but with a twist: Tehran would receive a research reactor core that would run on fuel converted from Iran's newly accumulated stockpile of low-enriched uranium. The LEU would be sent abroad, converted into fuel in Russia and France, and then returned to Iran in the desired form of a research reactor core. The United States would provide political and financial support.

It was ingenious. After all that had passed, an opening had been found for the United States to elegantly reengage with Iran. By removing most of the accumulated LEU from Iran, tension over Iran's uranium enrichment would be defused, or at least postponed. Iran would be demonstrating that its enrichment program was being applied to peaceful purposes. The international community would receive reassurance that Iran's LEU stockpile was not being reserved for or channeled toward nuclear weapons. Diplomacy would at last get its foot in the door.

Then, on September 12, 2009, I received a call from President Obama. He began by graciously saying that he admired my work and believed we shared a vision on many issues. He wanted personally to invite me to speak at the UN Security Council Summit on Nuclear Non-Proliferation and Nuclear Disarmament, where he would be presiding as president of the council.

I was elated by the invitation and of course accepted. The conversation then shifted to Iran. Obama said he was committed to addressing the concerns about Iran's nuclear program while respecting fully Iran's rights under the NPT. The fuel proposal, which, he added, also had Israel's support, would be a way to defuse the current crisis and gain time for diplomacy and negotiation.

When I had learned that President Obama was going to call, I had touched base with Ali Salehi, who had replaced Aghazadeh as the vice president of Iran and the head of its Atomic Energy Organization.[14] I had asked Salehi whether the Iranian leadership wanted to convey anything to Obama. A message had come back from Ahmadinejad saying that he was "ready to engage in bilateral negotiations, without conditions and on the basis of mutual respect." There were additional details, related to Iran's willingness to help in Afghanistan and elsewhere.

I now passed these messages along and gave Obama my view that the United States should focus as soon as possible on the bilateral track, rather than reaching out purely through the mechanism of the P-5+1. Obama listened and thanked me for my advice.

The next day, I invited Salehi and the Iranian ambassador Ali Asghar Soltanieh to my home for a briefing. Vilmos Cserveny was also present. I gave the Iranians a copy of the U.S.-Russia fuel proposal and explained its multiple benefits. Iran would be using its own LEU for its own reactor fuel—an implicit recognition of Iran's right to enrich. The United States would be sending a strong signal of its readiness to help Iran in the peaceful use of nuclear energy. And Iran was not being asked to stop or suspend its enrichment; on the contrary, this proposal would help defuse the enrichment standoff and provide time for negotiation.

On the other hand, if Iran refused the proposal, I said, it would raise concerns. They now had a significant quantity of LEU. Why would they refuse to use it for their own research reactor?

Salehi smiled as he read the paper. "This is a very smart proposal," he

---

14 I was told that Aghazadeh had resigned because he was apparently quite close to Mousavi, Ahmadinejad's primary opponent in the 2009 presidential elections. Salehi was later appointed as foreign minister in December 2010.

said. "I wonder, would they give us yellowcake in return?" He asked this rhetorically, not really directing the question at me.[15] He also mused that the Iranians could be independently clever by enriching their own uranium to 20 percent and then manufacturing their own fuel. "But we will not do that," he added quickly. He knew that such a move would inflame the issue. He was clearly intrigued and, from what I could tell, trying to consider all the possibilities at once.

"You should not look at this only as a technical proposal," I told Salehi. "It is that, but it is also a political gesture that could open the door for negotiation."

Salehi agreed, saying he would wait to answer until after he returned to Tehran. Worried about getting a negative answer over the phone, he wanted to explain the proposal in detail, in person, to Ahmadinejad. The atmosphere in Tehran, according to Salehi, remained tense.

I recalled that a senior Iranian official had recently told me in confidence that a power shift had taken place in Tehran. Ahmadinejad had challenged Ayatollah Khamenei on a number of fronts. While Khamenei remained the Supreme Leader in the public view, Ahmadinejad had really taken charge of the executive power.

The good news, from my perspective, was that Salehi had direct access to the Iranian president. I knew Salehi well, and as a former ambassador to the IAEA and graduate of MIT, he was sophisticated both in his technical background and his cross-cultural diplomatic skills. He knew Iran's nuclear issues intimately. While an absolute loyalist to Iran, he was also determined to find a solution to the nuclear issues. From what I was told, his appointment to the vice presidency had been a surprise, since he had worked closely with Rafsanjani and Khatami before Ahmadinejad's rise to power and was considered part of the liberal faction.

If ever there was to be a breakthrough, I thought, now was the time. With Obama and his team in the White House and Salehi acting as chief nuclear negotiator, both sides were genuinely interested in rapproche-

---

15 The Iranians were always on the lookout for ways to increase their stock of natural uranium, since they had very little of their own, and it was unlikely that anyone would sell them more under the current circumstances.

ment. Ahmadinejad was the wild card. The constant flux in Iranian domestic politics meant that he would remain sensitive to every perceived slight. And the passing of the Bush administration did not mean that neoconservative ideology had gone away to die. Its advocates would still do their best to wreak havoc on any deal.

But at least, I thought, we finally stood a fighting chance.

News of the first wrench being thrown into the works came from French ambassador Florence Mangin. At the IAEA General Conference she told me that France agreed to fabricate the fuel for Iran after Russia would enrich it to 19.5 percent. But she said that because of its relevance to the sanctions, the fuel proposal should go to the Security Council and be woven into the political framework of the P-5+1's deliberations. I groaned inwardly but said nothing. The approach was excessively legalistic, sure to gum up the process.

At my first opportunity, I appealed to the new U.S. ambassador, Glyn Davies, who had replaced Greg Schulte. Davies was an experienced career diplomat with a broad worldview and common sense. "Please," I pleaded with him, "take care of this. We need this operation to go smoothly." The provision of fuel for a research reactor, I told him, fell under the IAEA's technical cooperation mandate. As such, there was no requirement to make it part of additional discussions at the Security Council or with the P-5+1.

Davies agreed. He said he would try to have Washington talk to Paris.

My next stop was New York: the UN Security Council Summit on Nuclear Non-Proliferation and Nuclear Disarmament, hosted by Obama. When I arrived on September 21, there was a request from U.S. undersecretary of state Bill Burns to see me, together with his colleagues Bob Einhorn[16] and Gary Samore.[17]

I had first met Burns when he was ambassador to Russia and had

---

16 Special adviser for nonproliferation and arms control at the U.S. State Department.
17 Special assistant to the president and White House coordinator for arms control and weapons of mass destruction, proliferation, and terrorism.

quickly realized why he had a reputation as one of the finest career foreign service officers in the United States: he was sharp, humble, soft-spoken, and straightforward. I had also worked closely with Einhorn and Samore for over twenty years, both when they were part of the Clinton administration and when they were in think tanks during the Bush era.[18] They were two of the top U.S. experts on nonproliferation, in addition to being close friends. I went to see them at the Waldorf Astoria, where Obama was staying. The customary buzz of the Big Apple was subdued. Everything was in lockdown bunker mode because of security concerns for the summit.

Burns opened candidly: the United States was "stuck" on Iran. They saw the proposed fuel deal as an escape route; if it failed, they would be forced to move on further sanctions. Burns was keen to set a date to meet with Iran on the proposal. I told him I was working to pin down the logistics.

Then I mentioned that at Schwechat Airport in Vienna, just before flying out, I had received a cryptic letter from Iran. The gist of the message was that Iran was constructing another pilot enrichment plant. This was prefaced by an odd statement about Iran's need to exercise passive defense and protect its human resources. I showed Burns, Einhorn, and Samore the letter, and Einhorn took a few notes.

An urgent request came the next morning: Gustavo Zlauvinen, head of the IAEA's New York office, had gotten a call from Einhorn, who needed to see me that night at my hotel together with Samore. I was jet-lagged and preparing for the summit, so I called Einhorn to ask the reason for the proposed visit.

Without preamble, he said they had known for two years about the Iranian facility under construction. A team representing the U.S., French, U.K., and Israeli intelligence agencies was preparing to go to Vienna to brief the Agency's technical experts. He thought that he and Samore should tell me what they knew ahead of the Vienna briefing.

---

18 Einhorn had come to see me with Tom Pickering—another fine career diplomat—during the Bush administration, when they were working on the report of the bipartisan Iraq Study Group led by James Baker and Lee Hamilton.

I asked why the IAEA had not been told before. It was yet another example of information being shared with the Agency selectively, at the time of the supplier's choosing. They had not been sure of the nature of the facility, Einhorn said, which sounded like a bogus excuse. I suspected they were hoping to catch Iran operating the facility, giving the United States a "gotcha" situation to bolster their accusation that Iran had a nuclear weapons program. I was not pleased. Einhorn and I agreed to meet the following day, after the council meeting.

The new Iranian facility was located at Fordow, roughly thirty kilometers north of the city of Qom. The Americans claimed it was small, built to house just three thousand centrifuges, which, in their view, meant that it was not intended for industrial use and was therefore designed for military purposes. Iran, they said, had known since the spring that Western countries were onto the facility. This, they believed, was why the Iranians had finally decided to declare it to the IAEA.

The news was immensely disheartening: The Iranians' failure to declare the Fordow facility to the IAEA at the time of beginning construction, as they were obligated to do, would only add to international distrust of Tehran's intentions. Still, I resolved to press on with the fuel proposal. I held several telephone conversations with Salehi, in New York and then in India, my next stop on a multicountry visit. I was trying to pin down the Iranians on two dates: one for inspecting the new facility and one for the meeting on the fuel proposal. I also wanted some assurance, before the next P-5+1 meeting, scheduled for October 1 in Geneva, that Tehran agreed with the proposal in principle. Salehi was keen to move things forward, but he was waiting for a green light from Ahmadinejad. The new facility, he said, was not an industrial plant. It had been conceived as a backup enrichment facility during the Bush administration, when the threat of a military strike at Natanz seemed serious. The Fordow plant was carved into a mountain, designed for maximum protection from aerial attack. There was no need for it to be large, Salehi said. It was an expression of Iran's resolve to preserve its nuclear enrichment technology and knowledge base, regardless of external threat.

As a date was finally set to discuss the fuel proposal, Salehi confirmed that the Iranians were generally in agreement with the plan, but he could not say so officially before the meeting. That was good enough for me to convey to Washington.

A few days later I was told that President Obama wanted to speak to me by phone. He began by thanking me for taking the time to meet with Burns and company on the day of my arrival at the summit in New York. I was impressed, as before, by the sensitivity of his approach. In his view, he said, it was extremely important for the Agency to gain early access to the new facility. "I do not want to interfere with your Agency's work," he said, "but I hope you will report promptly to the Board once you visit the facility and have made your own assessment." He was pleased that we had a date for the fuel proposal meeting and that the Iranians had reacted positively.

While in India, I spoke to CNN-IBN about the revelation of Iran's new enrichment facility as an unfortunate "setback to the principle of transparency, and to the effort by the international community to build confidence about the Iranian nuclear program." I explained Iran's argument about needing the facility as a backup in case of an attack, which is why "they could not tell us earlier on. Nonetheless, they have been on the wrong side of the law, you know, insofar as informing the Agency about the construction—and as you have seen, it has created concern in the international community."

The Fordow facility notwithstanding, the signals from all sides indicated a desire to conclude the fuel deal. At the P-5+1 meeting in Geneva on October 1, my primary concern was to prevent the discussions from getting sidetracked, particularly by a loose statement from the French, who continued to speak provocatively about Iran's nuclear program. We put great effort into ensuring that prior to the meeting all parties had a clear understanding of their own position as well as the stands that others might take. We wanted no surprises.

The meeting went off without a hitch, referred to by Obama as a "constructive beginning." Regarding the fuel proposal and the inspection of the new facility near Qom, the participants largely restated the terms I had already mediated between the United States and Iran. The meeting served as public articulation of a private agreement. Not all the participants realized that things had been precooked.

Just before the end of the meeting, Solana called, reaching me in Kathmandu. The P-5+1, he said, had confirmed that the inspection of the new facility should take place within the next couple of weeks. He wanted to check whether this was all right. The timing was fine, I said, but it was not up to them to set inspection dates. Solana apologized, saying they had not meant to interfere.

I said no more. But the behavior struck me as typical: the Western countries involved in the process always wanted to be perceived as being in charge—to push, to prod, to put pressure, to set deadlines, to dominate the debate, to inflict punishments—which inevitably gave them the appearance of the schoolyard bully and undermined precisely the objectives they hoped to achieve. Solana added that they had gotten the Iranians to agree in principle on the fuel offer. I did not volunteer that this had been prepared in advance, set up through a patient series of discussions with Salehi. I just said I had heard as much in my conversation with President Obama.

At a press conference after the P-5+1 meeting, Obama discussed the progress made. "I have been in close touch with the head of the IAEA, Mohamed ElBaradei, who will be traveling to Teheran in the days ahead. He has my full support." I marveled at how the world had shifted, in just a few months. After years of being either ignored or attacked as the archenemy of the United States, the IAEA was once again a partner, treated with confidence. It was an unexpected but welcome finale to my tenure with the Agency. I had hoped to last long enough to see a move away from the Bush administration's policies. But I had not expected to encounter a new president in full command of the issues, reachable by phone, who spoke with appreciation for our work.

From Kathmandu, I arranged to fly on short notice to Tehran on October 3. Meeting me at the Esteqlal Hotel, Salehi reported that Iran was ready to let IAEA inspectors visit the new facility at Fordow. However, there would be a slight delay. Given the public statements by Obama and the West that the inspections had to take place within two weeks, the IAEA would have to wait until after that deadline. Tehran did not want to appear to be taking instruction, whether from the United States or anyone else.

The fuel proposal concept was now also facing a lot of internal opposition in Tehran, yet Salehi had managed to convince Ahmadinejad to go along. The Iranian president, he said, wanted dialogue with the United States, and if anyone could make it happen, it would be Ahmadinejad.

I tried to probe Salehi on what issues Iran might raise at our upcoming fuel proposal meeting. He mentioned a number of possibilities: asking for assistance with refurbishing the Tehran Research Reactor, which was forty years old and had originally been supplied by the United States; alternatively, asking for help with purchasing a new research reactor from the West; or asking the P-5+1 to let Iranian engineers receive training abroad.

Salehi also mentioned a long-standing, contentious issue: uranium Iran had paid for but that, after the 1979 Revolution, had never been delivered. He said Iran might ask France and Germany about finally receiving this uranium. This was not a good idea, I told him. Bringing more uranium into Iran at this stage hardly seemed like a sensible way to defuse the crisis.

On the fuel proposal, I told him the arrangement might call for twelve hundred kilograms of LEU to be shipped out to Russia, where it would be further enriched, and then to France, where the fuel for Iran's research reactor core would be fabricated.

"This quantity assumes that we need a core for ten years," Salehi responded. "We might be asking for a core with only a five-year life, which would require less LEU."

My advice was to get as much LEU out of Iran as possible, to calm the enrichment situation and create an opportunity for negotiation. While this was a technical issue, it had huge political implications.

I also asked whether there was there any chance that Iran might now reconsider a time-out or freeze-for-freeze agreement, to get the dialogue under way. The idea would not sell in Tehran, Salehi said frankly. With all the condemnation from the West, enrichment had become a sensitive matter of national pride. The room for compromise on this was limited. From my discussions with Iranian officials, however, I understood that Iran might be able to implement an undeclared de facto freeze, letting the news reach the public via IAEA reporting.

We discussed how Iran might pursue dialogue bilaterally with the United States. To some extent, success on a bilateral front would alter the P-5+1 negotiations, making the multilateral efforts easier. But bilateral dialogue needed a pretext to begin. Perhaps "technical discussions" with the United States—advice on how to renovate the research reactor's control room, for example—could furnish such a pretext?

Salehi was noncommittal. It had been quite difficult, he said, for him to achieve even the progress made thus far.

My next meeting was with Ahmadinejad. I had requested a one-on-one conversation, with only Salehi present to act as an interpreter. I explained to Ahmadinejad the political value of the proposed fuel arrangement and said it would be good for the IAEA to inspect the new facility at Fordow as early as possible, suggesting—as agreed with Salehi—that the inspection take place soon, before October 25. I was mindful of the conclusion of my term but, more important, I wanted to stanch the buildup of speculation by the West. "You should know," I added, "that Western intelligence agencies were aware of the facility for a number of years."

Ahmadinejad smiled. "If they really did know," he replied, "Obama would not have said"—as he had, in a press conference—"that it is possibly a military facility." Ahmadinejad made no reference to my own statement on CNN that Iran was on the wrong side of the law, in terms of its failure to inform the IAEA about Fordow.

He added that Obama should stop lecturing Iran, stop saying "you must do, you must do" and reproving Tehran in public. Ahmadinejad should understand, I said, that Obama had domestic constraints, to which he replied, "So do I." Clearly, for Ahmadinejad and for Iran as a whole, respectful treatment by the West was critical. Ahmadinejad was especially dismissive toward Sarkozy, who he said had been "impolite" for some time. He was also insulted that Obama had not responded to his congratulatory message after the U.S. elections. The key to progress in bilateral relations with the United States would be a matter of tone, making Iran feel more like a partner and less like an outcast.

When I mentioned that the application of the Additional Protocol would help Iran's case, Ahmadinejad said this would not be a problem, but he felt that Tehran needed some sort of positive gesture from the West. Perhaps, I suggested, once the fuel agreement was concluded, the Americans could provide spare parts for Iran's aging fleet of civilian aircraft. "Spare parts are not so important. We need," he said, "to get past fifty years of animosity."

This led me, indirectly, to the sensitive topic of Ahmadinejad's statements about Israel and the Holocaust.[19] "You should not give your detractors an opportunity to misuse your statements," I said. He understood what I was referring to immediately; nobody in the Arab and Muslim world, he said, was ready to accept the "Zionist regime."

After the meeting, Salehi passed on that Ahmadinejad appreciated my efforts to help resolve the Iranian issue and had told him, on his next trip to Vienna, to bring a nice present for my wife. Thus Aida received a traditional Iranian vase and a lovely framed verse from the Koran. On leaving Tehran, I myself was given some first-class pistachios. Such are the perks of international civil service.

Although the stage was set for progress, the situation remained delicate. One misstep in any direction could upset the precarious structure we had built.

Two weeks before the fuel proposal meeting was scheduled to take place, on October 21, Hillary Clinton weighed in with a provocative statement. In a press conference with David Miliband, she expressed impatience with the Iranians: "The international community will not wait indefinitely for evidence that Iran is prepared to live up to its international obligations," she declared. What came next was worse: "With Iran, it is tragic that a country with such a great history, with so much to give to the rest of the world, is so afraid of their own people. The way

---

19 I had discussed this with Salehi ahead of time. He said that if I wanted to approach the topic, I should only do so in a convoluted way. Apparently, in Farsi it is customary to make any critical remarks in a roundabout manner.

that they are utilizing secret prisons and detentions, show trials, is a reflection of the discontent that they know people feel toward the current leadership."[20]

Ahmadinejad and his colleagues were irate. The Iranian ambassador came to inform us that Salehi would now not come to the fuel proposal meeting. I called Glyn Davies. Clinton's statement, I told him, had been completely unnecessary and was undermining our efforts to create an environment conducive to negotiations. If such provocations continued, I would give up. I asked him to call Washington to see whether Clinton, who was in Moscow to meet with Foreign Minister Sergey Lavrov, could at least make a separate, more positive statement.

The response was prompt. At a press conference with Lavrov on October 13, Clinton toned down her stance, saying that the United States had a "dual-track approach" toward Iran: "We believe it is important to pursue the diplomatic track and to do everything we can to make it successful. We believe that Iran is entitled to peaceful nuclear energy, but that it is not entitled to nuclear weapons."[21]

Lavrov helpfully added that Russia was convinced "that threats, sanctions, and threats of pressure in the present situation are counterproductive."[22]

I called Salehi and Ambassador Soltanieh. I told them I had informed the Americans of Tehran's angry reaction and pointed to Clinton's more positive tone. I asked them to convey a message to Ahmadinejad, urging him to take the moral high ground rather than rebutting the United States through the media. Most important, Iran should not squander the opportunity presented by the fuel proposal meeting. The Americans had agreed to discuss the issues Salehi had raised in Tehran: refurbishing the reactor, training Iranian scientists, and the possible sale of a new research reactor. This would be the gateway to a broader dialogue.

Salehi said he could not approach Ahmadinejad again about attending

20 Jeff Mason, "Clinton Warns Iran of Need for Nuclear Progress," Reuters, October 11, 2009.
21 "Remarks with Russian Foreign Minister Sergey Lavrov," October 13, 2009. Transcript retrieved at www.state.gov/secretary/rm/2009a/10/130505.htm.
22 "Don't Pressure Iran, Says Russia," BBC News Online, October 13, 2009.

the meeting because the Iranian president was quite upset by Clinton's remarks. Still, Soltanieh promised he would pass on my message.

"This may be my last chance to help you get engaged with the United States," I said. I threatened not to hold the meeting if Salehi or someone of his level did not come.

I was not, in the end, required to carry through with my threat. The critical fuel proposal meeting convened in Vienna on October 19, as planned, with Soltanieh present. Dan Poneman—U.S. deputy secretary of energy and a friend of long standing who had worked for many years with Brent Scowcroft and at the National Security Council during the Clinton administration—headed the U.S. delegation. Poneman was a breath of fresh air: bright, modest, a big-picture thinker, always eager to find solutions. The Russian head of delegation, Nikolay Spassky,[23] was also a first-class diplomat.

The French, on the other hand, came across as hard-line and legalistic. Headed by Frédéric Mondoloni, representative to the IAEA, the French delegation arrived with scores of proposed amendments to our prepared draft agreement.

During the meeting, Iran dramatically announced that they did not want France to be party to the agreement. As their reason, they cited France's failure to deliver the fifty tons of uranium Iran had bought before the 1979 Revolution—exactly the point I had asked Salehi not to raise. I suspected, though, that the undelivered uranium was not the real reason for Iran's antipathy toward the French, recalling Ahmadinejad's complaints about Sarkozy being "impolite." Sarkozy always found ways to insult Iran. In late August, for example, he had reportedly said, "It is the same leaders in Iran who say that the nuclear program is peaceful and that the elections were honest. Who can believe them?"[24]

---

23 Deputy head of the Russian Federal Atomic Energy Agency.
24 James Mackenzie, "France's Sarkozy Raises Iran Sanction Threat," Reuters, August 27, 2009.

The Iranians were using this opportunity to get back at the French, even though Sarkozy had offered Obama his support for the deal. Indeed, France was one of the only countries with the technology to manufacture Iran's research reactor fuel. A call to Salehi was in order. "I think you have made your point vis-à-vis the French," I said. "You will need them in the future for technology—both for power and research reactors." I suggested that I could keep the French in the agreement as my own proposal.

The Iranians could live with that, Salehi said, and asked me to have the French send their ambassador in Tehran to see him the next day. In a sidebar meeting with the French delegation, I explained how we had worked to keep them in the deal. "You have to ask your people in Paris to control the rhetoric," I said. "You cannot publicly accuse people of lying and then expect them to trust you as a partner." Our next hurdle arose when the Iranians moved to bargain over the modalities for shipping the uranium abroad. The understanding in the P-5+1 meeting in Geneva had been that all twelve hundred kilograms of LEU would be removed in one go. Iran now insisted that they first had to receive the fuel, manufactured from some other source of LEU, and only then would they release their own stockpile of enriched uranium, in two batches. This, they said, was because of the stated lack of trust and their past experience.

As a way out, I suggested that the Agency could take custody of the material from the time it left Iran until it was returned in the form of fuel, thus giving Iran the guarantee it needed. In any case, Iran's risk would be fairly low: its enrichment capability remained intact. As I told Soltanieh and his colleagues, the timing and amount of LEU to be delivered was, in my view, a red line for the Americans and other Western countries.

We were at an impasse. I called on Salehi, who, to my surprise, said they would deliver the entire twelve hundred kilograms if the United States were their counterpart in the agreement, instead of Russia or France. It was a brilliant stroke. By bypassing the third-party countries, the Iranians would open the door to direct bilateral dialogue with the Americans. This is what Ahmadinejad had told me they wanted all along.

It would also send a message of trust and confidence in both directions, from Tehran to Washington and back again.

On receiving Salehi's message, the Americans were flabbergasted. Poneman and his team scrambled to call Washington for guidance at around four o'clock in the morning, D.C. time. They finally responded with a counteroffer. The United States would not be a partner in the agreement, but they would issue a political statement of support and would commit to helping Iran upgrade the safety of their old research reactor. This was a giant step forward. I suggested that the commitment from Washington be annexed to the fuel agreement and signed by the Americans. They agreed on the spot.

Poneman got authorization to see Soltanieh in a bilateral talk. Soltanieh said he could meet Poneman only if I were present. I took them both into my office. Poneman expressed, on behalf of the U.S. government, their goodwill toward the Iranian people. The conclusion of this fuel agreement, he said, could open the way to a broad range of cooperation between the two countries, including providing Iran with new research reactors, which Iran was keen to have. The meeting was cordial and friendly. Soltanieh took careful notes to report to Tehran.

We were balanced on a high wire, somewhere between a momentous breakthrough and failure. Late that night, I called Salehi, promising to email him a copy of the U.S. statement. I asked him to impress on Ahmadinejad that this deal would empower both sides to change completely the terms of their dealings. I explained that according to Poneman it was too difficult for the Americans to accept bringing the Iranian material to the United States for further enrichment and fabrication. There would be too many hoops to jump through because of sanctions and domestic restrictions vis-à-vis Iran.

We spoke again early the next morning. It was now October 21, the final day of the fuel proposal meeting. Salehi was sitting with Ahmadinejad, who had another idea. He suggested that the Americans be the counterpart to the agreement but with the work subcontracted to the Russians and the French. The LEU would not need to go to the United States at all. Salehi added that he needed the Iranian team to come back to Tehran, so that he would not seem to be the only one advising the Iranian president. They would need a couple of days, he said, to provide a response.

I reconvened the meeting. I presented the proposal in the form discussed with Poneman and Soltanieh at the previous day's meeting: Iran would ship out the full twelve hundred kilograms of LEU, and the Agency would take custody of it, with the United States giving a statement of political support. I told the participants that they had until Friday, October 23, to give their final approval. I urged them to approve it, noting the doors that would be opened by the agreement. I was of course addressing primarily Iran; the other three participants, the United States, Russia, and France, were already on board.

With the meeting concluded, I made a short, upbeat statement to the press. The U.S. delegation dropped by to express Washington's appreciation. Obama called later in the day to thank me personally. "If this agreement is approved," he said, "it will change the dynamics here for me." It would give him the space needed for negotiation with Iran on many fronts. More than once, for so many reasons, I felt the need to pinch myself.

The celebrations were premature. In Tehran, attitudes within the political establishment had been hardening since the P-5+1 Geneva meeting at the beginning of the month. Critics on all sides, including the liberal faction that had recently lost the presidential election, were accusing Ahmadinejad of selling the store. Ali Larijani, who had seen his efforts to achieve a de facto suspension vetoed by Ahmadinejad, was now chairman of the Majlis. It was political payback time. He had joined the ranks of those criticizing the fuel proposal as an "insult to the nation." Why, they asked, should Iran not be able to buy its fuel on the market like any other country?

Ray Takeyh, an Iran expert on the U.S. Council on Foreign Relations, summarized the situation eloquently: "There's been a breakdown in the country's foreign policy machinery. Iran doesn't have a foreign policy

right now. It has domestic politics, and its foreign policies are just a sporadic expression of that. It's not sinister; it's not duplicitous; it's just
incompetent."[25]

I had just over a month left at the IAEA. I was in daily contact with
Poneman in Washington and Salehi in Tehran, trying to hammer out a
deal. Salehi kept floating and then retracting a number of add-on proposals to sweeten the arrangement; he was consumed with trying to
find a way to sell the deal in Tehran. Eventually he came back with an
answer: Ahmadinejad could agree only if the LEU remained at home
until the Iranians received the research reactor fuel. They proposed
storing the LEU on the island of Kish in the Persian Gulf, under IAEA
custody and control. Iran would be ready to swap the material as soon
as the fuel was delivered.

I began to draft an agreement to that effect, but Poneman called to
say that Obama was "very uncomfortable" with any agreement that
would keep the nuclear material in Iran. They were ready for any other
creative solution, including making the United States the sole party to
the agreement, as Salehi had earlier proposed. They also suggested storing the uranium in a third country, such as Turkey or Kazakhstan,
where Iran would have complete trust in the host.

I checked in with Salehi. Unfortunately, domestic politics had once
again shifted. The United States as the sole party to the agreement would
no longer be sufficient. The bottom line was that the LEU had to stay
physically in Iran until it was time for the swap.

We were watching the brightest of opportunities sink into the mire
of domestic politics in both Washington and Tehran.

Salehi rang on November 5 to say that he had been asked by President Ahmadinejad to see Khamenei to discuss the fuel agreement.
Salehi was surprised; he had expected the Iranian president to make
the decision himself. The Supreme Leader told Salehi that the international treatment of Iran's request for fuel for its research reactor was
becoming an indignity. Iran, he said, would deliver the LEU as a swap,

---

25 Doyle McManus, "Talking with Iran—and Sending a Message," *Los Angeles Times*,
November 1, 2009.

but only in batches of four hundred kilograms, and only upon receipt of the fuel.

Only days earlier, Hillary Clinton had insisted in the media that the deal would not be changed,[26] which upset the Iranians even as they acknowledged Obama's more conciliatory and friendly statements. Salehi was dejected. Even the idea of storage at Kish Island was no longer on the table. Khamenei's last response was "the final word." This new condition would not fly, I told Salehi. He knew that and asked me to urge the Americans to be patient.

In an interview with Christiane Amanpour, I attempted to put subtle pressure on the Iranians, urging them to look at the big picture and suggesting the idea of Turkey as a third country where the LEU could be stationed. I called Poneman after the interview, to let him know the latest. He called back shortly thereafter to say that Obama was comfortable with Turkey and Turkish prime minister Erdoğan taking this role. Salehi meanwhile had discussed the option with Ahmadinejad, who in turn had briefed Khamenei. Through the Turkish ambassador, I sent word for Erdoğan to speak to Ahmadinejad about the idea during the latter's upcoming trip to Turkey.

My final visit to the United States as IAEA Director General was like nothing I had experienced there in the past eight years. In Washington, I met with an exhausting lineup: James Jones, the national security adviser and his team; Hillary Clinton and her team; the Senate Foreign Relations Committee, chaired by Senator Kerry; and many other officials from the Department of Energy and the State Department. Wherever I turned, I found expressions of thanks. I had come back home to the United States I knew. It was a good conclusion.

In New York, I delivered my final address to an appreciative General Assembly. It was hard not to recall the vociferous criticisms that had not so long ago been leveled at me for partiality and the old chestnut,

---

26 "US Will Not Alter Iran Nuclear Deal," Al Jazeera, November 3, 2009.

speaking outside of my box. But for all the sweetness and gratification of this conclusion to my tenure, the unraveling possibilities of rapprochement with Iran weighed heavily on my mind. We had come very close.

The Iranian fuel proposal did not die when I left office, continuing instead to take its twists and turns. On February 9, 2010, the Iranians declared they would begin enriching LEU up to 20 percent to provide the fuel for their research reactor. Two days later, Ahmadinejad rather inexplicably declared that Iran had become "a nuclear state." By midmonth, IAEA inspectors verified that Iran was enriching uranium to 19.8 percent in Natanz.

But a more positive development was evolving behind the scenes. After several months' delay, Tehran was warming to the suggestion of a fuel swap that would feature interim storage of Iran's LEU in Turkey. In April, Obama wrote directly to Brazilian president Lula da Silva—in a letter that was later leaked to the press—urging that any fuel swap include the measure of storing the fuel "in escrow" in Turkey. I remained in occasional contact with the foreign ministers of Brazil and Turkey, fully supporting this new arrangement.

On May 17, 2010, in a joint declaration, Iran, Brazil, and Turkey announced they had reached an agreement on a fuel swap. Iran would send twelve hundred kilograms of LEU to Turkey, in a single shipment, to be held in escrow while Iran's research reactor fuel was being fabricated. It was a leap forward—particularly because it signaled the willingness of new players, Turkey and Brazil, to take an active role in resolving the diplomatic impasse.

But the very next day, in a masterstroke of diplomatic futility, the P-5+1 announced that they had reached agreement on a fourth Security Council resolution to escalate sanctions on Iran for not bringing its enrichment program to a halt. Hillary Clinton called the fuel swap deal with Turkey and Brazil a "transparent ploy" on Iran's part to avoid new sanctions.

I was dumbstruck and, to say the least, grievously disappointed. Once again, as I noted in an interview with *Jornal do Brasil*, the West had refused to take yes for an answer.[27] Brazil and Turkey were out-raged. Ahmadinejad urged the United States to accept the fuel swap as a move toward openness and dialogue. At the Security Council, Brazil voted against the sanctions—to no avail. The Western powers once more had touched a solution with their fingertips, only to brush it away.

When I had first proposed the fuel swap, Iran had produced about fifteen hundred kilograms of enriched uranium, so the agreement would have removed most of Iran's inventory from the country. By the time of the agreement with Turkey and Brazil, the stock had risen to about twenty-five hundred kilograms, which of course made the agreement less attractive to the Americans as a diplomatic point of entry, since Iran would be retaining a "significant quantity." Iran also had not committed, in the agreement, to stop enriching to 20 percent, although Ahmadinejad had hinted that they would do so.

The Western powers were not happy about these aspects of the deal, but it was obvious to me that they could easily and successfully have addressed these issues in the early stages of negotiation. It was incomprehensible and somewhat naïve to ask Iran—or any country, for that matter—to give up everything before the start of talks and expect a positive response. But the pattern was familiar: nothing would satisfy, short of Iran coming to the table completely undressed.

---

27 "ElBaradei Slams West's Rejection of the Iran-Turkey-Brazil Deal," *Jornal do Brasil*, June 3, 2010. English transcript retrieved at www.campaigniran.org/casmii/index.php?q=node/10263.

CONCLUSION:
THE QUEST FOR HUMAN SECURITY

The yearning for security is a universal human quality. But for nations as for individuals, the definition of security and the strategies for how to attain it vary greatly, whether the quest is to secure food, water, health care, or freedom from want—or other basic human rights (freedom of expression, freedom of worship, freedom from fear). To nations, security might mean the achievement of economic, military, or ideological dominance, or the projection of power and influence. In too many regions of the world, long-standing tensions block the path to security, and the quest to attain it must begin with their resolution.

Despite this range, it would be a mistake to think of global insecurities as disconnected. Repeatedly, we see the links: poverty is often coupled with the abuse of human rights and a lack of good governance, which in turn begets injustice, rage, and humiliation—an ideal environment for breeding violence of multiple sorts: extremism, civil strife, wars. And it is in regions of long-standing conflict—irrespective of the nature of the regime in power—where countries are most frequently driven to undergird their defenses or enhance their status through the pursuit of nuclear and other weapons of mass destruction. Survival is central to every regime whether democratic or authoritarian.

In the era of globalization, it is more apparent than ever that these insecurities are threats without borders. We cannot comfort ourselves that a security menace half a world away will not affect us, whether in the form of a cyber attack, a financial meltdown, a pandemic, or a theft of nuclear material. Such threats cannot be countered effectively by any one country or organization; by their nature, they demand cooperative multinational, multidimensional responses.

In the case of nuclear weapons, if the danger is to be mitigated and ultimately eliminated, it must be seen in this broad context. The threat will persist as long as the international community continues to address only the symptoms of each new nuclear proliferation challenge: waging war against one country, making a deal with a second, issuing sanctions in a third, seeking regime change in still another. So long as nuclear weapons remain a security strategy for a limited few possessor countries, with umbrella arrangements that extend that security to a secondary circle of "allied" countries; so long as others are left out in the cold, the proliferation risk will be with us. With the emergence of sophisticated extremist groups, for whom the threat of retaliation is irrelevant, the nuclear deterrent has become no more than a temporary if not delusional security strategy. Security is indivisible.

Fundamentally, this means that the international community needs to develop an alternate system of collective security, one perceived not as a zero-sum game for a given country or group of countries, but as a universal imperative rooted in the notion of human security and solidarity broadly writ. This shift in thinking is not only a moral or ethical obligation, but also one of practical necessity: as the planet's population grows and resources become more limited, human survival will depend on how effectively we manage our interdependence.

An alternate system of collective security must be, in every respect, equitable and inclusive. We must develop strategies to share the wealth of the planet more equally—recognizing that poverty, too, is a weapon of mass destruction. We must invest deliberately in advanced science and technology to meet development needs, rather than creating products that generate more wealth for the wealthy. Current investments in technology are overwhelmingly profit driven; greater emphasis should be placed on scientific discovery and technological innovation to address hunger and disease. Only when we begin to alleviate poverty will we be able to generate momentum, in affected regions, for effective governance.

When basic human needs are met, the environment is conducive for citizens to turn their focus on gaining their political, civil, and social rights.

A multinational security paradigm must rest on strong, responsive multinational institutions. If nothing else, the crises and challenges of nuclear nonproliferation that the IAEA has dealt with in recent years have revealed both the flaws of our existing multinational institutions and the contours of how to fix them. The UN Security Council, the international body charged with keeping world peace, must redirect its attention to the root causes of conflict rather than only the symptoms of insecurity. This would mean far greater emphasis on peacekeeping and peacemaking; on the early identification and prevention of disputes; on agile, effective mediation and reconciliation; and on taking ownership for resolving conflicts. Correspondingly, the council, dominated as it currently is by one or a few members of the P-5, ought to lessen its emphasis on after-the-fact coercive measures, which invariably victimize vulnerable civilians, as occurred in Iraq before the second Gulf War. The council also needs to rebuild its credibility based on consistency and fairness, eliminating the double standards linked to geopolitics or moral relativism.

On the nuclear front especially, the multinational structures for preventing, detecting, and combating proliferation require strengthening. The IAEA, as the de facto custodian of the Nuclear Non-Proliferation Treaty, can be more effective in verifying nuclear programs worldwide—including detecting clandestine nuclear activities—if it is given the necessary authority, technology, funding, and, where applicable, available intelligence and other information.

Legal authority is the first step. A unified effort is needed to bring comprehensive safeguards agreements—and Additional Protocols—into force for all parties to the NPT. This could be completed relatively quickly. The international community must also face up to the limitation of the Agency's existing verification mandate, centered as it is on nuclear material. If the IAEA is expected to detect and pursue clandestine nuclear weaponization operations, it must have the corresponding legal authority.

To keep up with the pace of technological changes that facilitate nuclear proliferation and to maintain its credibility as an independent verification body, the IAEA must have the necessary financial support to be able to acquire and maintain its own state-of-the-art technological capability and train and renew its inspection workforce. Dollar for dollar, the Agency has proven to be an extraordinarily sound investment. But at its current level of funding and with the dilapidated state of its technology infrastructure, the IAEA sooner or later will be unable to fulfill its nuclear verification mission.

All states should recommit to sharing relevant information with the IAEA about potential nuclear proliferation concerns, consistently and promptly. This is a legal obligation under the NPT. Deception on the part of would-be proliferators cannot be countered effectively if countries with relevant intelligence selectively bypass or support multinational nonproliferation structures according to political whim.

Moreover, when countries with such intelligence deliberately strike first and share information later—in direct contravention of international law, as in Israel's 2007 bombing of Syria's facility in Dair Alzour and Iraq's Osirak research reactor in 1981—condemnation of these actions must follow, and, more important, must come with consequences. The rule of law is meaningless if we apply it only selectively.

Two multinational initiatives already under way should be strengthened. The first is to provide the highest level of security for nuclear and radioactive material, to keep it out of the hands of extremist groups. The second is to move from national to multinational control of the nuclear fuel cycle. In December 2010, the IAEA Board adopted a decision to authorize a fuel bank of low-enriched uranium, under Agency control, to provide an assured supply of fuel to bona fide users—a measure for which I had pressed for years.[1] This is an enormously important first

---

1 The vote on this measure passed with twenty-eight in favor. Six countries abstained— Argentina, Brazil, Ecuador, South Africa, Tunisia, and Venezuela—and Pakistan was absent. The abstentions reflect a remaining vestige of distrust about the purpose of the fuel bank, stemming from the early proposal from six Western countries that had asked participants to give up their fuel cycle rights as a condition of fuel supply. Hopefully, this distrust will dissipate over time.

step. The ultimate goal, however, should be the full multinationalization of the fuel cycle, in parallel with moving toward universal nuclear disarmament.

From my front-row seat to the nuclear dramas of the past two decades, I have seen over and again how the lack of a sense of fairness and equity in negotiations is guaranteed to sabotage even the most commonsensical, desirable, and just resolutions. The road to win-win bilateral cooperation is strewn with casualties, the victims of disrespect, distrust, self-defeating domestic politics, and painful historical legacies that do not fade overnight.

Still, improbable as it might seem, after the frustrations and even outrage of these years at the helm of the IAEA, I continue to believe that diplomacy has the capacity to resolve problems that might seem intractable. A key reason for optimism is the recent progress—both ideologically and concretely—on nuclear disarmament: a complete change of face, driven by the awareness that, with the spread of nuclear technology, the rise of extremism, and the increase in cases of proliferation, continuing the status quo is a formula for self-destruction. In a landmark essay, four seasoned veterans of the cold war—Henry Kissinger, George Shultz, Sam Nunn, and William Perry—declared the world to be "on the precipice of a new and dangerous nuclear era" and were bold enough to advocate, as a realistic goal, "a world free of nuclear weapons."[2] The response was overwhelming. In the year that followed the article's publication, I had the opportunity to touch base with each of these gentlemen. They spoke about the enthusiastic reception of their call for disarmament, which was far more than just a well-written op-ed; they each saw it as the start of a collective campaign to change the global outlook.[3]

---

2 "A World Free of Nuclear Weapons," *Wall Street Journal*, January 4, 2007.
3 In the lead-up to the 2008 U.S. presidential primaries, Bill Perry and Sam Nunn told me that, among the four of them, the two Democrats were working on the two remaining Democratic candidates, and the two Republicans were working on the Republican candidates, to ensure that, regardless of who made it into office, the next U.S. president would be committed to working toward a nuclear-weapon-free world.

On the anniversary of their first essay, the same four men published a second essay, following a conference at Stanford University's Hoover Institution. This time, they gave concrete recommendations for how to achieve disarmament.[4] That these stalwart cold warriors have moved in this direction is a stark indication of a new urgency animating disarmament activism.

Margaret Beckett, the British foreign secretary, added her voice to this call for disarmament, indicating her government's approval and outlining steps to be taken:

> What we need is both a vision—a scenario for a world free of nuclear weapons—and action—progressive steps to reduce warhead numbers and to limit the role of nuclear weapons in security policy. These two strands are separate, but they are mutually reinforcing. Both are necessary, but at the moment too weak.[5]

A number of similar efforts are under way. A major international campaign was launched in Paris in December 2008 under the name Global Zero. It has been joined by more than two hundred public figures from all walks of life: former heads of state, military generals, Nobel Prize winners, ministers and parliamentarians, influential writers, and other civic leaders. Using their influence and contact networks, these individuals have sought to advance and expand the diplomatic dialogue among key governments, advocating a phased drawdown of nuclear arsenals by all countries possessing such weapons.

On April 8, 2010, U.S. president Barack Obama and Russian president Dmitry Medvedev signed a new Strategic Arms Reduction Treaty (START) in Prague. The limit set on deployed strategic warheads under the new treaty is 1,550, well below that of the 2002 Moscow Treaty—and this time the numbers will be verifiable and irreversible. Even before ratification of the new treaty by the U.S. Senate, the United States started

---

4 George P. Shultz, William J. Perry, Henry A. Kissinger, and Sam Nunn, "Toward a Nuclear-Free World," *Wall Street Journal*, January 15, 2008.
5 Shultz et al., "Toward a Nuclear-Free World."

to implement its provisions. The State Department's published statistics at the end of 2009 showed a total of 1,968 deployed strategic warheads. According to the Federation of American Scientists, "the last time the United States deployed less than 2,000 strategic warheads was in 1956."[6]

This movement on the part of the United States and Russia—the two countries with the greatest responsibility to show leadership in disarmament, since together they account for more than 95 percent of the nuclear warheads in existence—has sent a quite positive signal to the global community. But it is not enough. Both countries must speed the pace of dismantling the thousands of undeployed weapons and downgrade deployed weapons from their cold war alert status, to allow more time for the leaders of each country to verify and respond to reports of possible nuclear weapons use. In addition, the new START treaty must be followed and strengthened soon by other multilateral arms control agreements, such as the Comprehensive Test Ban Treaty and the Fissile Material Cut-off Treaty, both of which have long been in the works. But it is gratifying to see substantial movement in the right direction. By demonstrating their irreversible commitment to achieving a world free from nuclear threat, the nuclear-weapon states can greatly contribute to the legitimacy of the nonproliferation regime and gain the moral authority to detect, deter, and defeat any cheaters in the system, with the support of the entire international community.

Another reason for hope, as I read the situation, is in the potential for a negotiated agreement in the U.S.-Iran standoff. Having watched what has and has not worked in complex nuclear diplomacy scenarios, I believe the elements for a solution are finally in place. Both sides are motivated to achieve a partnership. This does not mean every individual is so motivated; there are hordes of detractors firmly planted in both governments—not to mention pundits who prowl the media airwaves and populate various editorial boards. But the key individuals are keen to find a way forward.

---

6 Hans M. Kristensen, "United States Moves Rapidly Toward New START Warhead Limit," Federation of American Scientists Strategic Security Blog, May 2, 2010, retrieved at www.fas.org/blog/ssp/category/hans_kristensen.

The change that took place in mid-2009 is without precedent. To an audience whose customary window onto such goings-on consists of the *Washington Post* or the *Financial Times*, it is difficult to convey the nature of this behind-the-scenes shift in attitude. But in the frenetic final weeks of my tenure, the efforts to identify creative solutions, along with the reassurances of goodwill and respect passed back and forth between Iran and the United States, were all but unheard of during the previous eight years. The subsequent breakthroughs, admittedly, have been small—a few discussions between officials, exchanges of letters behind the scenes, and the reconvening of the six parties in negotiation, with the United States finally represented at the table. Progress is always tentative. Long periods of 2010 were frittered away with additional posturing and delays. But as such small steps alter the notion of what is possible, the concept of renewed ties between the two countries is no longer quite so unimaginable. Whatever the outcome, this change is a testament to the shifts that are possible when the necessary political will is present, with fairness and equity as the starting point.

Of course, Iran is not the only nuclear game in town. North Korea's nuclear weapons capability, even if not fully defined, has long been a major source of regional insecurity in East Asia. The complex political maneuvering that emanates from Pyongyang is historically difficult to read. But on this front, too, the seeds have been sown for a peaceful resolution of nuclear proliferation concerns and other insecurities on the Korean Peninsula. Whatever the hurdles, past lessons tell us that any solution lies in helping North Korea move away from its pariah status and return to the community of nations.

The final reason not to lose faith that diplomacy and dialogue can prevail as the strategy for dealing with nuclear crises is based on a point of logic: the alternative is unacceptable. Of course, optimism is a far cry from certainty. Nuclear diplomacy is a tedious, wrenching business. But the road ahead is clear. Ultimately, we are a single, conjoined human family; like it or not, we are in this together. The only quest that makes sense, the only quest worth pursuing, is toward collective security.

ACKNOWLEDGMENTS

Nuclear diplomacy is a complex and long-term undertaking. Yet the world is a better place because of the intensive labor and sustained commitment of people throughout the international nuclear community: diplomats, inspectors, scientists, lawyers, lab workers, journalists, activists, and academics, leaders from every sector and at every level, and in particular my colleagues, the dedicated men and women of the International Atomic Energy Agency. Many have been a source of inspiration and encouragement in the writing of this book; many of their ideas, observations, and anecdotes have enlivened and enriched these pages and, while it is impossible to name every person, each one has my sincere gratitude.

A few people deserve special mention for their contributions to this project.

I am especially indebted to Laban Coblentz, my chief collaborator in the conceptual development and writing of this narrative, without whom this book would not have been what it is. An extraordinarily gifted writer, an innovative thinker, and an unfailingly cheerful and loyal friend, Laban found ways to burn the candle at more locations than should be humanly possible. I must also single out his most valuable asset, his wife, Angeline, a former IAEA colleague, without whose patience, support, and discipline this book could not have been completed.

The writing also benefited greatly from the assistance of a number of

IAEA colleagues—Jacques Baute, Vilmos Cserveny, Olli Heinonen, Herman Nackaerts, Tariq Rauf, Laura Rockwood, and David Waller—who, graciously and on their own time, supplemented my memories of what happened when and where, adjusted and clarified my lawyer's explanations of nuclear technology, and answered many questions to ensure the accuracy of the accounts. Eva Moosbrugger, my longtime dedicated assistant and confidante at the IAEA, generously donated countless evenings to carefully transcribe my rambling reflections from recorded dictation into intelligible text, and prodded me to record my thoughts even in the busiest of times. Ewelina Hilger, researcher par excellence, made similarly exhaustive efforts on her own time to track down supporting documentation, confirm coordinates and chronologies, and follow up with various IAEA and industry experts on important details. Stephanie Zupancic, my current assistant, followed me uncomplainingly to Cairo; le Gers, France; and many other places, helping me stay in touch no matter how remote my location or how challenging my schedule.

Most of the themes and concepts explored in these pages were first articulated in speeches and writings during my tenure as IAEA Director General. In addition to those already named, key contributors to the molding and expression of these ideas include Richard Murphy, Melissa Fleming, Graham Andrew, Geoffrey Shaw, and Ian Biggs.

Noah Lukeman, my agent, approached me years ago with the idea of writing this book, understanding how important it was for these messages to reach a broader audience, and gently refused to let it drop off my radar screen. I am especially grateful to Noah for helping to find the book a genuinely supportive home at Metropolitan Books. Metropolitan's publisher, Sara Bershtel, has been an energetic and caring advocate, supplying crucial advice and encouragement, while my editor, Riva Hocherman, proved to be an ideal partner in shaping and sharpening the focus of the manuscript. Riva is, hands down, the finest editor a first-time author could hope for: her intelligence in grasping what I wanted to convey, her uncanny craftsmanship, her passion for getting the ideas just right and staying on message helped to turn the narrative into a finely tuned, compelling read.

No author could wish for a more supportive and loving family. My wife and children, as well as my mother, brothers, and sisters, have always been there for me during the highs and lows of my time as Director General. My son, Mostafa, in his thoughtful and understated way, was always present to gently challenge my intellectual ability, and when I needed him to fix an Internet connection or come to the rescue of my rudimentary software skills, his "geek" IT talents were always available. My daughter, Laila, and my son-in-law, Neil Pizey, unfortunately both lawyers like me, read multiple versions of the narrative, churning out pages of perceptive questions, helping me to tease out the technical details that needed more explanation for the educated lay reader—Laila in her direct and irreverent way and Neil in his more soft-spoken and probing manner.

Nothing I put into words will be sufficient to describe how very fortunate I am to have Aida, my wife, as my partner, friend, and alter ego. Throughout the emotional, mental, and physical stress that came with the episodes described in this book, as well as the labor of its writing, she has been my unwavering ally, my honest advisor, and my sanctuary.

Finally, I would like to pay homage to my late father, who, even in his absence, remains an inspiration to me for many of the values I hold dear.

INDEX